"Cal Bombay has certainly experienced a
walks us through his multi-faceted life with
reflections marked with wisdom, humour, compassion, and faith. As is true of
all his writing, you move easily through the book, enjoying humorous anecdotes
while being drawn into the experiences and meaningful life lessons provided.
Enjoy!"

Rev. David Wells
General Superintendent, The Pentecostal Assemblies of Canada

"A man deeply committed to God and family, Cal answered the call to missions
with the same passion and desire to impact others that has marked his entire
life. I've had the privilege of knowing Cal for many years through our ministry at
100 Huntley Street. His efforts to free hundreds of Sudanese lives made a mark
on history and profoundly inspired all of us with his commitment, even at the risk
of his own life. What a pleasure to read about his adventures and discover many
scary details that he *conveniently* did not tell us at the time!"

Lorna Dueck
Consultant, LornaDueckCreative.com
Former cohost with Cal and retired CEO of Crossroads Christian Communications

"Cal Bombay's commentary, which he did regularly on Canada's daily Christian
television program *100 Huntley Street*, balanced out guests who made life
appear as exciting as their rather close-cropped snapshots. Cal does it again
here. His detailed brushing brings realism to the landscape, actual stories of
his own walk. Chapters are short, each giving a slice of life; humorous and
charming, he never takes himself too seriously. I found myself agreeing when
his experiences seem close to mine and yet learning about life in ways I had
never considered. This is a book about life intertwined by faith. To Cal these two
aren't binary; they are integrated. One flows to the next. It may be that this book

will be a starting point for your memoirs. For many of us, it will be an offering to another, a simple and profound reflection on what matters in our walk of faith. Cal so creatively reminds that our lives, too, are worth living."

Brian C. Stiller
Global Ambassador, The World Evangelical Alliance

This is a story that had to be told! For years, thousands of *100 Huntley Street* viewers enjoyed slices of Cal's life in his daily TV commentaries. Spiritual lessons "from the chicken coop" were especially endearing. But here is the journey that shaped the humble hero so many came to love, weaving through decades of fascinating history and unexpected global adventures, told with his trademark warmth, humour, and honesty. You will want to return to the life principles that conclude each chapter and will be left heartily affirming the book's title!

Moira Brown, author, broadcaster, former co-host of *100 Huntley Street*

A LIFE
WORTH
LIVING

Cal R. Bombay

THE CAL YOU NEVER KNEW
CAL BOMBAY
FOREWORD BY JIM CANTELON

A Life Worth Living
Copyright ©2021 Cal Bombay

Published by Castle Quay Books
Burlington, Ontario, Canada and Jupiter, Florida, U.S.A.
416-573-3249 | info@castlequaybooks.com | www.castlequaybooks.com

Printed in Canada.

Edited by Marina Hofman Willard
Cover design and book interior by Burst Impressions
Printed in Canada

978-1-988928-51-7 Soft Cover
978-1-988928-52-4 E-book

Library and Archives Canada Cataloguing in Publication

Title: A life worth living : the Cal you never knew / by Cal Bombay.
Names: Bombay, Cal R., author.
Identifiers: Canadiana 20210265779 | ISBN 9781988928517 (softcover)
Subjects: LCSH: Bombay, Cal R. | LCSH: Missionaries—Africa—Biography. | LCSH: Religious
   broadcasters—Biography. | LCSH: Christian biography. | LCGFT: Autobiographies.
Classification: LCC BV3505.B66 A3 2021 | DDC 266.0092—dc23

Dedicated to my wife, Mary,
my son, John,
and my daughter, Elaine

CONTENTS

FOREWORD

CAL BOMBAY CALMLY reports, "People have wanted to kill me from time to time" as almost an aside in this captivating memoir. His casual approach to what for most of us would be utmost crisis is indicative of the character of the man.

He writes about miracles, camping in his car in African bushlands, encounters with wild-eyed militia soldiers (gun barrel at his temple!), sleeping in mud huts, eating indigestible food, rescuing blood-soaked terror victims, hugely successful evangelistic meetings (some with thousands in attendance), encounters with snakes, and on and on, with a sense of detachment that is staggering.

But most intriguing of all is the pioneering role Cal has played in South Sudan. He has literally been a saviour to thousands of desperately enslaved people, not only in regaining their freedom but also in providing shelter and farm training in thousands of acres of formerly dormant land.

His Sudan incorporated Savanah Farmers Cooperative NGO is providing farms of refuge unlike anything ever seen before in that stricken part of the world.

Cal's accounts are totally engaging, full of candid detail and humour. The book is truly a page-turner.

I have known Cal Bombay for years as a colleague and friend. I can vouch for the integrity of the man. And, after you read his memoirs, you will too.

Jim Cantelon
President, Working for Women and Orphans
Host, *Jim Cantelon Today*

ACKNOWLEDGEMENTS

MY FAMILY DESERVES credit for living through all this together. Mary, my wife, and John, my son, who lived a lot of this with me in Africa while working at Crossroads, were patiently supportive. John's wife, Karen, and their children, Josh and Tori, provided much joy and refreshing in times of rest. Josh, married to Rachel, presented me with our first great grandson, Oliver. My daughter, Elaine, did some outstanding editorial work on this book.

Friends and colleagues who corrected and stimulated memories: I thank you sincerely.

Chief editor Marina Hofman Willard of Castle Quay Books was both an inspiration and an expert in catching many blips and giving wise advice. I thank her for her enthusiasm.

I must give *some* credit to my keyboard for putting up exclusively with two forefingers and a thumb thumping on it for many hours.

INTRODUCTION

I QUITE GRUDGINGLY surrendered my life to God's service—I had my reasons for hesitation. My dad, grandfather, four uncles, and some cousins were in ministry. I didn't like the idea of being at the beck and call of a mob of people with problems. I figured I'd make enough troubles for myself.

But eventually, I surrendered to God's call. And what a ride it has been!

I serve a miraculous and personal God whom I have tried to obey. God took me with all my weaknesses to accomplish some astonishing things, despite me, and He alone must receive all the glory. (I hope you'll blame me when you realize how outlandishly I sometimes acted. I'm just barely smart enough to take God at His word and obey Him.)

My father once said, "What God does needs no exaggeration!" Indeed, I have no need to embellish the truth. I've stuck to the facts to the best of my knowledge; and yes, I left out some of the bone-chillingly stupid things.

God has done many miraculous things, as I've detailed here. Yet, don't imagine that my life was a continuous string of exciting and miraculous incidents. Sometimes life was just tedious and boring. But I concluded that I have lived a life worth living, full of thrills and chills, almost beyond my belief.

My hope is that you encounter our God, who can take a life and bend it profitably to His will. I hope, too, that you will let God bend you.

What I have to say in this book is my story—the experiences of my wife, my family, and me—and we are all still moving forward. More to come, I expect.

1 STARTING THIS LOOK INTO THE PAST

THE DRIVE WAS familiar, almost too familiar. One era passed, and another began.

It was out of the driveway of the Crossroads Centre in Burlington, right on North Service Road, then merging onto Highway 403, trying to get to the outside passing lane before I went under the first bridge.

It was my last time to do so. It was just coming up to December 2003. The back seat of my dodgy old Oldsmobile was filled with personal stuff. Seasons!

I've had some time now to think of seasons, the seasons of my life. This last season at *100 Huntley Street* lasted longer than any of the others—almost 25 years.

I was leaving with nothing but a few small RRSPs in which I had invested some money. I had little else but memories. Oh yes, one other thing: a contract to be a consultant to the Missions Department for the year 2004. For some unknown reason, I wouldn't collect a retirement benefit to match the over 24 years I had served the Crossroads ministry. I decided it didn't really matter. I had memories, and most of them were pure, refined gold.

I drove up the long mountain road through Hamilton, which flattened out as I continued to Onondaga, where I had lived with my wife, Mary, for 15 years. The same stuff was still there. Red lights, fields, potholes, barns, and houses slipped by as I cut off onto old Hwy 2/54 to White Swan Road.

I remembered the other seasons. Memory is a glowing thing. Over time, it has a way of dropping off the chaff of life and capturing only the golden kernels. Experiences that at one time left a bad taste now could become memories, polishing away the grit of disappointment. Refined gold! Sometimes amusing.

I tried to figure out how many actual seasons I had experienced. Could I really separate childhood from my teen years? Was there that much difference between those younger years and college? Were my almost four years of pastoring long enough to be a life season?

Seventeen years in Africa as a missionary qualified as a season, a season with hundreds of memories. Then there was Crossroads and *100 Huntley Street*. That, too, was a season with more than enough memories. Now here I was, not quite out of a job but at the beginning of a new season, one that would turn out to be every bit as interesting, exciting, challenging, frustrating, and dangerous as all the previous seasons. I might even manage to earn a few death threats.

As I pulled into my driveway and pressed the remote in my car to open the garage door, I realized that more than just a garage door was opening. A whole new life was before me. I was 66 years old. I had just registered a new charity named Cal Bombay Ministries, Inc. I had a clear goal in mind.

Never would I have dreamed … but I'll not waste my time on dreams. I'll relate the reality.

I have been told that I began my life by crying, screaming.

My parents told me that on December 8, 1937, at 2:00 a.m., the doctor held me upside down by the ankles with his left hand and gave me a swat on my tiny little butt with his right. I screamed. That was not the welcome a little person should expect when entering a different source of oxygen!

The new place was North Bay, Ontario. More specifically, at home in the parsonage, where Mom and Dad already had a 19-month-old son, called David. Dad was worried that the doctor would drop me on my head. Gruffly the doctor said, "Wouldn't hurt him a bit." Nobody asked my opinion!

Mom told me that Dad, looking at my red and wrinkled face and body, asked, "Is he all right?" The doctor again answered, "Perfect specimen. Good shaped head!"

My father, Rev. Richard A. Bombay, was the pastor of a growing Pentecostal church in North Bay. A large portion of the congregation was Italian workers with the railroad, a major employer in town.

I don't remember anything of those two years in North Bay. Dad told me that he took me fishing at a dock on Lake Nipissing once. He supplied me with a stick and some bait to hang over the edge of the dock while he cast out into the lake. The muskie caught me before I caught it. But Dad caught both of us before we could be dragged off the dock. I have loved fishing ever since.

I hesitate to relate another bit of history, but here goes. I had long, brilliant, blond curls that hung to my shoulders when we were still in North Bay. This was long before the hippie world. It becomes doubly embarrassing when I look at the pictures that prove this detail. It also appears that I am dressed in a girl's winter coat. It went well with the long blond curls. A poorly paid pastor's family must make do with what they can get.

When I was about two years old, my father was called to Oshawa to become pastor of the Pentecostal church on King Street West. The church was just east of the city centre, on Hwy 2, the main east/west highway in Ontario in 1939. I tagged along.

Oshawa was built around the McLaughlin Buick Eight. Robert McLaughlin had developed and begun building that car. His plant amalgamated with General Motors. Most of the industry in town was auto related.

King Street was the only Pentecostal church in town. At that time, many people still thought of Pentecostalism as a cult, a strange aberration from traditional Christianity. But people came, were saved, filled with the Holy Spirit, and healed.

The church did not look like a church. It was an oblong two-storey cement block building. The front entrance had an overhanging roof slung by chains, which also served as a balcony. It was six feet square and without rails, other than the chains that held it secure. A second-storey door gave access to it. That door was always locked. I remember the one time we were ever allowed out on that balcony. It was during World War II. Dad took my brother David and me by the hands to watch a massive flyover of war planes from Trenton. It was a thrilling sight. Dad was a warden for the city of Oshawa. He was also chaplain to the very secret Camp X on the lakeshore on Oshawa's west side. He never talked about it, even in later years. It was many years afterward when I learned that the spy "Intrepid" was trained in espionage there.

We lived upstairs, above the big room that served as a sanctuary. My sister Ruth was born in that apartment while Dad took Dave and me out for fish and chips, a rare occasion on his salary. It was done mainly to get us out of the way, and probably to avoid our hearing the sounds of childbirth. When we got home, we had a sister. We stood in awe at the sight of this little red and wrinkled screaming thing.

When I went missing once, my mother became frantic. She finally found me because of a deep sigh I made as I slept—on a wide windowsill behind heavy curtains. My brother David was much better at that than I was. He slept outside the window on the sill. Mom was able to grab him before he fell onto a pile of rubble outside two storeys below.

David and I shared a room on the west side of the apartment. David loved to scare me about the dark. He had two special scares for me. He told me that if I opened my eyes in the dark, they would fall out. Ha, he had to start wearing glasses long before I did.

The other scare was the claim that when the closet door opened at night the floor disappeared into a pit that had no bottom. I trembled my way to sleep many a night. If I fell in that hole, I would break everything in me. He got his reward for this too—he was in bed for six months with casts on both legs with osteochondritis. The smartest guy in his class came around every day after school and gave David the lessons of the day. He and David stood at the top of their class at graduation. He had an IQ that was too high for my comfort.

David and I had the usual sibling rivalries. He was 19 months older than me, so he took it upon himself to be my boss, chief instructor, and occasional defender if someone intruded into our territory. Like most siblings, we argued. "Don't argue" was the frequently issued command from both Mom and Dad. There came an occasion when David was not ready to accept my disobedience to him. I argued back. He sternly warned me, "Don't argue!" I answered back with deep feeling, "Don't arg ME!" I think I won that one.

Our rivalry usually found its expression when we were on opposite teams. One particularly wonderful winter with an abundance of packing snow, we built two forts in the backyard. With neighbourhood kids and Dad, we started our war with snowballs. It was suddenly over when one snowball lodged right in my wide-open excitedly screaming mouth. The excitement stopped, as did my breathing. I was choking. Dad squeezed my cheeks, crushing the soft snow; then he dug my mouth empty with his fingers. Our team lost as I went choking and crying to Mommy! That same snow made wonderful snow taffy.

I remember when a tree had been cut down in our backyard. My father had cut it up and set up a chopping block for splitting the firewood. David somehow had got hold of a hatchet and was chopping off chips of wood from the end of a short piece of firewood. Wanting to be helpful, I used my mitt-covered hand to brush the chips off into the snow. The hatchet descended just as my right hand was brushing chips away. I yelled as the hatchet came down on my fingers. My mitten filled with blood. There I was again, screaming.

I was getting good at screaming.

I thought that I was dying, of course. So much blood, and it looked worse as it spread in the snow. Mother soothed the terror, removed my mitten, and stuck my hand in the snow, slowing the bleeding. Then we went inside, had a wash-up, and two tight bandages. I suspect Mom wiped away more tears than blood.

We had a beautiful collie dog called Lassie. She was the pet of the whole family. She barked and bounded around in the backyard with us. We loved her. We had neighbours on both sides, and our back fence bordered on a graveyard. One day we came home to find Lassie lying dead in the yard. She had been healthy and happy just hours before. It turned out someone had thrown a piece of poisoned meat to her. It was one of the sadder days of my young life. Dad figured he knew who had done it but never would tell us. Not everyone liked "those Pentecostals" in those days.

Living above a church can be an interesting experience. Midweek services drifted up from below, and we were often sung to sleep while Zelda Sutton babysat us. Mom played the piano as Dad led the service and preached.

Dad had an old Model A for visiting his congregation throughout Oshawa. I recall the ratty materials overlaying the roof of the car. It was tattered in several areas. But that old black crate that Dad called "Pearl" (he called most of his cars Pearl) was a faithful old thing, even though you had to crank-start it.

The church/apartment faced onto King Street. At night, long before Highway 401 was built, transport trucks going west would growl loudly in low gear as they hauled their loads up the hill past the church. We got used to the sound.

Once, David and I imagined we had been abandoned. This may have been another one of David's terror tactics—one that he began to believe himself. Looking back, I think that may have been my first slight brush with terrorism. There were more to come.

We both ended up sitting on the curb crying our eyes out while trucks crawled by just a few feet from our little feet. A group of people had formed by the time Mom and Dad returned from a short evening stroll. They thought we were safely asleep. They really were embarrassed. We did our best to keep Mom and Dad on their toes. It's not always easy to train parents!

From my earliest memories, good humour was a part of our life. Occasionally it was at each other's expense. Most often it was a spontaneous general remark. We were not into structured jokes very much. Something from within the family worked best for us, and it kept us close to one another.

Although we apparently did not have much money at all, we kids did not know it. As far as we were concerned, we had the best family on God's earth.

That's something I still believe!

Wisdom Gained: Parents have a divinely appointed obligation to close doors of dangers yet open wide their children's minds and hearts to everything good and godly.

2 I CARRIED HUMOUR THROUGHOUT LIFE

I WAS RAISED IN a home full of humour. We children from that home took it everywhere throughout our lives. We were five, in this order: David, Calvin, Ruth, Lois, and Rick.

When my youngest brother, Rick, was conceived, it came as a bit of a surprise to Mom and Dad. Dad found an interesting and humorous way to announce the coming event to the older four of us.

Lois, the youngest at the time, was seven when Dad took us aside to break the news. "Your mother is going to have another baby." We were all taken slightly aback, since he was really going to be a latecomer.

After Dad got us used to the idea of diapers and crying and all that comes with it, he appeared to turn serious. He said, "I'm a little concerned about this baby." We were all old enough to know that at Mom's age there could be some complications. But that was not Dad's real concern as it turned out. He went on, "I read some facts recently in the *Reader's Digest*. They seem to be true."

By this time, all four of us were fidgeting and somewhat concerned, not knowing what to expect. Then Dad delivered his punchline: "I read that every fifth child born into the world is Chinese!" A totally mischievous use of statistics.

It took a moment to sink in, but then we got it. Statistically the Chinese population was growing at such a rate that one out of every born around the world is Chinese. We laughed with a combination of relief and great hilarity at Dad's way of announcing the news and making it start out on a happy note.

Dad was the source of many a laugh in our home as we all grew up together. That same sense of humour, perhaps in an even more intense form, has been passed on to all of us. That fifth child, Rick, had an almost irreverent intensity eventually—the Reverend Richard Stanley Bombay!

When Mary and I were courting during college, it was that fifth child that we pushed around the block in a stroller in Oshawa whenever we came to my home for the weekend. It was an excuse to be almost alone together.

Later, when Rick was about eight, he came to visit Mary and me in Wellington, Ontario, where we were pastoring. It was shortly after he had been involved in a car accident with our parents. The car had flipped down a hill when a country road in Muskoka had collapsed.

As a result, Rick was having nightmares and could not seem to settle down. After a particularly bad nightmare Mary went into his room and stroked his head until he went to sleep. She fell asleep beside him. When Rick awakened in the morning, both astonished and scandalized that Mary was in his bed, he woke Mary with a loud "What are you doing in my bed?" Mary tried to explain, but he was not buying her story. She fled! Of course, since then he shocks people by telling them that he slept with his brother's wife shortly after we were married. His humour always had a strange twist to it. That is the irReverend part of his personality coming through.

Our father had a reputation as being extremely strict as a father and pastor, but it was always tempered with his humorous streak, which brought both fun and understanding. It appeared both at home and in the pulpit.

To this day, when our family gathers, we start talking on any given subject, and suddenly someone makes a humorous aside. Then someone else adds a remark, and it builds until we all have aching sides from laughing.

We talked shop a lot since we were in Christian ministry. It was at a time when churches were changing their names to such things as "The Gateway" or "The Gathering Place" or "Search's End" and dozens of other names with little implication of "church" in their title. It was also a time when fraudulent Christian leaders were being exposed for financial exploitation of their naive followers. This was rich fodder for the Bombay imagination and creativity.

Lois's husband, Fred, has a rare sense of humour and suggested we start a church called "The Church of the Holy Cassette." That grew into a highly complicated structure of mail-order religion and a mission program called "The Bombay Children's Fund." By the end of that imaginative episode, in our silly joking, we were a fiction that had millions of dollars coming in through the mail, and our children could all have retired by age 12.

It was all imagination and humour, yet we concluded that there were enough naive people in North America that it would probably succeed if someone was unscrupulous enough to launch such an idiot venture. I have lived to see scams using religion as bait for naive donors, making millions for the unscrupulous perpetrators of similar schemes.

We could joke about these things, but there was not one among us who could countenance the frauds who were bringing disrepute on the church and the name of Jesus Christ by using such scandalous methods to dupe the gullible public.

The same held true on the mission field on which Mary and I served. Cross cultural living requires a good sense of humour. With no television, email, or reliable radio reception, all we had was books and each other. Any incident at all became fodder for fun.

Amoebic dysentery was common. Everyone suffered from it from time to time. One of our missionaries, Paul Twigg, a printer in Evangel Press, was out preaching on a Sunday in a church near Nyang'ori, the mission station in Kenya. All went well until he was driving home from the service. The cramps and pain and pressure hit him suddenly. Kip Rotich, an employee of Evangel Press, was with him as interpreter and guide. Paul struggled mightily to contain himself, driving at high speed to get home before he lost control. That was when he hit a rough railway crossing. He lost it, quite literally. I can't imagine what was going through Kip Rotich's mind for the rest of the drive home. Anyone in their right mind would have just stopped at the side of the road to take the problem behind a bush and be done with it. Everyone travelled with a roll of toilet paper, "missionary Kleenex."

When Paul got home, he dropped Kip Rotich off near his home, then tore into his yard right up to his front door and yelled at the top of his lungs for his wife, Marjorie, to "Bring me a blanket!!" Of course, we never let him forget it, and the very inclusion of that incident in this account is designed to remind him once again. He told it to us himself, so we had to assume it was not to be kept secret.

Paul Bruten was a guest of missionaries Wilbur and Ruby Morrison on one occasion. Paul was a missionary working on the Kenya coast. Late one night I heard him laughing outside Wilbur's house across the mission station. His laugh was one of the most distinctive laughs I have ever heard. It was a sort of barking high-pitched blast that carried some distance. I had learned to imitate it quite well.

When I heard it, I answered it in like manner. Silence. Wilbur and Paul continued their obviously humorous conversation, and Paul barked out his laugh again. I imitated it again. This went on a few times. At some point, Paul asked about that "noise" following his laugh. Wilbur was aware of what was happening but didn't want to embarrass Paul or me, I assume. Personally, I wouldn't have minded. The next morning, I asked Wilbur how he had managed it. He said, "When Paul asked, I just told him we have some very unusual night birds that live on this station." Paul accepted the explanation.

On the same station, Keith and Eleanor Morrison were teaching in the secondary school. Keith was the principal. A bunch of us would occasionally get together to play Rook. Mary invariably would bring along a plate of wonderful gooey fresh Chelsea buns as a dessert. Keith would invariably take his out of the centre of the 12 sections on the plate. You know, the one that had the most goo, nuts, and raisins and no hardened edges. We claimed he felt it was his "divine right" to have those particularly coveted centre pieces. It became a joke.

Once, after finishing a game, Keith had to leave for some school business. When he came back, all four centre pieces had been claimed, and the ring of outer buns was all he had for a choice. A broad grin spread across his face, and he simply said, "You guys!"

It was shortly after that when, during an electrical storm, lightning hit our closed-circuit telephone system and blew his set right off the wall. Those old wall-mounted phones had a mouthpiece on a big brown box, with a black earpiece to be held in one hand and a crank to wind with the other, to generate enough power to make the other telephones ring. It would be a collector's treasure these days. Sometimes they even worked.

Without the humour, the games, and the fellowship, both socially and in prayer, living in the fish-bowl closeness of a mission station would have been nearly unbearable.

I seem to have built a reputation for bringing humour into almost everything we did. There were times when a well-placed bit of humour changed what could have been a tense and even rancorous atmosphere into a much more calm and bearable experience.

I still use humour as both a weapon and a balm.

Wisdom Gained: A well-balanced sense of humour often heals, calms, and defuses the most acrimonious atmosphere, even in committee meetings. It often curbs bad intention. "A cheerful heart is good medicine, but a crushed spirit dries up the bones" (Prov. 17:22).

3 BREAKS I HAVE HAD

I BREAK THINGS.

My sleigh was already broken, but it went down College Hill in Oshawa smoothly, right into a big maple tree! I broke my face and my right arm. It's a wonder I didn't break my neck.

My face was my main concern limping home that day. Too much blood and funny movements under the skin and in my nose. My arm really didn't get my attention until later. It was broken and eventually had a cast put on it. I learned to write with my left hand. Everything seems to have a good side to it. I am now somewhat ambidextrous.

I had mechanical interests. I was fascinated by my father's portable Underwood typewriter. He was off visiting the sick, and I was alone in the house. I took it apart to see how it worked. When my father got home, I had a table covered with parts and no idea whatever how to get Humpty Dumpty back together again. My father was not amused; neither was I later …

Sometimes I broke rules. When I was in high school, I decided, since Dad and Mom were off with some other ministers at a convention, I could pretty much have the run of the house and the car. I had no license, but Dad had been teaching me to drive. So, I borrowed the car. It was winter, and the roads were icy, but I wanted to see my cute little heartthrob on the other side of the city.

On the way to her house was one particularly steep and unsanded hill. It led down to the street where Little Miss Heartthrob lived. I got down the hill much faster than planned. Suddenly my thoughts of romance turned to survival. Fortunately, I didn't hit anything. I crept home and parked the car, and no one ever found out until you just read it now. Sometimes you're just plain lucky.

I think confession time is over.

When I got to high school, I found I liked both football and basketball. I didn't break any ankles, but I was often limping around on sprained ankles. My ankles had the most beautiful shades of purple, chartreuse, and yellow sometimes. Our doctor told me not to play basketball. But basketball was my favourite sport, so I played anyway and occasionally got my friends to help me limp home.

My granddad, Rev. Reuben Sternall, prayed for my sprained ankles. The amused twinkle in Granddad's eyes as he came to sit beside my bed before he prayed will always stick with me. "Boys will be boys," his eyes seemed to say. "Let him be a healthy boy, Lord," he prayed as he laid his hands on my black and swollen ankle. I was up the next day. I was able to continue playing with far fewer and less serious sprains.

I had decided to get involved in boxing as a sport. At the local gym I began my career with a knockout. When I came to, the ceiling above me spinning in an interesting pattern. Dizzily I finally got to my feet and wobbled to a bench. There I made a life decision: I'm going to try to stop breaking things, especially if they are a part of me. But later in life …

Wisdom Gained: Help your children find the humour in every situation, even the ones that might seem like a setback or adversity.

4 THE STICK

MY DAD WAS an unusual man in many ways. He was a good father, a good preacher, and a man whom people admired for his integrity. He was always fair, although my siblings and I would often question that quality, as most children do with their parents.

Dad was a man I wanted to be like. I hung around with him as much as I could. I'd ask to go with him when he was off to do almost anything. I was, of course, excluded when he and my mother would visit in the homes of parishioners.

I was never excluded when he went to pick apples at an orchard just west between Oshawa and Whitby. He would pick apples for pay for a few hours to get a little extra income to supplement his pastoral stipend. He would also pick up "grounders" that had fallen from the trees and were bruised, pay for them at a reduced price, and bring them home for Mom to convert into pies, applesauce, pies, apple butter, and more pies.

There were times when Dad would drive out into the country where a church member had kindly offered him space for a garden where he could grow his own vegetables. There were long rows of potatoes, some carrots, beets, and a few other root vegetables, all of which were stored in a cold corner of our basement, in slightly damp sand. They lasted right through the winter.

I remember with relish the day we drove from the centre of the city of Oshawa in Dad's beat-up old hand-painted car (you could easily discern the brush strokes) down Simcoe Street, following a small white frame house sitting on a big flatbed truck. It had been sold to make room for Oshawa's new city hall. Dad had bought a lot in the College Hill area of the city and had built a foundation for the house. As a little kid, I felt like a king as part of the "parade" preceded by a police car, slowly leading the house on the truck as it inched down the street. Hydro workers disconnected wires crossing the street before the house came and reconnected them after we passed. It was an exciting journey. To me it was exciting to know that my dad could activate the whole city. It never occurred to me that it was a normal procedure.

On Sunday afternoons, I enjoyed going to the Genosha Hotel just east of the "Four Corners," where King and Simcoe Streets intersected. The hotel did not have the best reputation, but it was, at the time, one of the tallest buildings in town. Because of this, it had Oshawa's radio station and transmitter on the top floor and roof. I'll never forget sitting in utter silence as my dad would talk to Oshawa over CKDO radio. A simple yet profound Bible teaching, some Christian music, and a prayer, all of which he spoke into a large silver microphone sitting on the desk in front of him.

Dad was also the administrator of justice and punishment in our home. He and Mom shared the administration of much love. Often our punishment would be our forced "withdrawal" from society in the solitary confinement of our bedrooms. At other times it was "the belt" applied to the most teachable part of the human anatomy. It was never too hard but always, in our childish opinions, too much. Sometimes a little lilac switch was applied, never in anger but always with words of advice about the future. We called it "The Stick."

I was often with Dad at the door of the church after Sunday morning services as he greeted people leaving the church. My right hand was in his left as he shook people's hands warmly. I was just there. Not everyone even noticed me. Some said "Hello, Cal," and some would pat me on my very blond head.

One man took the time to shake my hand too and commented, "You're a well-behaved little fellow!" Dad glanced at me with a look that betrayed a deeper knowledge of my behaviour but with a glimmer in his eye and a grin. He said nothing. The man continued, this time with a question: "What is it that makes you such a good little boy?"

I'm sure he expected me to come out with some deep spiritual answer, like "Jesus makes me good," with a giggle. I'm afraid I disappointed him and possibly embarrassed my dad by answering, "The Stick!"

In later years, I often felt that when it came to discipline in our home, the verse that best describes my father would be Psalm 85:10: "Love and faithfulness meet together; righteousness and peace kiss each other."

In the last days of my father's life, Mary and I felt that we should skip church and drive to Oshawa to visit my father. We took our daughter Elaine as well. The same impulse hit my younger brother Rick and his wife, Wendy. The older of my two sisters, Ruth, was also there with her daughter Barb from Detroit. We did not know it at the time, but Dad would suffer heart failure the following Wednesday and pass into the presence of Jesus, whom he served for so many years. That brought an end to the many times when I would go to my father like a magnet to just talk about life, the things of God, and family history.

The older I got, the more I truly understood and appreciated "The Stick."

Wisdom Gained: A disciplined child, given quality time with a parent, even if in silent companionship, develops emotional and mental stability—and acceptable conduct.

5 PAIN AND OBEDIENCE

ABOUT A MONTH before my fourth birthday, I learned a lesson about pain. In fact, years later, I wrote an account of it, in the old King James style of English, which I occasionally use in a sermon on obedience to God. You might as well enjoy it.

> And his mother denied him and said, touch not the pot that boileth on the stove, for thou shalt be burnt and thy skin shall scar for an everlasting remembrance against thee. And Calvin heeded not the words of his mother, Olive. And Cal reached with a mighty stretch and took the handle of the pot in his hand. In his own hand took he the handle of the pot. And boiling water poured forth, and the skin was lifted from Cal's little pot—and the scars remain on Cal's big pot even unto this day as a memorial against him. For Cal was stupid in disobeying the voice of his mother, Olive. (1st Calvin 3:11)

That's not Scripture, but neither is it unscriptural. I learned something about obedience that day. Obedience, especially to God and His laws, brings both protection and blessing. Obeying Mom often protected me from the discipline I would otherwise have cashed in on from my father, had I disobeyed.

The little wood frame house at 52 Mill Street was the second house we lived in in Oshawa. It was in the middle of a block, with a Red and White grocery store about six houses down on the corner to our left. To our right, uphill, were more houses, and at the top was College Hill. It was there one winter that I ran into a tree on my sleigh, mashed my face, and broke my right arm.

That was a painful experience. But it was not the only one. To a child, life can seem to be one painful experience after another. The neighbourhood into which we moved was lower/middle class, but with a few exceptions.

Several houses away there lived two brothers. Ed was a little older than my brother David, and Gord was a little older than me. The day we moved in we knew we were in trouble. They stood off to the side watching David and me while the movers lifted and carried.

Through words and gestures, we were clearly assured that we did not belong and therefore had no rights on Mill Street. Within two days of moving in, both David and I came running home with bloody noses.

Dad talked to the father of these boys. From what little we overheard of the account, he was fortunate to come home without a bloody nose himself. The family clearly demonstrated that they were firmly entrenched in violence and disregard for everyone else's behaviour and thoughts on our street. A beer hall was not too far away, where the father had full visitation rights.

Others on the street had suffered at the hands of Ed and Gord as well, so we suddenly had friends. We belonged to the serfs and peasants, while Ed and Gord were the ruling class. However, their rule came to an end quite suddenly in two separate episodes. One fellow on the street had his heart set on revenge. While he waited for his chance, he practiced, somewhat gently, on the rest of us. When his chance finally came, it came out a little more violently than any of us expected. He wanted to come out of his revenge unscathed. He did!

Ed, the older of the two boys, walked past a thick hedge, and our friend, who shall remain unnamed, stepped out of the hedge behind Ed, grabbed him by the shoulders, with his knee in Ed's back, and pulled hard. Ed's head hit the sidewalk. We had practiced on the lawn. Ed was out like a light. He survived with a well-earned headache. One down, one to go!

Several days later, Gord was coming home from school alone. He decided to give me an overhaul. I had already been whoomphed and intimidated, so he figured that I was easy prey.

What he didn't know was that my preacher dad had given me a bit of counselling. "The next time you are attacked, get your fist into the attacker's face first, and so hard that it's all over before you get hit!" Strange but welcome advice from a preacher. I thumped Gord good! Surprisingly, I managed to knock him down. I was sure his face was sore, so I took pity on him and stuffed his head into a snowbank to assuage his pain. Well, I never really thought of it that way until long after. We never had any more problems with Ed and Gord. Bullies just need to know that they can't get away with it forever.

But it wasn't all pain! We had some good friends in the neighbourhood. Some were the children of members of the church Dad pastored. Others became friendly over time.

My sister Ruth, a young and assumed hairdresser, used a pair of scissors to play "hairdresser" with the daughter of the lady next door. Instead of very long, curly, and beautiful blond hair, she had strange sprouts and tufts pointing out in all directions. Her mother was not amused. They got over it. Ruth, well ...

One of our friends and I were walking home from school. We went down the hill, past the wonderful smell of the bakery, and over the bridge that led uphill to our houses. On the bridge, we found a complete, perfectly round, clean, and unused cigarette.

Ah, the daring of youth! We got a match from somewhere and broke the cigarette into two halves: one half for each of us. We went under the bridge and lit up. Not being very smart about those things, I sucked a whole big lung full of air through those burning tobacco shreds and began to cough and choke and sputter. Tears came to my eyes. I sat for some time trying to recover. As soon as I recovered some semblance of normal breathing, my conscience kicked in. Too late!

I went home. I couldn't handle the idea of supper and went to bed. I pretended I was sick. Nay, I was sick, and I missed a few days of school. I fought guilt until I won, then went back to normal foolish childhood stuff. It was years later when I confessed that little episode to my parents, but I never touched another cigarette.

These were the days when a loaf of fresh bread cost eight cents. Every time we walked past that bakery down by Oshawa Creek, we drooled. Between Murray and me, we decided to save up four cents each until we could buy a loaf on the way home someday. That day finally came. There is nothing like the soft, creamy centre of a freshly baked loaf of bread. Of course, we threw away the crusts—what normal kid wouldn't. My mom wondered why I was off my food again that night. I confessed this one right away since I had plans to commit this sin again.

Kids can be so dumb. I was. I knew where my mother kept a little broken teacup in the cupboard with some loose change in it. There was never very much, but I knew it was there. Every day, on the way home from school, we had to pass the Red and White grocery store.

One of my great weaknesses was potato chips. We seldom had them. I stole a nickel out of the teacup, bought a package of chips, and sat on our front porch eating them. It never occurred to me that my mom might see me and wonder where I got the chips. She found out after some very professional interrogation, and I once again found out that children occasionally have painful experiences.

Some years later, we moved into a beautiful brick house located at 37 Fairbanks Street. It was constructed by the owner, who was a builder by trade. It had oak floors and built-in leaded glass bookcases around a fireplace. David and I shared the room upstairs on the right, our sisters had room beside ours, and Mom and Dad's room was across the hall. I remember the horrible dark rose colour Mom painted the bathroom. It guaranteed that no one would stay in there long. It was just repulsive.

My youngest sister, Lois, was born on my father's birthday, which caused quite a stir. I don't remember her birth as well as Ruth's. Lois just seemed to appear and be there one day—Dad's birthday.

One day, while Mom was preparing dinner, Lois was in her highchair in the dining room next to the kitchen. Lois clambered up onto the tray, then fell to the floor. Mom rushed to rescue her but tripped and fell herself, sliding across the floor, kicking Lois into the corner. By this time, Lois was screaming her head off, and I was crying because I thought Mom had killed Lois. I finally figured she was still alive when her screaming never stopped. Calm finally returned, and supper was served, followed, as always, by family "altar" with all of us kneeling and praying after the meal. Peace!

I lived in that house until I went to college. It was from the front porch of that house that my brand-new bicycle was stolen when I was about ten or eleven. I'd had it for only three weeks. Unnecessary pain for a kid.

My first job was as a newspaper boy for a few years. Then I delivered groceries all over the city from Clark's grocery store. One summer, I painted all the venting on a tannery a neighbour managed. The next job was fitting shoes in one of the two classy shoe stores in the city. Our neighbour owned it. I attended Centre Street Public School from that home.

In a successful attempt to teach me a bit of money management, Dad bought me a costly Gruen self-winding watch for Christmas by putting 20 percent down. The balance was to be paid by me. It worked. I began to understand the value of money. And in our family, that was an essential.

It took some years, but Dad had proven to the other ministers in town that he was neither a fanatic nor a heretic. Eventually he became president of the ministerial association in Oshawa. He was well accepted and respected and had great fellowship with the other pastors in town. He was deeply involved in civic responsibilities as a minister. He participated in Youth for Christ and a dozen other activities outside of our own church on Simcoe Street South. I didn't comprehend it then, but he was an outstanding man of God. To me, he was just Dad!

Dad was not well paid. Dad was very not well paid! In fact, he was so underpaid that, except for Christmas gifts, there were few other treats. Both David and I bought many of our own clothes. Dad never made a big issue over his income. He was called to minister, and that's what he did. When he left that church after 24 years for higher office, he was making $85 a week. The minister who followed him was given $225 a week. Dad never complained. He simply trusted God and practiced good money management. We as children never even knew we were poor. He was a genuine example of Christian character and practice.

Wisdom Gained: As words to the brain activate the intellect, so pain to the body initiates a knowledge of right and wrong, good and bad, and guides to the right.

6 MY FAMILY

SOME RAILWAY STATIONS seemed to have fewer people pass through their doors than our home did when I was growing up. Pastors, evangelists, teachers, and many friends were welcomed. We had many of another type come to our front door begging. We used to call them "hobos": jobless and hungry people.

The stream of hobos coming to our front door began to increase dramatically. They would bypass every other house on the street and come to 37 Fairbanks Street. The hobo grapevine knew where they could get a handout. Dad would always try to give them something. He gave away more than anyone will ever know. But it began to be a serious drain on his personal and scarce resources. Many of the hobos, after getting a bit of coin in their hand, would make a beeline in the direction of the beer store.

After taking this to the church board, Dad arranged a deal with a little variety store down the street. It had a five-seat counter for fast food. Dad would hand out coupons for meals there instead of cash. He was later dismayed to find some of these coupons ripped or crumpled and discarded on the street. At least he was not aiding and abetting a life-destroying drinking habit.

Dad would have holidays, as anyone should. Two weeks a year, as I remember it. Sometimes, we would go to camp at the sandbanks on West Lake near

Picton. Eventually Dad was able to buy the old family homestead up north in Bracebridge where he was raised as a kid. It had been from that house that he first went into the ministry.

That ancient place elicited many memories in Dad that he shared with us as kids. I have recorded many of those in Dad's biography. One of those stories was about an unwanted visitor.

One summer, Dad and I renovated the old house. We slept on the floor, Dad by the window while I slept by the door. One night, Dad told me a story I'd never heard before about the door I was lying next to.

It seems the house was haunted. Years ago, Dad and his brother George were sitting in the living room with their father. The latch on this very door suddenly clicked open, and the door swung open. My grandfather told my dad to close and latch the door. This happened three times in succession. Finally, Granddad got out his toolbox and remounted the whole latch assembly to fix it. He was an engineer and knew how to use tools of any sort. He closed the door and latched it. He put his tools away and sat down again.

As he did, the latch lifted again, and the door swung open. Granddad glared at the door and, in disgust, got a hammer and a long nail and nailed the door shut. This time it stayed shut.

Although I never knew my paternal granddad, he seemed to have taken just about anything that happened in stride. Dad showed me the holes where the nail had been driven in.

Then he told me another story that involved my Uncle George and my grandfather. They heard the outside kitchen door open and close. George looked up and saw the treads of the stairs slightly depress and heard someone climbing the stairs.

They listened to the footsteps, looking warily at one another. The footfalls reached the upper floor and crossed into a bedroom. They heard the creaking of bedsprings as if someone lay down on a bed.

This was too much for George. He raced, yelling, up the stairs. Nothing and no one were anywhere. He scrambled back down the stairs and sat trembling.

Those stories that night led to a discussion about the spiritual realm and the powers of evil forces. This was all rather new to me. I knew my father was not a fanatic or a fool. He was a solid, stable, and intelligent man. He taught me a lot that night about things I had only guessed at before. It put me in good stead for some situations I would face in the future in Africa. He went on to tell me how through prayer those evil forces were expelled from that house, never to be experienced again. My grandfather was still not a Christian, but my grandmother was.

It was also in these relaxed moments when I began to realize some of the heritage I had, from not just my own father but the many kin we had. My Uncle George was a minister, and he and Dad often ministered together before they were both married.

I saw Dad's concern for people demonstrated. His ministry wasn't just from the pulpit. I saw his "extra mile attitude" when he would bring some young man about to stray from God to the Bracebridge cottage. They'd talk while they fished or explored the forests of Muskoka.

My mother was one of four sisters, all of them married to Pentecostal ministers. Their father, Rev. Reuben Sternall, was one of the founding fathers of the Pentecostal Assemblies of Canada, who himself had some odd interpretations of Scripture at times. Family came and went. Doctrinal discussions were an everyday part of our lives, but no one got rancorous or loud about any differences. We have always been a very close-knit family. Doctrinal differences were set aside rather than allowed to rupture relationships. The essentials of the Christian faith were all held in common.

Watching and listening to all this had a profound effect on me as a young person. The foundations of my faith were formed watching and listening to my extended family.

Bracebridge was the summer holiday place for our family. Muskoka seems to be in our genes. Our whole family still loves it. Dad wanted to build a cottage down the hill from the old homestead/cottage after we had renovated it. There were great pine trees on the hillside. My brother David and I went up with Dad one week in the summer to harvest the massive pines and prepare them for a sawmill. The lumber would be used to build the cottage down at the edge of the Muskoka River, across from Flat Rock, where everyone in the family had learned to swim.

After we felled and trimmed several trees, Dad got up on a particularly large pine to lop off some remaining branches. It began to roll downhill with Dad on top. He tried to jump uphill to let it roll away behind him but instead fell in front of the rolling tree. It rolled right over him. David and I stood back horrified, thinking he was dead. After a few minutes, he groaned and painfully got to his feet. With our help he got to the top of the hill. "Let's go home," Dad said.

After having been nearly crushed by the tree, Dad drove all the way from Bracebridge to Oshawa in pain. Had it not been for a slight indentation in the ground covered by a few pine boughs, he would have been a dead man. As it was, he suffered for weeks afterward. I saw the determination of a survivor that day.

The beautiful small cottage was eventually built. Dad also built a plywood punt to get to it from across the river at Flat Rock where the car was parked. I have many happy memories of that place, swimming, fishing, canoeing, and wandering the woods as far upriver as High Falls, where my engineer grandfather had built the first bridge over the Muskoka River.

In Oshawa, my maternal grandparents lived just around the block at 33 Quebec Street. We would often crawl through the neighbours' backyards and fences to go visit Grandma and Grandpa Sternall. There, too, we learned from their recounted personal histories and matters of faith and experience, which contributed to the spiritual growth of all my brothers and sisters.

Almost everyone we were related to or were friends with were either ministers or missionaries.

Ministry was not for this kid! I was going to get a high paying job. Well ...

Wisdom Gained: Good family relationships build character, trust, and healthy personal social attitudes. Most of a child's adult behaviour is established by the adults in that child's life, both good and bad. Be good.

7 SIBLINGS

BEING RAISED WITHOUT brothers and sisters must be a lonely burden. I did not have that burden. I had the other burden: four siblings. They also had a burden—me!

David, the oldest of us all, was born in 1936. He was a genius, though he would have denied that fact. Bell Telephone, with parental permission of course, took him out of high school and continued his training on the job. He started by digging holes for telephone poles and slowly worked his way up into quite responsible positions. He was posted to the far north of Canada on the Distant Early Warning (DEW) line during the years of fear of invasion by Russia over the North Pole. He and a co-worker were responsible for the development of the first direct dialing system in the world. He oversaw a $60,000,000 facility in Kitchener. He never talked about any of it. When we asked him what he did, his answer was invariably the same: "As little as I can!"

He was not allowed to visit certain countries and often travelled with a briefcase shackled to his wrist.

David was deeply involved in church life wherever he was posted. When he retired, he took a few post-retirement consultant assignments in both Holland and the USA. His retirement passion was the research of our family tree. I almost feared what he might have found behind the Bumby—Bombey—Bombay name evolution from England. I mentioned enough about it in my father's biography. He and his wife, Winona, had three daughters. His death by heart attack was sudden at age 66 and left our whole family devastated.

I came in second, as I have most of my life. I also got second-hand clothes. When David outgrew them, I in-grew them. Dad did not have a *new-clothes-for-all* income.

Ruth, the third of this group of five, a registered nurse, married Rev. Calvin Ratz. They pastored in Dorval, PQ, Abbotsford, BC, and Brightmoor Tabernacle, in Detroit, MI. Ruth and Cal had served in Hong Kong as missionaries. Then, when Mary and I were missionaries in Kenya, developing Evangel Publishing House, I wrote to our head office asking for a qualified editor. We needed someone badly. To my surprise and delight, they broke their own rules and sent family, Cal and Ruth, to fill the post.

They lived with us in the same small two-bedroom house with their two children and our two youngsters for months before they were finally given a house to live in at Nyang'ori Mission Station. It was rather confusing at times. Both fathers named Cal! Both sons named John! Just to be sure, everyone answered when anyone was called. The miracle is that we were still friends after living in such close quarters.

Lois was born on my father's birthday, September 4. *That* was a celebration! Lois met and married Fred Mott at Eastern Pentecostal Bible College. They went on to minister in Mactier and Collingwood, then went to Taiwan as missionaries. Later they moved to Frobisher Bay (now Iqaluit, Nunavut) to pastor. Fred went back to college, graduated, and eventually became head of the carpentry department at Conestoga College in Kitchener–Waterloo, Ontario, for many years. Somewhere along the line, Lois earned her LPN. Lois and Fred have a son and a daughter, both adopted, just as Mary and I have adopted children.

Rick was the latecomer, born in 1954. He was born the night that Hurricane Hazel ripped through Ontario. He's caused a stir everywhere he's gone. Rick met and married Wendy Towell at Eastern Pentecostal Bible College (EPBC). Some referred to it as Eastern Pentecostal Bridal College. They pastored in Chesterville, Port Hope, Montreal, Pickering, Havelock, and Oshawa. They had a five-year hiatus in ministry while Rick taught new Canadians the computer skills necessary for job opportunities. Rick was appointed secretary-treasurer of the Eastern Ontario District of the Pentecostal Assemblies of Canada, a position he held for about four years. He helped at Cal Bombay Ministries for some years before retirement. His sense of humour is hilarious and totally irrepressible. He leaves a trail of laughter behind him.

Ours is a very close-knit family. The tensions of childhood melted away to a closeness that is very much absent in altogether too many modern families. A great deal of credit belongs to our mother, Olive, who raised us with love — so much love, in fact, that each one of us thinks we were her favourite child. That takes brilliance. The bearer of these five children passed away approaching 97 years of age. She sat down to dinner one day, bowed her head, and quietly entered the presence of the Lord.

Everyone eventually dies, but the family still grows. I have a great-grandson who will keep carrying the name: Oliver Richard William Bombay.

Wisdom Gained: Family is the pinnacle of human relationships. Guard it with aggressive love. Cherish it so much so that only God's love can exceed it.

8 YOUTHFUL PRANKS

BEING A TEENAGER in Oshawa in the early fifties was both a challenge and a joy, especially as a preacher's kid.

We had a remarkably active youth group at our church. Dad had a special interest in the youth of the church and, indeed, the city. He participated in Youth for Christ, and thus so did I.

Our church youth meetings were held on Friday nights. Sixty or more would attend. There was always a mature man of the church who helped and guided, but the leadership was in the hands of the youth themselves. Scores of young people went to college and into the ministry from that church.

Arnold Bowler was the youth leader for a time. We would later serve together as missionaries in Africa. He was about seven years older than me. But there was a bunch of teens, all about the same age, that I hung around with. Two were especially good friends — Wayne Halliwell, who became a pastor, and his cousin Franz Russell, who became an actor. On Saturday mornings, we met in their grandfather's house and prayed together for several hours at a time.

We also got into some mischief together. Another of their cousins was Stan Weyrich. We often went hunting with bows and arrows in the forest in the undeveloped land near Lake Ontario. We were there when we heard a rifle shot and the ricochet of a bullet pinging by. Suddenly, I was bleeding from a bullet graze on my left shin. My parents never heard of these things until years later, of course. Why should I risk restrictions on an activity we enjoyed? I loved the bush. We never ever did put an arrow into anything but a tree or two. No rabbit was in danger while we were out hunting.

We were consistent in our attendance at the youth meetings. They were good, life changing, and had great impact on many. One Friday night, we heard the front door of the church slam shut and the sound of sirens pulling into the church parking lot. A young man came rushing to the room downstairs where we met, rushed right on through, and threw himself to his knees in the prayer room. Life became remarkably interesting for an hour or so. We could hear voices at the front door of the church. My father came downstairs and quietly asked someone where the guy was.

After a muted conversation, Dad walked through the meeting room to the prayer room without a word, retrieved the young man, and quietly walked back out to the front of the church with him. I never did find out what that was all about. Perhaps the guy had read a book about how people in a distant past were able to rush into a church for "sanctuary."

Most of us have rushed to God in a fit of urgency from either guilt or fear. I don't judge that guy too harshly. We have all been there to some degree! We sure did talk about it at youth group for the next few weeks. We imagined all kinds of scenarios and started all kinds of rumours. We were, after all, just a bunch of teenagers with active imaginations!

It was in those young people's meetings where most of us had our first opportunities to sing publicly or to speak, simply to share our testimony with the others about what God was doing in our lives. It was after those meetings that as a group we would spend long times on our knees in prayer. There much of the future of our lives and relationships was formed. Many a good marriage came out of that group of young people.

We were often mischievous. In the Sunday services, we sat together in the back row of the church. The deacons, ushers, and elders would sometimes feel the bite of our misdirected humour. One of my best friends mounted a pin in the toe of his shoe and stuck it into the leg of an usher. The usher jumped and looked around quickly but was met with pure innocence. He turned away puzzled, rubbing his leg. Some of the men in our church had more grace than our shenanigans could penetrate.

Once, while we were sitting in that same back row, not behaving entirely well, I heard my dad call me from the pulpit. My attention was quickly riveted to reality. Dad was announcing that I was going to come to the pulpit and sing a solo. I almost died on the spot.

Dad had heard my mother and me practicing a song earlier in the week at home. Mom was a very capable pianist and almost always played for the church services. I went to the front and, with knees shaking, sang my first solo in front of the whole congregation. It went right to the heart of the way we were acting during the service. The opening and ending words of the song were "If I have wounded any soul today, if I have caused someone to go astray … Dear Lord, forgive." Ouch!

That launched me on my "singing career." I eventually sang duets with George Bateman, a veteran and mature man in the church. I was in quartets and trios in college. But I always sounded best when I was drowned out by a full choir.

Wisdom Gained: Be involved. The most fun and the best experiences will help us understand our own nature and personality traits.

9 TEEN YEARS

LIFE CAN BE exciting for a teen. It can also stink!

Before the days of driving schools, Dad taught me to drive his car. A few weeks after I got my license to drive, a bunch of us were returning from Geneva Park where we had been swimming most of the day. As we rode our bikes past General Motors, we saw a big crowd in one of their large parking lots. Curiosity grabbed us. We stopped to see what was going on. It was a driving contest.

For a lark, we all decided all to enter it. I was given a 1955 Chevrolet to drive. I felt like a king sitting in the first car with a "wrap around" windshield and that wonderful smell that only a new car has. I came out of that driving contest first for that day. The finals were to be Saturday. I entered, and to my shock and joy, I won. I got a trophy, my picture in the *Oshawa Times* newspaper, and the whole bit! I was a hero in my own mind! I outdid my older brother David, which was always a profound joy, though seldom accomplished.

I chose to go to a vocational high school, Oshawa Collegiate and Vocational Institute. OCVI was north in the city near Oshawa General Hospital. I will never forget the first day I walked through the BIG doors of that big school. I was scared, and among total strangers.

I took as many technical subjects as I could. Drafting, machine shop, auto shop, carpentry, and of course the mandatory readin', ritin', and 'rithmetic stuff. I got involved in the Inter-School Christian Fellowship, where I met some fellow Christians and eventually became leader of the group. Our auto shop teacher, Mr. Lane, was the club's faculty sponsor. He was also a very committed Christian. He was my second auto shop teacher.

The first auto shop teacher was rather ill-tempered, and one day it reached a peak. When I handed in my homework a few moments late, he ripped it up and threw it in the wastebasket. Shy as I was, I told him he had no right to do that. He shouted at me, then threw a hammer at me. It missed me but bounced off one of the undergirding pillars of the three-storey school. The whole class was in a flap. The teacher sent me to the principal's office, where I gladly told all. I guess there must have been other incidents, since the teacher was not there the next week, or ever again.

Mr. Lane came to fill the vacancy Mr. Hammer Thrower left.

Because of my unwillingness to get involved in what, in those days, were questionable activities, I somehow earned the nickname "Pastor."

And I fell in love again. I'll never forget Hermina. She was a gorgeous blonde, with a long ponytail. She caused me a bit of grief—unintentionally of course. She couldn't help it that she was just totally beautiful! I got beaten to a pulp by the schoolyard bully because he liked her too. But I got to carry her books and even hold her hand on the way home from school. This was noted by a church member, who reported directly to my father, "I saw your son holding hands with a girl, and she had lipstick on!" Dad wasn't nearly as dismayed as the church member was. He did mention it to me though, chuckled, and forgot it.

The vice principal, Mr. Roberts, really embarrassed me one day. It happened shortly after the whole school had been given IQ tests. They called me back twice to retake the test, saying there must have been a mistake. But after three tests, they concluded that I had a much higher IQ than I was using. I really did not study too hard but usually came out in the top three in my class.

One day as I was crossing the street on foot with a green light, a car stopped beside me. The door opened, and out jumped Mr. Roberts. He was short. He ran up to me, right in the intersection, reached up and grabbed my shoulders, and shook me, saying, "You can be anything you want to be if you apply yourself!" Then he got back in his car as the light turned. People were watching, wondering what in the world I had done to deserve that. I did not stay around to explain. Red-faced, I ducked into a little restaurant and ordered a 29-cent hamburger.

Wisdom Gained: Being a teen is a difficult phase with conflicting emotions and biological upheavals. A child becoming an adult. Anything can happen unless proper parenting and socializing are established and consistent. Patience is needed for the teenager, but parents need a good dose too.

10 HOLY ROLLERS

AT HIGH SCHOOL, I was the preacher's kid. Not just the son of a minister but a Pentecostal minister. Everyone knew that Pentecostals were religious fanatics and given to strange behaviour at their churches. Or so it was reported by many. Not everyone in the school knew me. A thousand students just don't get to know everybody. A few knew me and either teased me or tried to make my life miserable. Most neither knew me nor cared to.

One incident was quite accidental but, in the end, comical. I saw a group of students on a Monday morning in the upper hall overlooking the school auditorium. This was not unusual between classes.

The centre of attraction was a student who was describing what he had seen in the Pentecostal church on the previous Sunday evening. He explained in detail how he saw people leaping up and swinging from the chandeliers in the church and rolling down the aisles.

A crowd was growing around him, hanging on every word. I suspect that none of them had ever been in a Pentecostal church and that few had been to any church. I listened for a while, then wormed my way closer to the storyteller. I started feeding him leading questions and he responded with crude but enticing details of ridiculous fantasies about the antics of the people in the church. After letting him commit himself to a great number of claims, I finally spoke up, loudly enough to be heard by everyone in his small audience.

I said, "I was there last night too … I didn't see any of what you claim you saw. I was there until the end of the service. In fact, my father is the pastor of that church, and I have never seen anything quite like what you've described. And I didn't see you there."

An awkward silence followed. The fellow turned quite an attractive deep pink, and the crowd walked away laughing. I gained a few friends that day. And those who knew me still called me "Pastor" in a kindly way.

Despite the claims at that time that Canada was a Christian nation, of the more than 1,000 students in that high school, our Inter-School Christian Fellowship rarely had more than 20 students turn up for our meetings.

Years later, I found that two other students from that school had become ministers, saying that one of the single strongest influences on them was my life and testimony. I found that hard to fathom since I was not particularly overt in my Christian witness. Perhaps it had more to do with the things I did not do than the things I did! Another student, many years later, phoned me at my office at *100 Huntley Street* to tell me he too had finally come to know Jesus Christ as his Saviour and wanted me to be one of the first to know.

We did have several Christian teachers, but even back then in 1956 to '68, schools had begun their inexorable move away from the teaching of moral values.

Quite often, it's what you don't and won't do that has more influence on others than what you say or claim. Words have more power when they are backed by a simple but biblical lifestyle. I didn't consider myself either holy or a holy roller. The most rolling I ever did was on a football field after being tackled. As a Pentecostal kid, I also learned to roll with the punches. In later years, the Pentecostal churches were almost eclipsed by the charismatic movement, and some Pentecostal churches have become almost an historical blip on the scene of world Christianity. Yet statistics do show that those who embrace Pentecost as a present-day experience are the leaders in world evangelism, no matter what denominational tag they tie to themselves.

Wisdom Gained: It is often how you act and what you do or refrain from doing that has great influence on your peers. Actions do speaker louder than words.

11 COLLEGE DAYS

MOTHER USED TO say about me and my brother Rick, "They were all right until they went off to Bible college."

Looking back, I realized that both our parents were strict with us five children. In the early 1900s, modern Pentecost was born from within the "Holiness" movement. The movement was known for its strict rules about how you should conduct yourself. Some of the rules had a clear biblical basis. Others were born from someone's personal convictions while the Pentecostal movement blossomed. We were born and raised within that box.

I tended to look at that box with a slightly different view.

I did not always listen too attentively at Bible school. I grew up in a pastor's home, so I had a good theological foundation by osmosis. There was a lot I already knew. And there were a few things I only thought I knew. Still other subjects which were both challenging and cause for some deep thinking. Was I really up to going into ministry?

Eastern Pentecostal Bible College was in Peterborough, Ontario, back in 1956 when I arrived. The fact that I even arrived there was somewhat of a miracle. You had to have the recommendation of your home church pastor. In my case, my father.

Right off the block, my father tried to discourage me from going into the ministry at all. He wanted to totally avoid the possibility of one of his offspring going into the same calling as their dad just to follow in his footsteps. The ministry was a serious and divine calling. He was concerned that there were already too many people filling pulpits who looked at it as a profession rather than true ministry. I have come to agree with him on that point. He insisted that I be certain that ministry was what God wanted me to do. I confidently told him it was.

Stage One—passed.

Stage Two. Scores of young people went to Bible college from the church in Oshawa while Dad was pastor. Dad, as an experienced pastor and church leader, had some standards by which he measured a person's suitability both to go to Bible college and to go into the ministry. One of them was church attendance and involvement. I just barely passed scrutiny on this one.

Yes, I attended church faithfully, both services on Sunday. Yes, I attended and took part in some leadership in the young people's meetings on Friday evenings. But with the Wednesday night prayer and Bible study I came in a little weak. That was his sticky point.

I participated in outreach and evangelism. I froze my toes one winter going from door to door on Bloor Street in Oshawa passing out invitations to an upcoming week of evangelism. I occasionally sang solos in both Sunday and Friday services. I sang duets with George Bateman in church, in retirement homes, and in prison ministry. I conducted services for the elderly in a retirement home in Whitby and drove a bus every Sunday afternoon for months to the northern extremes of Oshawa, helping to plant a church: first a Sunday school on the bus in a supermarket parking lot, then helping in the founding of the new Byng Avenue church.

Finally, and perhaps somewhat reluctantly, I was approved by my pastor.

Stage Three. Pack up and go. I was poor as a church mouse. Dad was not much better off financially. How was I going to pay for this? I had been working at Davidson's Shoe Store and had some money laid aside. I had heard that seasonal jobs were available to college students at the post office in Peterborough. I worked in construction during summer holidays, helping to build a Presbyterian church on Sheppard Avenue in Agincourt. Somehow, I scratched enough money together to pay tuition and board.

When I arrived, freshmen did not get the choice rooms. I ended up on the third floor of the old Nicholls Hospital, which had been bought and converted into a college with both residences and classrooms. My roommates were Murray Griffin and Bob Haskins. We did some mischievous things.

I did gain a great deal of unbelievably valuable information in those years, not all of it theological. In fact, some of it wasn't even logical. For instance, I found out that Norma-Jean Mainse had a pet name for her brand-new husband, David Mainse. Years later I used that knowledge to jokingly tell David that I'd reveal the name to the whole staff of *100 Huntley Street*. I never did that, of course. I mean, can you imagine what the staff would have done had they known that Norma-Jean called David "Poopsy-Doll" those many years before? Oops! Well, it's written now, and I can't seem to find the delete button.

We did some normal college kid things. Once, in the middle of winter, I received a bucket of snow and slush full on while I was taking a hot shower. That was cool. We also tried to make a classmate wet his pants by leaking warm water from a hot water radiator in the old classroom and dipping his fingers into a cup of it while he slept in class. It didn't work, so we poured it onto his chair strategically.

The college had previously been a hospital and was slowly following the fate of many of its patients. The morgue was where we used to store suitcases and travel trunks. We also made use of its imaginary ghosts from the past.

Bob Haskins was from British Columbia, and Murray Griffin and I were from Ontario. We three were also editor, sales manager, and business manager of *The Torch*, the college yearbook. This gave us special privileges of which we took excessive advantage. These privileges were never ever spelled out. We simply took them, if you understand what I mean. We had control of the dark room and the camera and were allowed to stay up late to tend to our duties.

Our class was called the Witnesses based on Acts 1:8. We were told years later that 72 percent of our class entered the ministry. Les Grant wrote our theme song, "Witnesses." Bob, Murray, Nathaniel (Nat) Vaters from New-foundland, and I formed the Witnesses Quartet. We were acceptable enough to be sent out on assignments to sing, preach, and promote the Bible college in local churches throughout Ontario and Quebec on weekends. Murray played the piano for most songs, and we often sang with no accompaniment. We had close harmony.

Murray, Bob, and I felt it was one of our duties to scare the daylights out of Nat. Bob sang baritone, Murray sang bass and played the piano, I sang tenor, and Nat sang lead until we exploited his superstitions one night.

Nat's dorm room was a former utility room that had space for one bed. One night the janitor, Pop, with whom we all had a friendly relationship, reached into Nat's room to turn on the light. The problem was that Pop had several fingers missing from that hand, and in the dim light, Nat saw this claw-like hand above his head and screamed as though he was being stabbed. It brought everyone to their dorm doors looking for the source of the blood-curdling scream. That offered interesting opportunities. Now please remember, we were college kids and had not quite reached maturity in some ways.

We decided Nat needed another night visitor. We planned well. Bob took a metal trash can, and Murray had the camera ready. I had a green towel over my head with two flashlights turned on to appear like big green eyes and was wrapped in a white sheet. We entered the room quietly. Nat was buzzing away rhythmically in a deep sleep. Bob said in an eerie voice echoing out of the trash can, "Nat Vaters, we've been waiting a loooooong time for this!" He repeated it several times. Slowly Nat's eyes opened and focused on me, with my two green "eyes"! Suddenly both Nat's legs kicked out and walloped me in the stomach, throwing me against the wall with a crash. Murray got a flash picture of the action. We fled.

In the morning, Nat was describing in detail, to anyone who would listen, the "visitation" he'd had had from the devil during the night. Finally, we confessed it was us. He didn't believe us! We were hurt! He didn't believe us, his friends! We travelled together singing! We studied together! We were friends! But he was sticking with the devil on this one.

Since Murray, Bob, and I were the staff of the school yearbook, we rushed down to the dark room and developed and printed the picture. It wasn't until we showed it to him that he abandoned the devil interpretation and blamed it on three other devils. Even that just barely convinced him. We remained friends for life, of course.

Within a week or two, all four of us as the Witnesses Quartet were sent to one of the larger churches in Montreal. Everything seemed to be going well. Murray was at the piano with a microphone, Bob and Nat and I behind the pulpit with microphones. As we sang, Nat began to go flat as lead singer. By the time we had ended the song, Nat was about two full notes flat.

Later, we had a horrible thought. We suspected the fright we had given him was traumatic to some degree beyond our plans. I really hope that wasn't the cause. The three of us could not seem to apologize enough to Nat. Though his singing was affected, Nat brushed it off with true Christian grace. I would like to forget that whole weekend. And thus was born the Witnesses "Trio."

Eastern Pentecostal Bible College has clear goals, an appropriate form of intellectualism, and a deep commitment to training people for Christian ministry. We prayed a lot.

The quartet (now trio) had to drive to a weekend assignment, and since the school provided no funds for such assignments, we had to pray and pay our own way. We prayed for gas for my old 1949 Chevy. The car been my dad's. When he traded it in, my brother David bought it back. When David later traded it in, I bought it again for $100. It was a family heirloom by then.

Two nights before our singing assignment, there was a $10 bill in a blank envelope under our dorm door. That was in 1957. To us it was a miracle. The gas was paid for.

Several school rules irked us. No radios or electrical appliances were allowed in the dorm rooms. Murray had an asthmatic condition that required him to put some menthol medicine into a pot and boil it into the air of the room. We all enjoyed the benefits of that hot plate. We also enjoyed its misuse. You cannot be a college student without taking some advantage.

One late evening, when we were taking advantage of Murray's condition, we heard the familiar tapping on the walls between rooms that warned that the dean of men was prowling the hall. Some students would sneak out past curfew for various reasons. Our problem that evening was that we were in. We were using Murray's medical device to pop corn and melt butter. What a delicious smell! When we heard the tapping on the wall, we took up our deceptive positions.

Tap, tap! Rev. Norm Schlarbaum, dean of men, "Force for God and Good," and former army sergeant, opened the door. With a puzzled look on his face he said, "I smell popcorn!"

We answered in innocence, "Yeah, it does smell like popcorn, doesn't it!" I got up from my desk and stuck my head out into the hall. "You can smell it out here too!" Bob was on his bed with a textbook in hand. Murray was sitting on the floor leaning against his bed, hiding the hot plate, with a textbook in hand. The "Force for God and Good" looked around, and everything seemed all right, even while a few more kernels of corn audibly popped under the bed behind Murray. The door slowly closed. The popcorn that night was especially tasty!

I must confess that, although we were getting good marks in our classes, we were also building a bit of a reputation. We admitted it with a certain amount of … dare I say "pride." I should also admit on our behalf that Murray's dad was a professor in the college, my dad was the assistant district superintendent, and Bob was related through marriage to the president of the Bible college. That gave us no special privileges. We simply gave ourselves the privileges.

Dr. Ratz was dean of the college. Occasionally, he would visit in the dorms with the students, just to get to know us all better. Everyone loved him. He came to our door one evening, tapped, and was invited in. As Dr. Ratz began to enter the room, he paused, and his jaw dropped. He stared at the wall, then at the ceiling, then at us, then back at the ceiling. The walls were yellow, and the ceiling was white—well, mostly. It was badly in need of paint. But before we painted it, we did some "decorating."

Since Bob was the lightest of the three of us, we smeared the bottoms of his feet with black shoe polish then supported him bodily as he walked up the wall, across the ceiling, around the light, and back down another wall. Dr. Ratz stood transfixed, his mouth open, his eyes wide, staring at those black footprints. Then he burst into laughter, closed the door, and left. Please note, none of us was related to Dr. Ratz yet. It wasn't until years later that his son Cal married my sister Ruth.

I think it was on that occasion, or it could have been another (there were so many), that we three were called to the office of C. B. Smith, the college president. He sat sternly behind his desk, with Dr. Ratz standing behind him on one side and The Force for God and Good on the other. All looked very solemn. We three lined up in front of President Smith's desk.

They looked at us in silence for far too long. C. B. Smith snickered, and then all three of them began to laugh uncontrollably. We joined in as well. When we had all regained composure, we were told it was a serious matter and not to repeat anything like it again, whatever "it" was that time. We left the room, dazed and unpunished. And we never did anything like it again—at least not quite the same. We did clean and paint the room.

Some people were in the habit of coming into our room without knocking. We decided to put an end to this intrusive behaviour by our lawless fellow students. We left the door partly open, with a plastic pail of water balanced on top. How were we to know that the first person through the door would be the dean of men, The Force for God and Good? As he pushed the door open, the pail of water came down in full flood all over The Force for God and Good. He was not amused, but he had broken his own rule of going into a room without the common decency of knocking or calling out. We were doing everything we could to train our teachers, but sometimes it just seemed futile.

That was our freshman year in college.

In second year, we could choose our rooms. We chose one on the second floor with a sink, a closet, and a few other amenities that none of the other rooms had in that ancient hospital building. No decorating was needed. The room was a former delivery room with white tiled walls. No decorating was possible! The floor was polished terrazzo. It was one of the elite rooms on the second floor, near enough to the two main classrooms that we could make a last-minute mad dash to be in class on time.

That room was the noisiest place in the college, but not because of the three tenants. Because of the terrazzo floor and tiled walls, it echoed and amplified the slightest sound. One night, Bob, Murray, and I were startled awake by explosions and the smell of gunpowder. We jumped out of our beds, terrified.

Finally, we discovered the remains of the firecrackers someone had thrown into our room. It took us a while, but we tracked down the culprits. It was David and Bob Smith, sons of the president of the college, and their cousins. They wanted revenge on us for picking the best room. David Smith would go on to become a respected lawyer and a minister in Pierre Trudeau's government. Bob experienced a lengthy revival while he pastored in London, Ontario.

Morris Fostrey came to class late one morning. This wasn't unusual. Rev. Herb Bronsdon was in mid-lecture when Morris opened the door, casually walked over to his desk, and sat down. Professor Bronsdon stopped lecturing and quietly stared at Morris as he made his way to his desk, his face stoic.

"Morris, why are you late?"

Morris stood and answered, "Sir, I had cornflakes for breakfast."

We all sat in stunned silence, replaying his answer in our minds. Finally, Prof. Bronsdon said, "Okay," and resumed lecturing. It was the joke of the college for days.

Our professors, teachers, and staff had as much fun as the students. C. B. Smith often sat in the foyer of the college in one of the big soft chairs. It was right next to his office, so he would take advantage to catch a few moments of respite. One time, he fell asleep, snoring quite contentedly. His wife, Beulah, came across him and signaled everyone to be silent. C. B. snored on in blissful ignorance. Beulah found a tape recorder and swore us all to secrecy.

The next day, in chapel, Beulah asked for a moment to play "a tape she had received from the mission field, of the sounds of wild lions in Africa." She then played the tape. C. B. listened for a few moments, totally unaware of the duplicity of his own wife. Like wildfire, the snickering became a roar of laughter. C. B. was confused, until his wife explained what it really was. C. B. turned as red as a face can get, but he was used to this kind of thing. He also wasn't above getting even.

Beulah taught music at the college. We were all gathered in the chapel to practise the "Hallelujah Chorus" in preparation for the upcoming graduation ceremonies in Toronto. Beulah was late that day. As she walked through the door everyone broke out in perfect harmony to the score of Handel's *Messiah*, "Hello, Beulah! Hello, Beulah! Hello, Beulah, hello, Beulah. Helloo-oo-oo, Beulah!" Some felt it was irreverent. Personally, I enjoyed it.

I could mention how my clothes and towel were stolen once when I was taking a shower. The fact that the men's showers were in the basement, near the old morgue under the women's wing of the college, made my escape to the safety of the men's wing a little more perilous, but I did it undetected.

As for Eastern Pentecostal *Bridal* College, many couples met and married, going into ministry together. Worked for me! Mary entered my life there. For that alone, I consider it "holy ground."

Mary was someone else's steady date at the time. The school had strict rules when it came to the boy-girl thing. No hand holding, no closer than a foot from someone of the opposite sex. We were allowed a monthly weekend at home and one date per week while we were at college—with written permission.

I had a previous love interest in Lansdown at the time, so I was not into any dating. I went skating with various girls on the Trent Canal, but nothing serious. I was being faithful to an idea. But that finally ran its course, and we decided that the relationship was not what God had for either of us.

Breakfast duty was a part of every student's activities. On a rotating basis, we had to serve the rest of the students breakfast trays, then have our own.

Mary turned up several times on duty at the same time I was on duty, both of us wearing sweaters of the same brilliant red. Several people remarked on how well we were matched. I noticed Mary more and more often, and not just at breakfast duty.

I learned that she too had broken up with her beau. Hmmm! But the competition was stiff. Now that she was free, it seemed all the guys in the college wanted to get to know her better. What a beautiful blonde! And smart! In the end, I won. We began to eat our meals together at lunch and dinner. We borrowed a rickety old Prefect car and took a drive on a Saturday up toward Lindsay. I learned that her father was a professional commercial photographer and her mother was the youngest of ten children, raised on a farm near Cannington, Ontario. Her dad was of United Empire Loyalist stock.

Before I let this relationship go much further, I had to find out something vital to me. I felt that God was eventually going to put me in missionary service. I asked questions all around the subject. As it happened, we were already both members of the Africa Prayer Band. Mary told me of a vision she had had as a child of 12. She saw herself under a tree, teaching African children. She stated that she was called to missionary work. I headed for the prayer room. I spent most of the night there. By morning, I was sure. So, I asked her if she'd be my wife, and she accepted.

Perhaps I'm of the old school, but I felt it necessary to ask her father as well. When I finally got up the courage to ask, he was silent for altogether too long. Then, with a twinkle in his eye, he said, "Well, you're the best of the crummy lot. Yes, you can marry Mary." Then he added, "You might just as well not support her as I!"

We tied the knot on January 17, 1959, in Willowdale Pentecostal Church, with my father and Mary's pastor, Rev. Willis McPherson, officiating. Two days later, my parents left for Africa as short-term missionaries.

We had a short honeymoon; then I went back to school. Since Mary had already graduated, she went back to Toronto to a job that paid some real money. She bought me my first heavy winter overcoat, and we lived on a shoestring. Meeting and marrying Mary was worth more than all three years at college, the tuition, room, and board, as well as the frustrations that beleaguer any college student. She is my most wonderful living memory of those years.

We had been called to pastor Wellington Pentecostal Church even before graduation. I would drive to Toronto, pick up Mary, then go to Wellington for weekend services. Then, after the Sunday night service, we did the whole drive in the other direction.

After graduation, we moved to Wellington. Along with all the fun we had in college, there was serious preparation for ministry taking place, not just in our heads but also in our hearts. There were weeks of intensive prayer. Visiting missionaries, pastors, evangelists, and teachers came and poured truth and their experiences into our lives.

Our school years were full of optimism, discouragement, and financial pressure. Weekends were often busy in assigned ministry, singing, and preaching. At times, I did not have money to buy gas to put in the car, but God answered prayer. You've already read about one time that God answered a quiet plea for funds. We were learning that miracles still happen. I did not find that hard to believe. I had seen a lot of it in my own father's ministry. But even more important, the Bible clearly taught the same thing, "until the end of the age."

We thought we'd learned everything there was to know, theologically, historically, and doctrinally, in relation to the distinctive doctrines of Pentecost and practical areas of ministry. As students, we argued and discussed the finer points of doctrine, eschatology, pneumatology, you-name-it-ology. We took strong positions on dichotomy and trichotomy, hardly knowing what the words meant at first.

We read. We studied. We listened. We even fell asleep in class occasionally. We learned how to run a Sunday school and how to perform a wedding. We even had to do extra practice preaching in front of the whole student body. This was perhaps the most difficult challenge since everyone knew everyone else so well, and everyone was quite willing to point out weaknesses. By graduation, we thought we knew it all. After our first few weeks in a pastorate, we felt like we did not know a thing. There are some things formal education just cannot prepare you for in ministry.

It was the godly elders in that first church who kept my nose above water. We had evangelists come and go, usually leaving good spiritual fruit behind and often an empty larder. Despite my callow youthfulness and some very stupid mistakes, God blessed our feeble efforts, and with all my weaknesses, the church grew. I learned some extremely important lessons in Wellington, some of which protected me in the years to follow.

In other words, school is never over.

Wisdom Gained: A college education is very useful, but real life can suddenly reveal how very little you actually learned and how much more challenging life in the real world can be.

12 FORCED MARRIAGE

ACCORDING TO THE rules, students were not allowed to marry during school terms. I expect it was based on the possibility, perhaps probability, that such college romances had no depth and might be in question in the long run.

Mary and I had already become engaged to be married, and we were planning on a June wedding in 1959. Something happened that changed all that. We suddenly had to fast-track our wedding due to circumstances over which we had no control. No, Mary was not "with child," as one malicious fellow student began to spread as a rumour. It was simpler than that.

By 1958, Dad was superintendent of the Eastern Ontario and Quebec District and assistant general superintendent of the Pentecostal Assemblies of Canada (PAOC). He was also a member of the general executive. As they sat in session one day, they were faced with a dilemma. There were problems on one of our mission fields, Kenya. A leader with some authority needed to go and address those problems. There was also a great need to gather many people who had accepted the Lord in a large tent campaign in Nairobi. Dad was the man they finally settled on, and after he talked with Mom, it was decided they would go to Kenya, leaving on January 19, 1959, for a two-year term.

As you can imagine, that was somewhat disappointing to Mary and me, since we wanted my father to tie the knot along with Mary's pastor from Evangel Temple in Toronto. The answer was simple. We'd get married on Saturday, January 17, two days before my mom and dad and my three younger siblings headed for Kenya.

There was only one problem. That school had a rule.

With fear and trembling, I decided to ask C. B. Smith for an exception to the rules, due to circumstances beyond our control. As I approached his office, I had an inspiration! I would simply tell him we were getting married on January 17.

Rev. C. B. Smith was a congenial man. I was friends with his firecracker-loving sons, David and Bob. I was hoping that C. B. Smith might have some of the same sense of adventure, daring, and good humour as his sons.

I stood before his desk. C. B. looked at me with questioning expectation. I finally blurted out that Mary and I were getting married on January 17 because Dad was leaving for Kenya two days afterward, and I sped on with the explanation. He was on his feet, around the desk, and shaking my hand in congratulations before I had fully explained. I fled with joy, before he remembered the rules.

So, we were married in Willowdale Pentecostal Church on January 17 in below-freezing weather. It was so cold that Mary's wedding gown froze to the church steps as we had our pictures taken. I had been standing on the hem of her dress, keeping the salt from melting the ice. She was rigidly attached to that church! It almost caused a disaster as we started walking down the steps to the waiting car. Mary's wedding dress almost decided to stay where it was.

The next day we attended the church service in Oshawa, where people for some strange reason said we were "so brave" to come to church the day after we were married. Brave? Our bravery continued as we had to bid farewell to my family the next day at Toronto International Airport. Their flight left early, so we started our honeymoon trip in below-zero weather. Great for cuddling! We borrowed Mary's father's 1956 white Chevrolet. My father-in-law was very fussy about his cars all his life, yet he did us that favour.

Two major incidents stand out in our memory during that honeymoon. As we left Canada for the USA it was well below freezing. It remained frigid until we were approaching Cincinnati, Ohio. Then wind and rain came in torrents as the temperature rose to 70 F degrees. We holed up in a motel, and in the middle of the night a 40-foot sign came crashing down into the parking lot, just missed the Chevy!

The next morning, we continued our journey south, we thought. As we approached the main bridge over the Ohio River, we saw flashing lights and a mass of cars. It was an awesome sight. The bridge had been closed because the waters had risen so high from the rain and melt. There was a barn with a dog spread-eagled on the roof, floating and just about to hit one of the main stanchions. Parts of houses and uprooted trees pounded on the bridge's stanchions. We checked back into the motel, where they were getting the fallen sign out of the way. Eight dollars a night was more than we wanted to pay, but we had little choice.

We never did get to our destination, for reasons neither of us can yet explain, although weather was a part of it. We headed back. It was on the return trip that our second notable and, for me, petrifying experience occurred.

In Pennsylvania, in 1959, they did not use salt on the roads to combat ice. Thus, the roads were ploughed almost free of snow, but what remained was packed into wonderful, slippery black ice. A big flatbed transport slid to a stop in front of us at a red light. I touched the brakes, but the car did not slow down a bit. I let up off the brakes and steered for the curb. I almost made it, but the front left fender was sliced open by the steel of the flat bed. It was a deep open cut, about 16 inches long. I thought I'd die. Mary's dad loved his car and had let us have it with some hesitation.

We drove back to Canada and straight to Peterborough, bypassing Toronto since we couldn't stand the thought of facing my father-in-law with the fender messed up. We took a motel room in Peterborough, and I looked for a body shop. When I explained what had happened, and all the circumstances, the owner of the shop, who knew me from church, said he could fix it "and you won't be able to find where it was." Well, he did the job. It cost me 13 dollars. I looked for the repair, and just as he had said, I could not find a trace of difference from the original state of the fender.

I breathed easier when I told my father-in-law, Bill Deacoff, to come and look at the damage I had done to his precious car. He searched and searched and could find nothing. I handed the keys back with effusive thanks and started breathing again.

I finally bought back my family's heirloom, the 1949 Chevy Torpedo. I sold it when two pistons disintegrated on the road between Peterborough and Oshawa. I just kept driving, engine clattering, until I parked it in our church parking lot. It never started again. I sold it as junk for 25 dollars. That was less than the value of all the fishing tackle I forgot about in the trunk of the car!

My next car was a peanut Volkswagen, and that was an experience too. That Volkswagen took Mary and me into our first pastorate in Wellington, Ontario.

Wisdom Gained: Make as detailed plans as you can, but always be ready for the unexpected. Life will unquestionably have those "It is what is" moments. Learn to develop perspective as a Christian. It eventually works together for good.

13 ME —A MISSIONARY?

FROM NINE YEARS of age, even before I had really become a true Christian, I had the uncomfortable feeling that I'd be a missionary someday.

·I had my escape route already worked out. I would go to Ryerson College, tuck some technical stuff in my head, then make my own quiet and prosperous way in life. Sure, I was just a teen, but I knew my own mind, and it had been made up!

I had even lived a Christian life! You betcha! My father was a preacher, so I had to behave like a Christian. But deep down inside there was no spiritual life at all. I prayed with the rest of the family around our family altar after dinner every day, but it was rote, nothing more. I had no sense of the presence of God or of His reality. I had to search for prayers that would be acceptable to my parents' ears. God could listen too if He wanted. That was in late 1951.

"But God." How often had I heard those words from both the Bible and Christian people? I had my own "But God" to manage. It was a Sunday night. I don't remember what Dad preached that night. I'd heard it all anyway, so I hadn't really listened. I came home and went to bed. That was the night when either a hurricane or a strong wind and rain came to our neighbourhood. I watched out my bedroom window as a foot-thick branch was torn from the trunk of a maple tree. I got scared.

I also got thinking. What if that other, bigger branch leaning toward the house and my window were to come crashing down? Was I ready to die? No, I was not! I crawled under the covers and began to think of all I'd heard about eternity, God's judgment throne, the Second Coming of Jesus Christ. I got sober. My brother was older and out with some of the church teens. Dad had not yet come home from the church.

I got out of bed and went down to the kitchen, where my mother was singing and washing the dishes. "I thought you were in bed!" she said.

"I was, but I want to give my life to Jesus. I want to know that I'm saved."

Mom and I knelt beside one of those ugly red vinyl chrome tube kitchen chairs and wept my way into the arms of Jesus. It is an experience I couldn't forget if I wanted to. Something deep inside of me changed and never unchanged. I don't know that anyone else noticed the change, because I had been putting on a pretty good act up until then. Yet I certainly experienced a difference.

But I still wasn't going to go into the ministry! No way!

Time passed.

I attended a youth rally with a friend of mine, Martin Hummel, an Austrian friend who had immigrated from Europe. He drove us in his father's paint truck to the rally 16 miles away in Port Perry, in a high school auditorium.

At the end of the service, I saw a young man for whom I had heard my father praying one day. I knew little about him other than he was married and had recently become a Christian. I felt a strange urge to go up to the front of the auditorium where he was standing and to pray for him. His name was Jack Mercer. I gently placed my right hand on his left shoulder. I began praying quietly. This was very much out of character for me. I was basically shy.

Suddenly and without asking God for anything at all for myself I found myself praying out very loudly in another language. This went on for a long time, and finally I quieted down. As I did, I saw flashing lights and thought perhaps I was going to have a vision or something of that nature. I opened my eyes, and to my utter surprise I was alone at the front of that high school auditorium. Martin was at the back leaning against the doorframe, waiting for me. The janitor was flashing the lights on and off. So much for my impending vision! But I was completely captivated with the reality and presence of Jesus. I'd heard about this and seen it often in the church where Dad pastored, but man, was I super-charged!

Acts 1:8 became my experience that night. I couldn't stop talking about Jesus. As I remember it, Martin got an earful about Jesus.

I was still adamant about not going to go into the ministry. I was 17 now, and my own plans were becoming clearer. I was going to go to Ryerson in Toronto.

I went to Lakeshore Pentecostal Camp for the youth camp like I did every year. I was as mischievous as anyone else. Slamming cabin shutters in the middle of the night, testing and teasing the camp "cops," was our normal before-bed activity. Then Wednesday night came. That experience is told in the next chapter. When I got off my knees that night, I knew the whole notion of going to Ryerson was cancelled and that I'd be going to Bible college to study for the ministry. And here I had spent four years taking technical courses in high school to try to under-qualify myself for the ministry. What a waste, I thought.

Wisdom Gained: You don't really have a life plan until it fits into the future and the hope that God has for your life.

14 THE CALL

ALL PASTORS START pastoring before they are really qualified. No exceptions. What is learned in Bible colleges, seminaries, and theological schools can't really prepare you for the totally unpredictable situations that a pastor must deal with. Certainly, theology is a big part of pastoral training, but it doesn't quite prepare you to deal with a husband walloping his wife while in a drunken rage.

I was asked to come "preach for a call" in Wellington, Ontario. Wellington is a small town in beautiful Prince Edward County near Belleville and Trenton. Mary and I went with some trepidation. It was March.

Our first impressions were not good. It was that time of year when the snow is melting. All the dirt and garbage that has been covered in a blanket of glorious white snow starts to show. The town looked run down and grey.

We got to the church a good half hour before the service was to begin. It was unlocked, so we went in. It was deserted. Within a minute or so, an older lady came and sat near the back. For the next 15 minutes, we listened as she mournfully kept repeating in a sing-song voice, "If we can't get along down here, how are we ever going to get along in heaven!" By the time more people began to arrive we were wondering how we'd ended up here.

I remember only a little about that service. The crowd was little. I felt little. The few who were there to hear me showed little or no reaction to my preaching. We had a little chat with a few people, including some board members. We left thinking we had made little impression. We thought, "Well, that's that!"

We drove out of town after eating a meal with the O'Brien family. We knew that the church had previously been a United Pentecostal Church, which did not believe in the doctrine of the Trinity, though they were committed Christians. It had come into the PAOC a few years earlier and was struggling. There were a few other things we did not know until later. It had changed associations with various denominations over the years. One day as I was searching the records of the church, I found that it had been associated with "The Fire Baptized Church of the Holy Ghost of the Hill of Kentucky." That gave me pause!

Word came that we had received a 100 percent vote. All 13 voting members wanted us. We did not know whether to be elated or deflated. Someone had told us that it was a "burnt-over field," without much of a future.

We accepted the invitation and the 25-dollar weekly stipend. We also received a 25-dollar monthly subsidy from our denomination's district office to help rent a house. We learned to trust God. We had to trust God. We lived out of town in a little frame house (very little) on Gore Road. The man who owned the farm next to our house, Bruce Wilson, told us to help ourselves from his tomato and corn fields. We often did. We had to!

Pastoring your first church can be a daunting experience. There were four other churches in the town of 1,050 people, two of them active. The pastor of the High Anglican church did not deign to speak to me, and we met only at the November 11 memorial services in the town park. The Roman Catholic church sat empty and derelict, with its cemetery overgrown. The Friends (Quaker) church had a beautiful red brick structure but no pastor. Some of their folk came to our church. Their building has since become a museum.

Over in the United church was an elderly man, godly and a truly sincere, genuine Christian. We had many conversations, one of which came about when I asked him about his own history and walk of faith. He had been saved in the Methodist church over 60 years previously and was now in his 80s. He told me the leaders of his congregation "restrained" him. He could not speak freely about the new birth or being born again; nor could he invite people to make public commitments to Jesus Christ as Lord and Saviour. He also recounted for me, with tears in his eyes, some of the phenomena he had seen and experienced in his earlier years at the altar of early Methodist meetings.

Wellington Pentecostal Church had few people, only five of whom had any enthusiasm for evangelism. I decided to invite an evangelist once a year. I advertised, put up signs in front of the church, put a sign on top of my Volkswagen Beetle, and visited home after home. People came. Wellington is a friendly little town, beautifully located on the shores of Lake Ontario and West Lake, where the famous sandbanks are to be found. People began to know me by sight and never crossed the road to avoid me. They also knew our dog, Bim. Once when Mary was walking Bim down the main street, she overheard a woman ask another, "Who is that with Mr. Bombay's dog?"

Over time some young people returned to the church. Some disaffected adults slowly came back too. My cousin Rev. Ken Bombay came with Rev. David Tonn as evangelists for two weeks during our first summer pastoring there. It was both exhilarating and interesting in many ways. When Ken preached, 13 people were baptized in the Holy Spirit, speaking with other tongues, just like in Acts 2:4. When Dave preached, 16 people came forward to accept Jesus Christ as Lord and Saviour.

Young pastors are either naive or nervy. I'm not sure which category fit me. My first funeral was for a suicide. My first wedding was a private affair in a home on the main street where I had to instruct the best man to put out his cigarette so I could get on with the ceremony. I will never forget the honorarium I received for that wedding. It was a two-dollar bill seriously blackened by grease. But it did buy food.

My first baptismal service took place at the inlet between Lake Ontario and West Lake. It was shortly after I had chosen to sing the hymn "Holy, Holy, Holy." The trouble came at the end of the chorus with the words "God in three Persons, blessed Trinity." Everyone in the church stopped singing when we came to that part of the song. They just stared at me as I led the only three others who did join me in singing those words. Mary, Walter Sprague, his wife, Juahita, at the piano, and I sang as a disjointed quartet for those seven last words. Huh?

There had been no baptismal service in the church for years since there was deep controversy over the baptismal formulae. Some wanted to be baptized simply "in Jesus's name"; others wanted to be baptized as instructed by Jesus, "in the name of the Father, and of the Son, and of the Holy Spirit." I knew I was in trouble. I consider the Trinity to be one of the clear and strong foundational doctrines of the Word of God. But I wasn't about to split a church over this difference. I have often wondered whether it was simple semantics, personality clashes, or a true doctrinal conviction that caused such schisms.

The Sunday afternoon of our first baptismal service arrived. I asked each one how they would like to be baptized. One somewhat naive but sincere young believer said, "In water!" Oops. I changed the question. Some said, "In Jesus's name." Others designated the Trinitarian formula. I baptized over a dozen people that day, and it was a bit of a spectacle for Wellington's residents.

I got around the doctrinal "problem" by baptizing some candidates as follows: "On your confession of faith in the Lord Jesus Christ as your own personal Saviour, I now baptize you in the name of the Father, and of the Son, and of the Holy Spirit!" For those who had asked to be baptized in Jesus's name, I added at the end, "In Jesus's name." Sounded biblical to me! And no one had a problem as a result, but they were all obedient in being baptized to represent their death in Christ and resurrection to new life.

Our training in ministry had further voids. For instance, how could I, never trained in marriage counselling, speak to people twice my age with any wisdom on the matter? As a result, I did and said some desperately stupid things. I asked for and received forgiveness more than once.

The ever-present tension between "Jesus's name" and "Trinity" always seemed to be raising its head. Mr. Frank Easton, a chicken farmer and elder in the church, was the Bible class teacher. We were using the normal Pentecostal quarterlies for our Sunday school program, both for adults and children. Frank taught well. But then a problem arose. The lesson for the coming Sunday was on the Trinity. Frank was of the Jesus's name tradition. I never even knew there was a problem until he turned up at my door much too early for either Sunday school or church.

He was red-eyed and looked somewhat disheveled. I invited him into the parsonage. He poured out his story. He told me he had never really studied the doctrine of the Trinity. The quarterly directed him to many passages of Scripture that reflect the three persons of the Trinity, none of which he had paid serious attention to before. He told me he really got hung up on the first reference in the Bible to the triune nature of the One True God. He read in Genesis 1:26, "Then God said, 'Let Us make man in Our image, according to Our likeness'" (NKJV). Then he studied the lesson more closely. Suddenly he realized that the word *Trinity* was simply a human term to describe the One God in His three persons.

He could not get away from it. Frank asked me what he should do. I told Frank to tell the class just what he told me and what he now believed to be biblically accurate. I offered him a razor, he shaved, and he prepared to give his simple testimony of his experience studying the subject.

He did it. The problem of the Trinity rarely surfaced again. Certainly, I never made a big deal of it. Though I believe in the Trinity, I was much more concerned that people come to know Jesus Christ as their personal Saviour. There are many more things that hold us together in the church of Jesus Christ than those things that often divide us. Frequently, our differences are matters of semantics or personality differences rather than doctrine.

Frank's change in belief and testimony gave him new biblical convictions that changed the attitude of the whole church. A few months later, we sang "Holy, Holy, Holy" without a sudden hiatus at the end of the song.

The church grew, and we built an addition onto the church building.

Mary and I had moved into a tiny house on the west end of town with electrical heating. I came apart at the seams when we got an electrical bill for 72 dollars on our small stipend. We moved again to a larger, poorly insulated house, right across the street from our church entrance. It had a pot-bellied wood-burning stove in the kitchen. With Buck Trumper, I cut enough wood to keep us almost warm. It was from that town and that house that we moved to Africa as missionaries.

I was rather young to be involved in domestic disputes. I received a call one evening from a distraught wife. Her husband was blind drunk and violent. "Could you come and help me, *please*?"

Well, I thought, since my father happened to be visiting, and he'd already pastored for 40 years, I'd take him along. He'd know how to deal with this. So, I suggested that Dad come along. His answer was simple: "You have to learn by experience. Just go!" I went, down past the railway tracks to their not-too-tidy house. As I entered, the drunken husband glowered at me from where he was sprawled in an old worn sofa chair. I talked for a while, reprimanded him from my "ministerial eminence," and was about to leave. The lady of the house said, "Would you please take these?" as she handed me several bottles of hard liquor. I nervously accepted them, and as I was leaving, I also took a packet of cigarettes from the man's shirt pocket, saying, "I'd better take these too. If you light one right now, you might explode." And I left. We disposed of it all by using it to clean the drain in our sink. The cigarettes provided a slight bit more warmth when I tossed them into the pot-bellied stove in the kitchen.

When we left Wellington, we sold our furniture and car and ended up with 12 dollars after paying off the loan we got when we bought our stereo record player. As missionaries we got a raise in pay. Mary and I both got 90 dollars a month as missionaries!

And we thought pastoring was a challenge!

Wisdom Gained: Pastoring a congregation of believers is the highest and most holy calling a person can have, if the pastor is a shepherd who truly loves people. Otherwise, chaos can cripple a whole congregation.

15 GOD PROVIDES WHAT YOU NEED

THE FIRST MAJOR setback was my pitiful little Volkswagen bug. Had it not been for a kindly local mechanic, Rolly Istead, this preacher and his wife would have been without wheels most of the time. It would be hard to forget those times in driving snow and freezing weather. Mary and I would drive to Toronto to Mary's parents' home. My parents were still in Africa at this point.

If the car started, we went. Our bare hands were the window defrosters. The heat that was supposed to be piped up to the windshield never made it. I would drive squinting through alternating frostless sections of the windshield left by Mary's hands or one of mine on the windshield.

Our first little white frame house was located on Gore Road, a few miles north of Wellington. Bruce Wilson, as mentioned, a neighbouring farmer, told us we could help ourselves to both tomatoes and corn from his fields all around us. We had to, since the 25-dollar-a-week income didn't quite stretch far enough sometimes. Even with gasoline at 25 cents a gallon!

Bruce was a happy man, 15 years older than his wife, Ruth. We talked to them about the Lord, but it was met with well-concealed tolerance. We became friends. Bruce occasionally baited us. At one point, standing in the middle of one of his tomato fields, he asked if we were planning on having children. We mentioned that Mary had had several miscarriages, but we hoped to.

Bruce, with a mischievous glint in his eye, said, "What you probably need is a new rooster!" at which he tucked his hands under his arms and flapped them like chicken wings.

Bruce and Ruth figured in our life in many ways over the years. Even though they were not born-again Christians at the time, we kept them on our mailing list while in Africa. We hoped that it might influence them toward God. It may well have done. But what really brought them to God was when a friend "tricked" them into going to a Full Gospel Men's Fellowship breakfast. Ruth was very crippled and using canes then. A string of doctors had made it clear there was nothing more they could do.

They wrote us in Africa to tell us what had happened. A Father Bob Mac-Dougall, a Jesuit priest, had spoken that morning. When the breakfast meeting was over, Father Bob was walking past Bruce and Ruth and noticed her canes as she was trying to struggle to her feet. He paused to pray for her, then kept walking, probably unaware of what had happened.

Ruth sat down again but this time let her canes fall to the floor. She then stood up and walked perfectly normally. She had been instantly healed. We saw her many times after, and she was always perky and healthy. The incident led to their putting their trust in Jesus Christ. We enjoyed their company, both at their cottage on Hay Bay and at their new home across from that first house we lived in at Wellington.

Sometimes the town was more kind to us than was the church. Ed Bailey, the town butcher, extended credit to us when we had no money for meat. He cut a frozen turkey in half so we would have something to feed a group of students from Eastern Pentecostal Bible College who were coming on assignment one Sunday. A member in the church, a chicken farmer, would not even sell a chicken to me, as he put it, "Unless it blows its vent!" I had no idea what he meant at the time.

Ed Bailey also delighted in telling us some of the local lore about the church I had come to pastor. At one time, the congregation had met just across the street from his butchery in a storefront on Main Street. People would sometimes gather to watch through the big store window as people fell to the floor in those early Pentecostal meetings. He told of getting sight of knickers on the women with the name of the sugar company still clearly legible on the sugar bags from which they were made. The church, he was telling me in a not altogether ambiguous manner, had a mottled past. There were a few other urban legends we had to live with.

The church grew, and an addition was built onto the church, and the crowd (now a legitimate word in the church) increased. Some startling incidents of salvation took place.

Allan Hennessy, an elder in the church, lived down the road in Bloomfield. One house separated their house from the graveyard. The man who lived in it was an abusive drinker. The family lived halfway between terror and hunger. One day Allan responded to a scream for help.

One of the boys was choking and turning blue. The family knew Allan as a Christian man. They were all in a terror as the boy writhed on the kitchen floor. Allan stooped and prayed for him immediately. The boy began to breathe normally. The family considered it a miracle. They came to church the following Sunday morning.

They came again Sunday evening, which was usually an evangelistic service. When I gave the invitation for people to give their lives to Jesus Christ, the husband and wife literally ran to the altar, where they wept, repented, and cried their way through to a relationship with God. I later heard that two of their boys eventually went into the ministry.

Good things happen when you have faithful elders.

Money continued to be scarce. Meat was seldom on our table. I had a Winchester .30-30 and a fishing rod. The woods had both deer and quail, and West Lake had bass, pickerel, and other edibles. My first hunting licence in 1959 brought me home a deer. But it was not my first shot that brought it down, nor was it the first deer I saw.

My first shot took a slab out of a tree 30 feet above the deer I thought I was aiming at. "Buck Fever," they called it. My second attempt was successful. It wasn't hard to keep it frozen through the winter. The winters were harsh.

Harsh winters meant trouble in our poorly insulated house. One morning we got up, and the toilet was glazed with ice. Why it did not crack the bowl and the tank, I can only guess. Perhaps the pot-bellied stove in the kitchen on the other side of the wall saved it.

I visited many homes. Sometimes I was welcomed; sometimes I was coldly turned away. I visited all who needed help or encouragement. Some people were highly intelligent; some had little or no understanding of life at all. But I decided that since God loved them all, so would I. And, believing that love is most often exhibited by action, I helped people do what had to be done, either on their farm or in the homes in town.

Fortunately, I was part of a large fellowship of churches. There were district rallies for youth, camp meetings in summer, and conferences, some of which we were able to get to when we had the cash.

One of our nearer neighbours and friends pastored the church in Brighton. David Mainse, who had graduated in the same class as me, would have us over there, or we would have them over to our home in Wellington on a social basis. It often depended on who had food in the cupboard at the time.

To this day, I am still in awe of how much milk David drank at one sitting at our kitchen table in Wellington. As it turned out, he was just strengthening his bones to take some of the hard knocks he would endure when he began Christian television in Canada. Our friendship endured.

Even when Mary and I moved to Kenya.

Wisdom Gained: If you commit your life to God, you will discover that God is even more committed to you!

16 MISSIONS AND REALITY

WE WERE GIVEN a house at Nyang'ori mission station. It had very thick mud walls, a red polished cement floor, and a tin roof, which amplified the racket of torrential rains.

I had two jobs: Learn Kiswahili, and teach some subjects in the Bible school. English and Kiswahili were the two official languages of Kenya. Kiswahili came easily to me, and within six months I preached my first sermon in Kiswahili. I was sent to the Church Missionary Society language school, where there were great teachers! When I was finished, they suggested I might want to join their staff and help teach Kiswahili. I thought not.

Mary and I were soon transferred to Uganda, where English and Luganda prevailed. The town of Mbale was a rather tough assignment to start with. Rev. Fred Clarke had been there for some time but was retiring back to Canada. Several comparatively new churches had been established by him in Uganda. When I realized we were the only missionaries of our denomination in the whole country, it seemed quite a daunting assignment for two 26-year-olds.

The mission house was located on a street rising toward the base of Mount Elgin. It was a genuinely nice house, lined with jacaranda trees. When the jacarandas are in bloom, everything turns a gorgeous mauve. Just up the street a few houses was one of President Obote's residences.

On the far side of the ravine behind the house were altogether too many local bars. The brawls, music, and general loudness kept us awake many nights. Our whole backyard was a rather steep incline with patchy grass. At the bottom was a fence that kept our dog Bom in the yard. (We also had another dog, called Bay.) One day we heard Bom screaming as if being beaten. He had been alone and sleeping at the bottom of the yard. Now he was yelping and rolling like he was having a fit. I ran down and saw that he was covered with biting ants. I grabbed him and ran up the hill to the house, getting a few bites of my own. It took quite a while to persuade those ants to loosen their pincer grips, especially on his belly. From that time onward, Bom decided that he preferred the front yard.

We were not there long before Mary developed a medical problem. Fortunately, there were two Scottish doctors working at the small hospital in Mbale. They were a husband-and-wife team. He was a gynecologist, and she was a neurosurgeon. Being a young husband and in a foreign land, I was nervous. We didn't have insurance to offset the costs of any medical procedures.

"Bring Mary in tomorrow morning. I'll treat her as an outpatient, and you can take her home later in the evening. No one will see a record of her being in any ward." I took Mary early in the morning and filled out some papers, and she was sent by a nurse into a room to wait. An hour and a half later, the doctor came by, saw her in the room, and asked, "Why are you here? We need you in the operating room." Quickly, Mary was taken away. A nurse took her down a hall behind closed doors. I sat in nervous apprehension. A seemingly long time later, Mary, looking somewhat dazed, was brought to me, and we gently put her in our little Volkswagen. It was just after sunset when we headed home.

On the way to our house, the trouble began when Mary began to see things I didn't see. "Watch out for the roadblock!" she yelled. I slammed on the brakes, "What roadblock?" I asked.

She pointed right in front of us. Nothing! I started again, and this time she saw a large group of Karamojong warriors dancing around a big fire. I stopped, and Mary turned toward me. Her pupils were so enlarged that her irises were almost gone. I frantically headed straight for the doctors' home.

Mary asked me to get her some ginger ale. I couldn't find any anywhere. She didn't remember asking me for it but was annoyed that I didn't get whatever it was she had asked for. In her still foggy stupor she said, "They can't do the operation until I have some ginger ale." Confusion seemed to reign. She saw wild tribal dancing around a fire outside her window. She was the only one to see it. A while later, she asked me, "Did you get it?"

I said, "Get what?"

"I don't remember, but you have to get it!"

Normally, Mary is very rational. But this …

After looking into her eyes, the doctor said, "She'll be all right." Then he added, "If her pupils stay dilated, bring her back in the morning." I thought I might personally need the doctor by that time. This was my darling, my wife! She was just experiencing the after-effects of the anesthetic they had used, but that look in Mary's eyes had scared me. The next morning, she seemed fine, though still in some pain from the procedure.

We had just barely gotten over that when, on a Saturday morning, we heard yelling and screaming approaching and entering our front yard, inside the thorn hedge that was supposed to hide our house and keep people out. We looked out, wondering if we might be under attack for some reason. We saw a gang beating a man, who was now on the ground writhing and trying to protect his head from the large pick-handles they were using to beat him.

I was a missionary, right? I was there to "save" people, right? I was scared, right? I ran out the front door, straddled the downed victim on our front lawn, and yelled for Mary to call the police. The people backed off but did not leave. Mary called the police, but they said they could not come until their Land Rover returned from wherever it was. I stood over the victim for a long time. The thugs didn't leave, even when the police finally did turn up. Then, of course, I heard the story through the police. This young man had defiled someone's wife, and in all too typical a manner, instant justice was to be meted out. The police took the bruised and bleeding fellow away, and that was the last we heard of it.

Fortunately, we met some Southern Baptist missionaries, Jim and Peggy Hooten, and their two children. They invited us to their home for a meal. We reciprocated and invited them over for a visit. Jim had barely crossed the threshold into the living room when he asked, "What kind of people are you? We've been here 30 seconds already and you haven't even offered us a coffee!" We knew that we had met our kind of people.

I was meeting with our African evangelists who were supported by Pentecostal churches in Switzerland, preaching almost every Sunday and often during the week. My interpreter, Francis Mutumba, spoke nine languages and was instant in his delivery. I didn't get to use my Kiswahili as much as I would have liked. Some years later, Rev. Bob Eames referred to Francis as "a man who had the wisdom to keep silent in all nine languages when it was necessary." Francis worked for me full-time.

It became a busy, busy time. It seemed we were on the go constantly, though I did find time to play nine holes of golf occasionally with Jim Hooten.

Once while playing golf (yes, there was a golf course in Mbale, Uganda, way back then), we saw another crowd of people screaming and cursing a young man who came from midtown, racing for his life. He had apparently grabbed someone's purse, and someone had yelled "Thief!"

The mob expressed its lust for immediate justice. He was fast, and he was smart. He led that mob around the golf course for a while and then headed straight back into the centre of town—and straight into the police station. Better to be in jail than buried, right? I'm still not sure how safe he was in there.

Life continued to get more interesting almost daily. Things were sailing along fine. I was beginning to get a grasp on the work I was to do. I was baptizing people who were being saved and filled with the Spirit. The work was thriving, and new churches were being established.

I saw God do many wonderful things in Uganda, some of which are recorded in this account. But the end of our time in Uganda was somewhat distasteful.

Wisdom Gained: In serving God, every step with God is a well-planted imprint on the soils and souls of the world.

17 THE BOY IN THE WHEELBARROW

SOME MIRACLES ARE startlingly obvious!

Mary and I spent six months in Kenya. We studied Kiswahili, taught at the Nyang'ori Bible College, preached on weekends, and generally tried to learn some of the customs and procedures of being missionaries. It was during those transitional years between colonialism and the independence that was coming to most African nations during the mid-sixties. It was a time of some tough adjustments, especially with conflicting recommendations and instructions from some of the senior missionaries.

Some were nervous about the coming independence. Others were anticipating it. We didn't know enough at that stage to know what we should think, though we were well advised. Perhaps overly advised in the various perspectives of others. So, we waited and watched.

Six months after our arrival, we became responsible for the work in Uganda. Some challenge for two 26-year-olds! It didn't take us long to see the opportunities and potential for church growth in Uganda. There were some incidents that God used to make it a lot easier for us to trust in Him rather than in any abilities we might happen to have. It involved a lot of preaching in some of the already-established churches. Some were big; most were small.

We taught courses for new pastors in the Mbale church. The number of churches was increasing so rapidly that it wasn't possible to send students for the three-year pastoral training in Nyang'ori, Kenya.

Paul Hhisa was a partially trained lay pastor in Uganda—tall, dark, and handsome, with a real love for people and a desire to lead them to Christ as Lord. He had begun a small church, built of mud walls and a thatched roof. It could not have been more than 15 by 20 feet, with a door and four irregularly shaped windows deeply shadowed by the grass thatch overhang.

While teaching the short course, I got to know Pastor Paul. He came from the Bunyole tribe. He was a very enthusiastic pastor and was aggressively building his new church. It was already too small. He asked me to come to preach and teach at this fledgling church.

It was a Sunday when I drove the 40 miles to his village where he had begun the church. After preaching, I gave an invitation for people to accept Jesus as Saviour and Lord. I remember several people accepted the Lord that morning, including the sub-chief of the area.

As is African custom, a dinner was prepared when a missionary came. The sub-chief, now a Christian, was also invited. We were fed chicken and *ugali,* a dense hot white cornmeal boiled in hot water until it becomes malleable. (I still love it!) As we were finishing eating, we heard someone call out, "Hodi!" It's common to call out *hodi* when approaching a house, rather than knocking on the door. A man came in and asked, "Will the missionary please pray for my son?"

I agreed of course and stepped outside the house. What I faced was a little daunting. There was a wooden wheelbarrow, hand fashioned, wheel and all. But even more intriguing was what was in the wheelbarrow—a small boy about nine or ten years old. His legs were folded under him, and he sat on the edges of his feet. His knees were oversized knobs on withered legs. They lifted him out of the wheelbarrow onto the ground. His legs didn't hang down but stayed in their twisted sitting position. They asked me if I would ask the Lord to heal him. I found out that he had had some disease, possibly polio, and had been this way for some years. Apparently, word got out that I prayed for the sick.

I must admit that I did not feel confident. I did not sense great faith on my part. I had heard of such healings taking place but had never actually seen one with my own eyes. We gathered around the boy to pray. When I laid my hands on his head and began to pray, I had no overwhelming sense of expectation. I just prayed that the Lord would heal him and make him walk. When I opened my eyes, he sat looking up at me with big brown pleading eyes. He continued to sit there.

I can't remember much of what happened after that other than having some questions in my mind about these things. I arrived back in Mbale with a heavy spirit. Did I lack faith? Was I really called to the ministry? Mary probably saw me in one of my rare morose moods that Sunday evening when I got home.

The following Wednesday, Pastor Paul Hhisa came wheeling into my yard, dropped his bike, and ran into my office in a side building. He breathlessly said, "The boy! The boy! You must come!"

My first thought was perhaps that the boy had died. Paul literally pulled me from my office toward my car. He unceremoniously plopped his bicycle on my car's roof, scratching it badly as he tied it down with strips of inner tubing. I went to tell Mary I was going to drive to Paul's village to see the boy. "I'll be back when I get here!"

I drove my little Volkswagen beetle as fast as I could. The roads were so poor that speeding could never become an issue. I parked beside a playing field near the school and church. Paul jumped out, pointing across the field and saying, "There he is!" I couldn't see anything but a bunch of kids kicking a football made from woven banana leaves.

Paul called out a name, and one of the kids peeled off and came running up to us. He stood there grinning. It was still early enough in my missionary experience that most African boys looked much the same to me. Black curly hair, dark skin, and big brown eyes! Paul said, "This is the boy you prayed for."

I looked at his legs. They looked perfectly normal. I asked Paul, "Are you sure this is the same boy?" For an answer, he instructed the boy to show me his feet. There was all the proof I needed. The outside edges of his feet were very heavily calloused. The soles of his feet were blistered and bleeding, unaccustomed to being used.

To say I was dumbfounded would be an understatement. But I joined in the praise to God for what was an obvious miracle. No one made any special fuss over me. That suited me fine.

I learned something important that day, something I had probably understood in a theological sense but had never experienced. Faith is not related to feeling, for I had felt nothing except a small measure of fearful apprehension. I found out that obedience is a much greater evidence of faith than anything such as feelings, sensations, or wordy prayer. I simply obeyed God.

"They will place their hands on sick people, and they will get well" (Mark 16:18).

That was the first of many similar miracles in Africa.

Wisdom Gained: When you see a genuine miracle by God's answering prayer, never turn back. Jesus is the same yesterday, today, and forever.

18 AN INFAMOUS SPEAR

FRANCIS MUTUMBA WAS my chief interpreter while I lived in Uganda. He was a very steady fellow, but he came to me one day very troubled. He wanted me to go to his village. I knew he was a Musoga but knew little about his tribe, family, and relatives. I was unaware of the reason other than to share the gospel with them. I learned that there were deeper reasons and that for generations they had been both afraid and very untrusting of white people.

To get to the village, we had to drive along a footpath. The children screamed and ran away as we approached. I jokingly asked Francis if they thought I was going to eat them. He answered "Yes! That's what they are afraid of." I didn't believe him until he told me that one of the threats adults used to make their children behave was "The white man will eat you if you don't behave!" It was his tribal form of a bogeyman.

We stopped in a well-swept yard, surrounded by many mud and thatch houses. For some time, no one was in sight. Finally, an old man shuffled from the largest hut toward us. The brush and trees around the village seemed to vibrate with apprehension. I stood, unmoving and unnerved, beside Francis. I had never come into a village with this kind of quiet non-reception before.

The man came and took hold of my right hand with his right hand, clutching his own right wrist with his left hand. I did the same. It was a sign to show that neither of us had hidden weapons in our left hands, a signal of peaceful welcome.

He led me to the centre of the well-swept compound where three small rocks were arranged around a firepit. We sat on bigger rocks around that fire spot. After Francis and the old man talked for a while, the old man called out. Other men appeared. They sat around us in a circle on the dry ground, leaving an open space in front of me. The old man called out again.

This time women began to appear at hut doors and shuffled on their knees from their huts to bow down before me, touching my feet with their foreheads. I was a little disconcerted at this sign of respect. Each wife backed off and sat silently on the ground behind the men. Next, the children were called, and I touched each one on the top of the head. When it appeared I wasn't going to eat them, they went to look at their reflections in the bulgy hubcaps of my VW. One of the men had pointed out the mirrors and the hubcaps. They had never seen themselves before, it seemed. I wondered if a white person had ever been there before. It was a long way from any road. It turned out I was right in that assumption. White man, car...

Through his nephew Francis, my interpreter, the old man told me the following story.

"Many, many years in the past, our ancestors were the first to see three white men who came to our land. They had heard about white people and knew that they would bring great trouble. They would kill our gods and teach us strange ways. The only way to stop this great evil was to kill the white people. So, they did. One of the old fathers of this village killed one of the white men!"

There was a long pause as the men of the village exchanged nervous glances. The old man went on. "Since that time, we have been under a great curse. All things go bad here ever since that time long ago. Your God has cursed us. We want you to ask your God to take away the curse. Our young men die too young, and bad things happen, and we have many troubles." He went on at length.

There was a long, quiet pause. I was about to answer that I would pray for them, fully intending to share the gospel with them as well. But it was not to be just yet.

The old man continued. "The white man's laws say that we cannot have spears. We have no spears, except one." He then pointed at another man and said something in Lunyole, and the man went to one of the grass-roofed mud-walled houses, got a rough triangular pole ladder, and climbed up the outside of the roof. Francis leaned over to me and quietly whispered, "They are getting the spear. It has been hidden in the thatch of many of our houses for many years." I was a little confused.

The spear was brought and put in the hands of the elder, who then continued, "This spear we have kept in our clan for many, many years. Our ancestors thought that it would bring us good luck, but it has always been a curse. Many families of our clan hid this in their new houses, but it is a curse on everyone in the village. We want you to take it away from here." I looked at the spear. It certainly looked old. The blade was perfectly shaped and razor sharp. The back of the spear was a thin shaft of beaten iron with a ring of hide and hair from a monkey's tail on it. It was a beautiful well-made spear. They handed it to me, and I took it hesitantly. Then the old man told me the rest of the story.

"This was the spear they used to kill the first three missionaries who came to us in our country! Please take it away from here so the curse will go away." As I held it in my hands, I was a little awestruck. I had read of the first three missionaries from the Church of England, who had come with the Church Missionary Society and had been killed when they came to Uganda.

It was Bishop Hannington and his two companions on their mission. The only discrepancy I detected might not have been a discrepancy at all, but perhaps the truth. I thought I understood it to have been the Baganda (the largest Ugandan tribe) who had killed those three missionaries. Yet, to get to Buganda (the territory of the Baganda—Luganda is the language) they would certainly have had to pass through this area, the land of the Bunyole, first. History does confirm they were killed on the eastern border of Uganda.

The men of the village looked at me expectantly. Finally, I said I would take it from the village. They relaxed and seemed relieved. Then I asked for the privilege of telling them the real reason those first missionaries had come. They agreed. I taught the simple truth of the gospel, which I suspected Francis had probably already shared with them. Then I prayed that God would remove the curse from their village.

Some of them became Christians, either while I was there or after. When I left their village, I took the spear with me, and eventually I took it back to Canada, where my family and I still have it. Some months later, although I never got back to that village, I asked Francis how matters were back at home. He smiled his crooked toothy smile and said, "They are happy now, and blessed."

The curse was gone, and many of them came to know and serve the Lord Jesus.

Wisdom Gained: No obstacle can stand in the way of God's grace and love. Whether a person has a real problem or just believes there is a problem, when Jesus comes into the situation, guilt and fear are dispersed.

19
DISCOURAGEMENTS

WE OFTEN HEAR glowing reports from the mission fields of the world. What seldom is revealed are the defeats and problems, the push and pull of cultural confrontations. The newer the missionary, the higher the risk of misunderstanding and discouragement.

I had been in Kenya only six months, studying Kiswahili and helping teach at the Bible college at Nyang'ori. On weekends, I was preaching through interpreters in three tribal areas, Luo, Maragoli, and Kalenjin, and generally learning the role of a missionary.

The early '60s were a time a political pressure and turmoil throughout East Africa. Africans were striving for independence from the colonial yoke of Britain. Similar political pressures existed within the various denominational church structures as well. The missionaries had to relinquish having the final say in church organization. They were days of transition and mostly carefully controlled tension.

It was my impression that the Pentecostal Assemblies of Canada was somewhere in the middle of the various moves around the world toward national church self-determination. I was often confused as to what I should think. Some of the older, more experienced missionaries advised that "They are not ready to run their own affairs!" Others, more often the younger missionaries, said that with a proper transition phase it could be done.

National self-determination was inevitable given the political atmosphere, both in the country and in various denominations. It was in this period that Mary and I were transferred to Mbale, Uganda, to take the leadership of the fledgling PAOC work there. The only other evangelicals in town were Jimmy and Peggy Hooten. We became friends. There was also a Christian couple, both doctors, who worked in the local Mbale hospital. One was a brain surgeon and the other a gynecologist. It was our good fortune to know them, and all of them lived quite near us in the small city.

While we lived and worked in Uganda, we saw the Lord perform many miracles. None of our work was easy, but the growth of the work outshone the problems. And problems there were, aplenty!

I had set out to do a week of teaching and meetings in the north of Uganda, at a village not far out of Gulu. I was still new to the country and did not know the geography. Maps were scarce, and even when a road was shown, it was not necessarily usable or even there! I set out in faith.

One road that was supposed to be there was not, and the next possibility was not passable. I was referred to a road that would take me to a ferry that was to cross a large area of swamp and the Nile itself. When I got to the end of the road and came to water, all I saw was a floating platform with 44-gallon drums under it—and a big bus on top. This was the ferry? I was told there was room for my little VW Beetle, so I hesitantly bumped onto the rail-less platform, which heaved and swayed even at the movement of my VW. I heard no engine.

Eventually, four "engines" walked out onto the barge and took their positions, two on each side. Using long poles, they began to push the barge through the swamp. Surprisingly, the swaying was not as bad as I had imagined. It took hours to get there, but finally we reached the end of another road that led in the general direction I wanted to go. About 13 hours after I had left Mbale, and over 400 miles later, I arrived after dark where my hosts were waiting.

Visitors are always fed on arrival. After dinner, my hosts led me to a grass-roofed hut with a diameter about the same as my height. No bed, no light, nothing but a flat dirt floor and plenty of mosquitoes. I tossed and turned and dozed a bit. Suddenly, and rather painfully, I woke up. My bowels were in an uproar. I had no idea where a toilet might be, so I just headed out. There was enough starlight to see general outlines of other huts and bushes. I hit the bushes. About eight times! I have no idea what was fed to me, but my uninitiated, weak, tender stomach was no match for the challenge.

By morning light, I was exhausted, spent, tired, and, quite literally, drained. I was supposed to teach that morning. I could hardly stand, let alone think clearly. When the local leaders met me to offer me a breakfast, tea, and some bananas, I explained my problem. I didn't even trust a banana, which came in its own wrapping. With profuse apologies, I dropped into my VW Bug and headed back to Mbale. It was a multi-stop trip, and I was ever so glad when I finally hit that final road, paved and pointing to where I wanted to be, at home with Mary! I got proper medicine, and three or four days later I lost the pallor and could eat again.

I have often wondered if the devil won that round. I was unable to contribute to the birth of a church in the Gulu area, and it wasn't until years later that another missionary was able to establish a church. I don't take defeat kindly. That one still irks me.

The devil turns up in many forms. We had built a new church of simple poles, mud walls, and a thatched roof not too far from the Kenya border. It began to prosper and grow. It was burned to the ground. We rebuilt it. It was burned down again. The devil was an arsonist. We built it again, and again it was burned down. We found out that some local Muslims took great exception to a church being built in their area. So, we built it again.

This time we used iron sheeting for the roof, and since mud and metal are hard to burn, it lasted and prospered, and the members even started another congregation a few miles away. My father used to use the term "stick-to-it-iv-ness," and I learned from him how to stick to a job until it is done.

While living in Mbale, I often preached in the large church that had been established by Rev. Fred Clarke, my predecessor there. It was a good mixed congregation from various tribes. All seemed well until some of the elders came to me with a complaint against the pastor, a Kenyan from the Maragoli subtribe in Kenya. They claimed the pastor was "committing adultery" with some of the women in the church.

When I asked them how they knew this, one of the elders said, "My wife is one of them." Another added, "Pastor Elam Kenyanga gives rides to some of the women of the church on the back of his bicycle!" This to them was a sure sign that some illicit relationship was going on. Men simply did not transport other men's wives on their bicycles.

At that time, Kenya, Tanzania, and Uganda were all under the authority of one central executive committee of the Pentecostal Assemblies of God (PAG). Some years later, each country would have its own superintendent and executive. I was stuck with the prevailing power structure, and I did not know what to do.

Since the church was now self-governing in East Africa, I decided to call the top three officers of the executive to come and deal with the matter. I was young and new, and the executive members were older experienced men. When they came, they called a public meeting of the whole congregation, including the accused. I also was asked to attend. The story slowly came out, and although calm prevailed for a while, eventually it got louder and more convincing, even though Pastor Kenyanga denied it all. He was not only accused of sexual sins but also of meddling with the offerings, and a few lesser thefts.

I never said a word. It was not my problem. I was there to plant churches, preach, teach, and spread the gospel. I didn't want the role of judge and jury. Elam Kenyanga was given his say. He denied everything. Then he began a verbal tirade against me. "Bombay has brought these accusations!" and "Bombay is responsible for stirring the church up over nothing!" And then an accusation came against me that I didn't even understand at the time. "Bombay insults this congregation when he preaches. He says they are all donkeys!" *What*?

I was deeply bothered by the accusation that I'd called the Ugandan congregation "donkeys." After reviewing what I had preached, I finally pinned it down. I asked a few of the men in the church what Elam might be referring to by "donkeys."

I had been preaching one Sunday on "The Joy of the Lord." It appeared that when I was preaching on joy, I referred to the unhappy look that some Christians wear on their faces. With my right hand, I drew my hand down over my face and said something about having long sad appearances, rather than living out the joy of the Lord. I thought Kenyanga was stretching it a bit, but I was finding out that gestures are sometimes very significant. This time it was interpreted that unhappy Christians were donkeys. Well, what can I say?

Word finally came from Kenya. Pastor Elam Kenyanga was to return to Kenya and pastor a church in his own tribal area. The executive members who had come to deal with the situation with Kenyanga were not only from the same tribe but were near kin. Tribalism?

Less than a year later, Kenyanga was attacked and almost killed by an irate husband whose wife he had abused sexually. He was cut up and slashed very badly by a *panga* (like a machete) at the hand of the husband.

Mary and I too had to move out of Uganda back to Kenya to be reassigned by the Missionary Staffing Committee. The African church appeared to be trying out its new authority. I had loved working in Uganda, but we had to bow to their decision.

We were feeling sorry for ourselves, but God can take such discouraging experiences and turn them into great joy. During our 17 years in East Africa, we moved 17 times. But this move brought us great peace and joy. The joy was my involvement in the founding and development of Evangel Publishing House!

Wisdom Gained: Circumstances do not control our lives. God does. He can take evil and turn it to good.

20 A THROW-AWAY TRACT

EVANGEL PRESS PRINTED and distributed millions of Scripture tracts long before I arrived on the scene. It had begun and progressed under Leroy Morrison, Arnold Bowler, and Bob Peel. At the time I arrived, Evangel Press was divided into two entities: Evangel Press, printing Christian literature for our own needs and the needs of other missions and churches, and a publishing department that was just beginning to publish substantial biblical books, tracts, textbooks, pastoral training materials, and even newspapers for our own and other denominations.

The job of developing the publishing house was handed over to me. The production of millions of tracts continued as a large thrust in promoting evangelism. Pastors and missionaries were encouraged to take them wherever they went.

Some tribes and subtribes had had nothing ever printed in their own languages. Since tracts were a relatively small translation work, many tracts were printed, some with simple picture illustrations. One of the most effective was entitled "The Wide and the Narrow Way."

Mt. Elgon straddles the border between Kenya and Uganda. A new translation was done for a tribe in another language on the Kenyan side of the border. It was the first ever literature of any kind printed in that language. About ten thousand one-page tracts were printed. All tracts had the name and address of Evangel Publishing House on them.

For a long time, there was no response. Then one day a letter in English came to my desk. It was written by a young student named John. He told how he had seen a piece of paper lying in the dirt of the road, and knowing how to read, he picked it up. When he tried to read it, he was very confused. He could not seem to understand it, even though he was able to read in both English and Kiswahili.

After slowly sounding out the words, it burst on his mind, "This is my own language!" It was so exciting that he ran home and showed it to everyone. He read it to others, often. The truth of the wide and the narrow way dawned on him as he read it, and he accepted the invitation on the back of the tract to ask Jesus Christ into his life. He knew a change had taken place deep within himself. He shared it until he had led seven others to the Lord through that one tract.

He wrote to ask for more copies of it, which we sent to him. Through further correspondence, we arranged to have a tent meeting in his area. Rev. Isaka Kaguli, a former school inspector who had been baptized in the Holy Spirit, had quit his work to become an evangelist. We decided to team up to do the preaching and teaching.

We had a large tent to meet in. We preached and prayed for two weeks. Many, many people came to know Jesus as Lord, Saviour, and healer. Some were baptized in the Holy Spirit. Isaka was a powerful evangelist. He preached salvation, healing, and the baptism in the Holy Spirit. Within the week the crowds had outgrown the tent. I did Bible teaching in the mornings, and Isaka preached and prayed for people from mid-afternoons until dusk.

One day a lady whose limbs were twisted and distorted came crawling crab-like into the meeting. She asked for prayer for healing. Isaka prayed for her, and immediately she was up and literally running. Word spread, and the meetings became well known and better attended.

In the six-month period right after those meetings, seven churches were established in the area, and a pastor was assigned to each. John became a lay leader in time, becoming a pastor after training at the Bible college at Nyang'ori.

In this present day and age, when fundamentalist Islam is forcing the conversion of many with violence, guns, starvation, and slavery, it is good to know that a strong truth still holds: "The pen is mightier than the sword!" And, as Jesus declared, "I will build my church" (Matthew 16:18 NKJV).

Wisdom Gained: When we recognize the reality and power of the Word of God and never hesitate in sharing all the Bible says, miracles follow those who believe.

21 THE SUDDEN CHURCH

WHILE STILL IN Uganda, I became friends with a very kind, gentle, and effective pastor, Gideon Okakale. He was a compassionate pastor and loved the people of his church. He loved to initiate new churches. But who could ever have contemplated how it would come about?

He and I had invited Evangelist Isaka Kaguli to come from Kenya and preach Christ at meetings in the town of Soroti just about 70 miles north of Mbale, where Mary and I lived. I was able to attend only one of the meetings because of other commitments.

Isaka had been a school inspector when he met the Lord Jesus. His education and position opened many doors for his ministry. I had the privilege of co-preaching with him on several occasions. As far as I was able to determine, he had only one odd belief. He believed that anyone who snored while they slept had a demon. Sleeping in the same hut as him, I had to listen to his rather loud buzz-saw type of snore. I never had the heart to tell him he snored. I snored too, but he seemed to get to sleep more quickly than I did, or perhaps he was forgiving of the demons that inhabited my nasal passages.

Isaka held the meetings in the open marketplace in Soroti. Hundreds came to hear the gospel, and many came to know Jesus as personal Saviour. Several remarkable healings took place and one that didn't *seem* very remarkable. For years, the old man had suffered from a constant pain in his stomach. He had tried everything he knew: traditional healers, herbalists, and witch doctors. He lived a few miles from Soroti but was in town and in severe pain. Isaka prayed for him, laying on hands as was his custom.

When the old man went back to his home his excitement knew no bounds. Everyone knew he was a sick man, but the man they had known was now healthy and active and without the pain he had suffered for years. He told everyone Jesus had healed him. The old man asked Pastor Gideon to have meetings out in the bush near his home.

Pastor Gideon came to Mbale to ask me to come to preach. He particularly wanted me to pray for the sick. The people were far from medical help, and all they had to turn to was traditional medicine men. The results of their ministrations were minimal, even though certain herbs had some curative effects. I scheduled three days in one week when I could drive to the meeting place, preach, pray for the sick, and still return home to sleep, Monday, Wednesday, and Thursday. I was already scheduled for other places and had duties for both weekends and that Tuesday.

When I arrived at the meeting place, about three hundred people had gathered under a massive mango tree. Pastor Gideon was there with three other pastors. The group sang for a while, and several pastors said a few words, none of which I understood, since it was in the Teso language. I was introduced to the old man who had been healed. He had one of the biggest smiles you can imagine. He seemed to have at least a dozen more teeth than is normal. God had done a miracle in his body. Everyone for miles around knew about it.

It was getting late into the afternoon when I was asked to preach. I first preached the gospel, pure and simple. When I asked how many would like to receive Jesus, at least half of those three hundred gathered there indicated they wanted Jesus in their lives. I thought they might not have understood, so I very carefully repeated the invitation to receive Jesus Christ, giving attention to what it meant in both the short term and the long term in their lives. Again, more than half the crowd raised their hands.

It took us so long to deal personally with everyone, and it was darkening quickly. The sun sets at about 7:00 p.m. near the equator. We had no time left to pray for the sick. We dismissed the meeting. I said I'd be back on Wednesday, and I would pray for the sick then.

When I arrived on Wednesday there were at least 450 people there. Pastor Gideon and four other pastors were also in attendance. I felt obligated to share the gospel again first, then pray for the sick later. Again, more than a hundred people said they wanted to become Christians. We prayed for each one individually. Once again, darkness fell before we could pray for the sick.

We arrived earlier on Thursday. I reaffirmed the salvation message and encouraged those who wanted to follow the Lord Jesus. Then I explained what the Bible teaches about healing. As the hundreds sat quietly under the tree, I offered to pray for anyone who had a physical need. Scores of people stood to their feet. We asked the people to spread out a bit so that Pastor Gideon, the other pastors, and I could move among them to pray for them. There was pandemonium. It seemed everyone wanted to be prayed for. We began, I with my interpreter at my side.

All at once, I heard a loud screaming. A young man thrashed around on the ground, apparently in the grips of a seizure. I approached the young man and joined the two pastors who were already praying for him. In a while he calmed down. I learned later that the local people considered him a lunatic. The pastors assured me he had been demon possessed. He was quite obviously calm and in his right mind now. He never reverted to his old condition.

We prayed for many, many people that day. Many claimed to be healed of things which were not obvious to the human eye. However, there were 17 obvious physical healings that took place under that massive mango tree, including crippled limbs made right, a blind man who saw, and the young man who had been called a lunatic.

Only a few weeks later, I was asked to go to the dedication of a new church building. It was just a few yards outside the perimeter of the big mango tree where the meetings had taken place. It had corrugated steel roofing and light steel pipe uprights to hold the roof up. The walls had not yet been finished. It was built for about 200 people, but it was a good thing that there were no walls, since the crowd would never have been able to get in.

Pastor Gideon appointed a pastor to lead this group of believers. A new church of well over 200 people was established within a fifty-day period. "And the Lord added to the church daily those who were being saved" (Acts 2:47 NKJV).

One Sunday, Pastor Gideon and his family were in a church worshipping God when some of Idi Amin's troops surrounded the church. With a shot from one of their rifles, they silenced the worshippers. The whole church was called outside into the open. The leader of the soldiers called Pastor Gideon to stand in front of him. After questioning him and threatening him, he finally told Gideon he could go back to the church. As Gideon walked back toward his congregation, the soldier raised his rifle and shot Gideon in the back, killing him instantly. Such a tragic end to a God-centred life.

Wisdom Gained: The most effective way of starting a new church is to simply preach the Word and believe that signs and miracles will do all the advertising necessary. But often there is a cost.

22 GUNS IN THE WRONG HANDS

SEVERAL YEARS LATER, as manager of Evangel Publishing House in Kenya, I went on several successful trips to mission stations, Christian bookshops, and secular bookshops throughout Kenya and Tanzania, promoting our books. It was Uganda's turn.

I packed up my Volkswagen station wagon, putting my mattress over the load of books in the back, along with some non-perishable food. During the day, I distributed books, recruited new authors, and drove many miles. So many miles.

As I swung around a dusty corner just inside Uganda on a dirt road, I had to slam on the brakes. A large tree had fallen across the road. I found out in seconds that it had been felled purposely to stop unsuspecting travellers like myself. Men in uniform jumped up out of the bushes from the side of the road and came at me with guns. One of these gentlemen leaned in through the window and placed the barrel of his gun against my right temple. To say I was nervous would be to understate what was happening in the region around my bowels.

They spoke to me in a language I did not know. I tried to answer in Kiswahili, in which I was becoming quite proficient. They either did not know any Kiswahili or wanted to keep me unnerved by refusing to speak it. They shouted and gestured at me. I tried what little Luganda I knew. No good. They really didn't want to talk. I was unsure just what they did want!

They were troops under the command of Idi Amin, the mad man who had taken military control of Uganda at the time. They kept the gun to my head. It was already a hot day, but by now I was really sweating. I'd heard what Idi Amin's troops had done to people, black and white, and I was not feeling good about my chances.

In the distance, on the left, I saw a Roman Catholic mission station on a hill. I pointed at it with one hand and at my own chest with the other. "Padre. Padre. Padre." I was willing them to understand what I was trying to communicate. They looked at the mission station; then they looked at me. I did not have a clerical collar or a robe. In my khaki shorts and sweaty shirt, I tried to look as Catholic as I could.

They conferred among themselves for a tense moment. Slowly they backed away from me. They laid down their guns on the side of the road and, with sheer physical grit and strength, lifted the tree from the road and waved me on. I didn't even stop to thank the Catholic mission for being there.

I slept in the car wherever I happened to be just before sunset. Sometime after dark I would cook with a little camping stove I had. I took along a few dozen eggs, fresh from my own chickens, and bought bread and fruit along the way. I'd often back the vehicle off the road into the bush, out of sight of the road, and crawl into the back of the car to sleep.

I had two bad experiences doing that. One night after supper, I cleaned up, backed into the bush, and went to sleep. A great roar awakened me. I sat up quickly, whacking my head against the roof of the station wagon. The car was vibrating. It was so dark I couldn't see what was happening. The world went quiet again, so I went back to sleep. In the morning I discovered I had almost backed onto a set of railway tracks, and the train speeding by must have just barely missed the back end of my car. At that point I almost gave up my book-selling career, involuntarily.

The other incident happened on the same trip under similar circumstances. I was in a deep sleep when suddenly the car was rocking from side to side. I had makeshift curtains on the windows, and I looked out the side windows, and on both sides I was surrounded by tribesmen with spears in one hand and a *simis* (a very sharp two-edged sword) hanging from each of their bare waists. They were chanting and grunting and shaking my car in unison. I was very edgy at that point.

I had no idea what their intentions were. I just buried myself under my blanket and began to pray. Slowly I realized the rocking and chanting had stopped. I finally looked out again, and I was alone. I went back to sleep. What else could I do? Where else could I go? I was too far from any town, in the middle of the bush just off the old unpaved road between Nairobi and Mombasa. I slept until dawn. It's a reassuring thing to be on good terms with the Lord!

Wisdom Gained: The most secure place you can ever be in this world is in God's hands, doing His will.

23 ACCIDENTAL MEETING WITH IDI AMIN

IDI AMIN WAS a Muslim. After his hajj to Mecca, he came back to Uganda with a strong anti-Christian attitude. A missionary who knew him personally once told me, "Before Amin went to Mecca, he was just a very clever military strategist with a grade four education. When he came back from Mecca, he was demon possessed." There were plenty of reasons to believe this. After Amin's return to Uganda, he committed terrible atrocities, including personally murdering Anglican Bishop Luwuum right in the state house in Kampala. I had met the bishop at the Pan Africa Christian Leadership Assembly just two weeks prior to his murder.

I know God was with me, and He had another purpose. God wins again! I was very grateful to be in His employ.

My office in Kenya was in Church House, in downtown Nairobi. I occasionally walked over to the Hilton Hotel for lunch. They had good fish and chips, and it only cost about 75 cents. Once as I walked up the broad steps into the Hilton, I noticed that a large crowd had gathered and was looking at the entrance. Curious.

When I mounted the steps and turned left to walk toward the restaurant, I turned to look again at the crowd behind me, wondering what was so fascinating. Hmm.

As I turned back to enter the restaurant, I walked right into Idi Amin's chest. Since his chest was just below my eye level, I got a good look at all medals he had given himself. We both politely said, "Excuse me." His bodyguards parted to let me through to the restaurant.

I was dumbfounded. I had come face-to-face with a president who was known for the slaughter of many thousands of Ugandan citizens. I got away without a scratch, just lost a bit of oxygen for a moment.

I thought much later, if I had "taken him out," so to speak, I could have saved the thousands of lives he was subsequently responsible for taking. Of course, I would have died too. Just a thought! Yes, even Christians can have fleeting stupid thoughts.

Wisdom Gained: Never overthink a problem; just keep moving forward, knowing that every step you take is ordered and known by the Lord.

24 MIRACLE RAIN IN DROUGHT

A MOST EXTRAORDINARY day began in such an ordinary way.

In 1963, two missionaries, a Southern Baptist and a Pentecostal, decided to plant a church together. The Karamojong were nomadic pastoralists tucked away in the far northeast corner of Uganda, bordering on both Kenya and Sudan.

The Karamojong were not a particularly welcoming people. They were suspicious of strangers. Their wealth was their cattle. Periodic raids against the Turkana in Kenya to steal livestock, and sometimes wives, were their stock-in-trade.

The men wore little or no clothing, sometimes only a piece of cloth draped over one shoulder and secured with a rawhide belt, with a short sword hanging from it. They all carried a spear and a stool/pillow carved from wood. Many men still packed their hair with clay to form great mounds on the backs of their heads. These were coloured with natural dyes of blue, red, and yellow and often decorated with ostrich feathers. Their hair must have been heavy with the added bulge of clay on the back. Their lower lips were pierced, and a large wooden plug was inserted as a mark of some status and, I assume, to avoid drooling. Their overall appearance was fierce and intimidating.

The women wore only a small loincloth made of rawhide and decorated around the edges with coloured weaving and beads. They usually had a clay pot on their heads, carrying either water or food of some kind or wood for their cooking fires.

The women did the work. The men fought the wars. They all resisted change from the outside world.

It had not rained in the area for 22 months when Jim Hooten and I set out across the semi-desert wilderness from Soroti. Before our many-hours way, we had picked up one of my occasional interpreters, Cornelius Eremu, who lived in Soroti. Cornelius spoke his own language, Ateso, as well as Kiswahili, English, the language of the Karamojong, and probably a few more.

We took the main road, dusty and dry, to the main town, Moroto. Neither Jim nor I had ever been quite as choked by dust as on that trip. It was hot—desperately hot. My little VW Beetle didn't have air conditioning, so we had to drive with the windows open. Cornelius, a rather tall man of about six foot five, had folded himself sideways into the back seat. He bore the brunt of the dust that came in through the windows and every other opening in the vehicle.

These were days of drought and terrible hunger. The rivers were bone dry. Jim and I stopped at one bridge and looked down into the riverbed of sand. The women had dug an ever-narrowing hole in the riverbed until they found some sludgy water about 15 feet down. There they dipped out dirty water with a calabash into pots they carried to their villages, for both themselves and the cattle and camels they owned. The water looked like pale cocoa. It was as undeveloped and arid an area as I had ever seen.

Jim, Cornelius, and I continued down the road. We saw a large cloud of dust. Assuming it was an oncoming truck, we slowed to a crawl. The dust on the road was as fine as talcum powder and just as slippery. As we approached the cloud, we realized it was not a vehicle but about 25 women and children dancing and shouting in unison. They were shaking small tree branches in the air as they chanted and danced. Cornelius explained to us that they were performing a rain dance to the god Edeke.

Rinderpest, or some other deadly cattle disease, had killed off many of their cattle many years before. The Karamojong believed it had happened because they had angered their god, Edeke. We stopped in the middle of the road as they chanted and danced in our direction. I said to Jim, "I think I'll tell them about

Elijah, who prayed for rain." As Cornelius and I were getting out of the car, Jim said to me, "You Pentecostals will do anything!" Yup.

I leaned on the front of the VW beetle, and the women quieted as they approached the car. After Cornelius spoke the greetings, I began to talk to them about Elijah and about his God. I told how Elijah had prayed for rain. I went into some detail as I recounted the biblical account. I kept it as simple as I knew how so they could understand. I told them that the God of Elijah was the one and only Supreme God who created the world, and even the Karamojong.

Then I tried to tell them about God having sent his Son Jesus to save us all. It was a hard concept to get across to people who might not understand what sin was and what God's law might be. I emphasized that the book I held in my hand was the words of the Supreme God. At that point things got dicey. They started shouting at me. I was a bit intimidated and wasn't sure what had touched them off. These were tough-looking women. Cornelius had already told me just how tough they were.

When it was decided that a couple should get married, they had a custom to ascertain whether the marriage should take place at all. It involved a knock-down drag-out fight between the prospective bride and groom. If the young woman won, the wedding was off. If the man won, it was on, as he knew he could control his wife-to-be. I daresay some women lost easily on purpose, approving the choice of husband. The elders judged whether the prospective bride was putting genuine effort into the fight. Some of these Karamojong women with some younger kids now stood in the middle of the road we needed to travel.

The women began to shout at me that I should pray for rain, Cornelius interpreted. Hey! I was here to share the gospel, not produce rain!

The shouting continued. I finally agreed to pray to the God of Elijah but asked them to be quiet while I prayed. They complied. I bowed my head and had every word of my prayer translated into their language. I kept repeating the name of Jesus, Son of God, and our Saviour. I worked the gospel presentation into the prayer. Then I asked God, in Jesus's name, for rain after these 22 months of drought. We got back into the car and drove on.

We went the remaining miles into the little village of Moroto, the "capital" of these nomadic wanderers. The first thing that caught my eye in that dry, dusty, and barren place was a battered tin sign advertising Coca Cola. It crossed my mind that Christians should be as thorough advertising the water of life.

A short, somewhat crooked dusty street with little dingy shops on only one side appeared to be the Moroto town. We drove around trying to find the district commissioner to discuss the possibility of getting land to build a church. After several hours we hadn't found anyone with any authority to do anything, so we decided to return home to Mbale via Soroti, the same way we had come.

I don't remember whether it was Jim or me who suddenly had a feeling of apprehension.

We looked down the only road back and saw "a cloud, as small as a man's hand" (1 Kings 18:44 NKJV). The air was a coppery haze of shimmering heat. A few light, fluffy rainless cumulus clouds hung around but held no hope, except for an occasional slightly cooling shadow. We waited hesitantly, partly because of the possibility of meeting some tough women, partly still hoping someone with authority would turn up to assign us a piece of land to build a church. There was nothing to delay us, and we really had to get back before dark.

In about two hours the sun would set. The little dark cloud was still there. With a great deal of uneasiness, I drove back out the road on which we had come. And prayed. The cloud had gone! When we approached the spot where we had previously preached to the women, we were awestruck.

For about a mile all around, rain had fallen, apparently a lot of it. I could hardly believe it, but the car slithered to a stop, and we got out. Not only was the ground slippery wet, but tiny little green sprouts had already begun to appear out of the earth. The only person in sight was an old man, sitting under a tree on his wooden stool/pillow. I asked Cornelius to go ask him about the rain. The old man related the story accurately. "White men came by and stopped a rain dance. They asked their God, Jesus, to send rain, and He did."

Jim and I had walked cautiously up behind Cornelius. When Cornelius told us what the man (who was blind) had said, we were more surprised than Cornelius. Our faith had been altogether too tempered by rationalism—probably less than a mustard seed. Their faith was uncorrupted by doubt. God is God after all! Why shouldn't He do such a miracle?

Years later, my father was in Dallas, Texas, where he was introduced by C. M. Ward, the famous Assemblies of God radio preacher, a fellow Canadian. C. M. Ward told the story of this miracle he had heard directly from the Southern Baptist missionary Jim Hooten. He then called on my father to preach, crediting him as being a "great man of faith." Dad set the record straight, stating that it was not him but his son who had seen that miracle from God. He went on to explain that I had written a letter home to my parents relating the experience in much detail.

That miracle of rain after 22 straight months of drought was one of the most remarkable miracles I have ever seen God do. It was certainly God who did it. So often we limit God by simply not asking. But, as I found out years later, that was still not the end of the story.

I was in Sudan in 2006 when I heard the rest of the story in Logobero, South Sudan! We were sitting around a campfire in the evening discussing the wonderful works of God, and I gave an account of the miracle I just described. A grin began to spread across Pastor George Taban's face. I thought he was just enjoying this account. He was almost always smiling anyway.

I had met this Episcopal priest because he was the manager of one of the seven farms Crossroads was sponsoring at the time with the Savannah Farmers Cooperative. I had known him for some years. What I didn't know was that his wife, Tereza, was a woman from the Karamojong tribe in Uganda. George was from the Bari tribe in Sudan. I had no idea that George had married outside his own tribe.

Apparently, Tereza had told George of this event. When I found that she was Karamojong, I requested that she come to the campfire. I asked if she had heard about that unusual rain that came when a missionary prayed for rain back in 1963. She lit up like a light bulb. "Oh yes!" she said. Then she related to me in remarkably accurate detail the incident as it had happened. She went on to tell me what I had never known. It had caused a real stir among the Karamojong. They had gone to a Roman Catholic mission to ask about this God named Jesus. Apparently, many Karamojong became believers because of that miracle.

When God does something out of the ordinary, word gets around. One sows, another waters, but God gives the increase. And it was certainly God who did it, despite our fearful lack of faith in returning by the road, which we thought might cause us trouble. It was years later that I heard that the Church Missionary Society of the Church of England planted scores of churches in the area.

Miracles such as this have a way of standing out in your memory. They remind us once again that God is all powerful and still answers prayer.

Wisdom Gained: Never let a cloud of doubt hamper your faith in the glory of His sovereign omnipotence. Read Job 38 for the four minutes it takes. Consider the greatness of our Lord!

25 WATER BAPTISM IN AFRICA

NO MINISTER'S LIFE would be complete without some insights into just how amusing a baptismal service can become!

The first water baptismal service I ever conducted was while pastoring in Wellington, Ontario. It involved some tensions and controversy over the baptismal formula and procedure. I had never had a dispute with the biblical form of total immersion. Under special circumstances I would have no objection to baptism by sprinkling, pouring, or otherwise, especially for those whose medical condition did not allow for total immersion.

But by floating? That became another story.

Mount Elgin straddles the border between Kenya and Uganda. The dirt road to Bulambuli weaves its way, snake-like, up the Ugandan side of the mountain. Many people live on the slopes of Mount Elgin, but few at that time had more than a bicycle. A church had been planted "way up there" by one of the PAG evangelists, and they wanted "the missionary" to come and baptize the new believers.

I was the only missionary in Uganda from our denomination at the time, so, on the appointed Sunday, Mary and I took our little Volkswagen for an upward drive. The Volkswagen made it most of the way. We were greeted by the elders, and they showed us a rather fast-moving small stream formed by melting snow coming down from the mountaintop.

There was a small pool in an almost flat little meadow where the church was located. They had deepened the stream a bit by building a small dam. The water was crystal clear and ice cold. I had to stand in that! Mercy! We had a short service where I explained the meaning of Christian baptism and, since we believe in it, baptism by immersion. When I stepped into the water, I pretended successfully that I could manage it, to a point. Cold!

After I had baptized several men and women, an old man, with a peaceful look of pure delight on his wrinkled face, came to be immersed. He must have been used to this water, since he waded in with no reaction, other than that beatific smile on his face. I positioned him, crossed his hands over his chest, put my left hand in the middle of his thin back, and with the words "On your confession of faith in the Lord Jesus Christ as your own personal Saviour, I now baptize you in the name of the Father, and of the Son, and of the Holy Spirit," I placed my right hand over his mouth and nose to protect him from breathing in any water. I then lowered him, feet upstream, into the water. Then the current caught him and took him away from my grasp.

He lay placidly and sublimely on the water, eyes closed, as it began to rush him downstream. His hands were still crossed on his chest. Perhaps he thought he was getting the A1 first-class baptism. He floated away, heading straight for a rocky rapid, headfirst. He was far beyond my reach. Suddenly some men jumped into action. With tree branches and sticks, they finally snagged his clothes and steered him to shore, where they helped him out of the water. The smile never once left his face, and his hands went up in the air, praising God. When the excitement died down. I baptized the remaining candidates with great caution and a firmer grip. I came out of that stream shivering.

They offered me chai. Something hot would do me good, so I accepted. When they brought it to me, it already had milk in it. That's the way they make chai. They boil the water, tea leaves, sugar, milk, and masala spice together. That is good chai. I took a gulp and suddenly forgot how cold I was. It tasted like sewage, not that I've ever really tasted sewage. It was coffee!

I have never liked coffee, ever! Whatever they did to this was designed specifically to confirm that I would never drink coffee again, ever! I found that they grew the coffee themselves, dried it in the sun after taking the husks off, then roasted and ground it themselves. I can't remember whether Mary drank that coffee, even though she likes the stuff.

Two other baptismal services stand out in my memory.

One was in the Luo tribal area, on rather low and flat land. The congregation had dammed a small slow-moving stream. There was a pool of rather dirty water, deep enough for full immersion baptism.

As I stepped into the stream it barely covered my knees by a few inches, but that was not the problem. It was the wiggly little creatures that distracted me. Bites, bugs, and bilharzia were more on my mind than the task at hand. I think I baptized that small number of new Christians in record time.

But perhaps the most memorable occasion was in the Embu area of Kenya at the base of Mount Kenya. I had been invited to preach at a rather large youth convention organized by a trans-denominational Christian youth association in Kenya. I was astounded at the crowd that came, numbering several thousand.

I had been asked to speak on an assigned subject, "The Fat Is the Lord's." A rather odd topic! I found the phrase repeated in Leviticus but had trouble trying to come up with a subject that could be applicable to a gathering of high school students. Finally, I settled on the thought that, as Christians, when we have more than enough for ourselves, the excess, "the fat," belongs to the Lord. It's a sermon I still preach from time to time on giving out of our plenty.

After the service, I was asked if I would assist in baptizing young people who had decided to follow the Bible's instruction. They wanted to declare publicly their witness by demonstrating their death to self and renewing of life in Jesus Christ through the sacrament of baptism. I had not come prepared for this. A change of clothes would have been handy.

I could hardly believe the number of young people wanting to be baptized.

Two African pastors and I stepped into this extremely cold water running down from snow-capped Mount Kenya. I cannot be sure of exactly how many I baptized, but it was nearly five hundred. The two African pastors each baptized about the same number also. Having stood in the cold water for such a length of time, I was almost unable to walk as I came out of the river. I was taken to a hut where I could dry out by a fire, and when I looked, my legs were an unhealthy looking blue. It took several hours of shivering before I felt anywhere near normal.

Yet, at the same time, I could not help but rejoice that so many Kenyan young people were turning to God and unashamedly giving witness to their new birth in Jesus Christ.

There are moments in Christian ministry that are sheer exhilaration. This was one of them!

Wisdom Gained: Life is full of chilling challenges, both large and small, but with the right attitude and the Lord by your side, they too can be turned into heartwarming delights.

26 FURLOUGH

BEING ON FURLOUGH is a trying experience. You try to spend time with family and friends. You try to raise funds for your support for the next term on the field. You try to get some real holiday and rest. You try to get used to a different bed every night while travelling across Canada. You try not to be concerned over-much with where you really should be (Africa). You try to live frugally in a rich culture, knowing what the rest of the world lacks. You try to keep your conscience under wraps as you eat a T-bone steak that costs too much. And I always tried to eat as much blueberry pie as possible.

I still have all these trying moments from time to time.

Furlough, though tiring, is also invigorating. As you promote your mission and call in life, you also constantly remind yourself of the need and the call. It becomes inescapable. Your calling and election become more established. One of the privileges is occasionally travelling with missionary statesmen like Clare Scratch, Jack Lynn, and any one of the Skinner clan. They were mentors to younger missionaries.

Occasionally a service will stand out in memory, either because of the pastor and people or because of the startling response to the challenge of missions. One meeting I will never forget was with Pastor Marvin Forsyth in

New Westminster, BC. This was prior to the present system that calls on every missionary to raise their own personal support. Back then, we raised missions' offerings for a general fund from which all missionaries received their allowances and their project support. It was more generic. It was also easier than asking people to cover your personal needs.

The church was full, and there came a very real sense of the presence and power of God in the service. As I preached and presented the need, the congregation was very attentive. When I finished, Pastor Forsyth stood to ask for the offering. His remarks were few, but he did mention that in Canada we have so much more than we need, and people around the world, and in Kenya where I was serving at the time, have little or nothing.

The people were hushed as the ushers received the offering, sometimes waiting in the aisle to give folk a chance to write a cheque. When the offering was brought to the front, the offering plates contained much more than cheques and cash. There were written notes and jewelry, rings, and necklaces. One diamond ring was so large it had to be worth about eight thousand dollars. Others were going to sell some possession and bring the money when it was sold. There were IOUs written and signed. A true "spirit of giving" had descended on that church. I had never been so astounded or seen anything like it, before or since.

Camp meetings were often a challenge. They had set a goal for the offering at Cobourg Camp in Ontario for the missionary service. Some folk may think it is easy for a missionary to ask for money for missions, even for general offerings. I find it somewhat easier to ask for support for "missions" or a specific project rather than for myself as a missionary.

In this service, it was a general missionary offering. I sensed God's help as I presented the need for world missions. The offering, I was told later, was by far the largest missionary offering ever received at that camp until then. There is a strange psychology at work sometimes. When a certain missionary was able to raise a larger offering, they were expected to do it every time. The fact of the matter is, unless the Spirit of God is present, the offering will be based on only an emotional response or a sense of duty felt by the givers. When God moves, money moves too.

I had been travelling for months from church to church, but for a change, I not only had a night off, but I was also at home in Toronto with Mary and our children. We had adopted our two children. John was adopted during a furlough in Canada. Then Mary made a special trip home to Canada, with John, to adopt a baby girl, Elaine. They became the delights of our life.

I had never heard our missionary Larry Ulseth preach or make an appeal. He was to preach in Stone Church in downtown Toronto. I wanted to hear him on that Wednesday night, so I went. Larry preached well. I listened well and enjoyed his presentation. Then the Lord spoke to my heart, and I wasn't ready to listen well. I felt a strong impression that I should empty my savings account of its $430 and give it to missions. I had been saving that money for my two children's future education! How could God ask me to surrender that?

My aim was legitimate. I wanted my two children to have a better chance at higher education than I had. Besides, I didn't have my chequebook with me. I went home a little under the weather. Should I do it? I struggled with that for days. When Saturday came, I realized I had to preach the next day, asking people to sacrificially support missions overseas. How could I ask people to do what I was not willing to do? I sat down, wrote out a cheque for the full $430, and sent it in the mail to our International Missions Office. A heavy weight lifted off me. I felt free to preach the next day.

A few weeks later, I was called by my cousin, Ken Bombay, to come to Kamloops and preach a weekend of evangelistic services. Ken knew nothing about my struggle two weeks previously, and I had no idea of the financial arrangements other than that my plane ticket would be paid. We had wonderful meetings and times of refreshing. In the last meeting on Sunday night, Ken decided that he would ask for a "love offering" for the speaker—me. I had been in Africa long enough that I wasn't familiar with the term "love offering." Perhaps I would get some hugs from people? The offering was over eight hundred dollars and was specifically for me, not missions. I was beginning to learn that obedience always brings blessings. It's not always financial, but some form of blessing follows, always!

There were occasions on furlough when it was just too demanding. I had preached in North Bay, Ontario (my birthplace), on a Sunday morning. During the service, it had begun to rain, freezing rain. I was expected to be in Sudbury for the evening service. I had a quick lunch and a slow and dangerous drive ahead. The road to Sudbury was slick. There were no cellphones in those days. What would people think if I didn't arrive? So, I crawled on. The long hill down into Sudbury really made me nervous.

I finally made it, slithering into the parking lot of the church moments before the service was to start. I realized the parking lot was empty but for one car. The pastor was there. I didn't know what to think. He said, "I don't know how you made it! We cancelled the service."

We had church at the pastor's house that night. All three of us! As usual, we sat up and talked of missions until early the next morning. It's amazing the number of questions and the depth of interest people have in missions when you are in their homes as a guest. Sleep was the last thing on their minds, though the first on mine. A bed rarely felt as good anywhere as that bed that night.

I had one unscheduled furlough. I was given a free ticket on the inaugural flight of Pan Am from Nairobi to New York and back. As a result, I spent a wonderful week with my father, travelling around Ontario as he filled his duties as district superintendent. I had heard of the death of Jomo Kenyatta just as I was leaving New York. I authored the following poem about him during the flight back to Kenya.

It was printed on the front page of one of the two English newspapers in Kenya a day after I got back. Here it is:

HIS EXCELLENCY, MZEE JOMO KENYATTA
Very few men on the face of God's earth
Have proven their wisdom, and shown us their worth
As Jomo Kenyatta, this continent's son,
Who ruled us with love, despising not one.
He had reason to hate and to look for a way
To get back at the white men who'd locked him away.
But rather than propagate evil and wrath,
He showed us the way down the *Harambee** path.
His way was of unity, justice, and love.
He seemed to be tutored by God from above.
For often when races and tribes disagreed,
For unity, justice, and love he would plead.
He nurtured this nation of people with hope.
He inspired us all to widen our scope.
The freedom he won us will live on secure,
He established forgiveness, the national cure.
Freedom of worship was one guarantee

That was given by law to you and to me,
For clearly, he saw from God's Holy Book
That for guidance and Truth, to God we must look.
His body is dead, but his spirit lives on.
The strength of his wisdom will never be gone.
His soul from his body has found sweet release,
But he gave to us all, that we live on in peace.
Cal. R. Bombay
Nairobi, Kenya
Sept. 1, 1978
* *Harambee* means "all together" in Kiswahili. It was a common rallying cry.

When in prison as a ringleader during *Maumau*, the national uprising for independence in Kenya, Jomo Kenyatta had a Bible in his cell throughout his incarceration.

Wisdom Gained: Never ever underestimate the power of the Holy Bible. It alone can accomplish what human effort can never accomplish. God's Word is unparalleled, everlasting, and powerful in its impact throughout history.

27 MIRACLES NEVER CEASE

JUST AFTER MARY and I were shifted out of Uganda at the behest of a tribally oriented decision, Mary and I were asked where we wanted to go. We gave our answer. They sent us somewhere else. Mary and I were told we would be taking over the development of a new publishing operation attached to Evangel Press that had been founded many years earlier. We would live at Goibei and work at Nyang'ori, two mission stations that were about 13 miles apart.

To Mary and me, that was bad news. Me, a publisher? Yeah, sure! Someone somewhere must have been kidding. I like reading, but I knew nothing whatever about what it meant to put a manuscript into the form of a printed book. Heaven help me!

And heaven did. Work had already begun on a large addition to the printing plant, which would become the publishing offices. Bob Peel was an older missionary experienced in the printed word and a great advisor to me.

A lot of people pitched in and got the place ready. The publishing branch would be a separate operation from Evangel Press. Until then, Evangel Press mostly produced literature to be given out freely but also printed jobs for other missions. The publishing department was to become a commercially viable entity able to survive on the sales of books and other publications. The only sales I had ever done was selling of shoes for often bad-smelling feet at Davidson Shoe Store in Oshawa as a teen before college. Now I had to produce *and* sell books.

The first decision I made was to name the new entity Evangel Publishing House, considering its origins. I chose—plagiarized, I suppose—as our symbol a drawing of a cross held in a hand like a standard. It came from an American Christian magazine. I was unaware of the worldwide copyright laws established in Helsinki, Finland, the same year I was born. But they would come in handy later in my life.

The front of the new building became a bookshop, with my office just off to the left. The only unusual piece of furniture in my office was a drafting table. Someone had to design covers for the new books, so I did it.

Many of the publications we put out were not hard decisions. A newspaper for the Pentecostal churches was a no-brainer. Tracts that had been published by Evangel Press were transferred to the Evangel Publishing House. We then had to assess what the needs of the church were in East Africa. It became apparent quite quickly that pastors needed study materials, church members needed good educational Christian reading, and students at the Christian schools needed textbooks. Decisions were made and action was required.

Now the big question: Who would write all these books? A good question with no immediate answers. I trolled the high schools' teachers, the Bible colleges, and fellow missionaries. No bites! Everyone was already too busy. Missionaries work hard and long hours. But, as the Bible says, "Of making many books there is no end, and much study wearies the body" (Ecclesiastes 12:12). I soon was living proof of that.

Finally, it began to come together. I wrote more than half a dozen books. I recruited African leaders who authored books. We built up an editorial staff and created a bookmobile, and missionaries carried books with them when preaching in various churches. We began publishing in many languages.

We had the inestimable help of Dr. Fred and Grace Holland, who coordinated the writing of a whole series of books called Theological Education by Extension (TEE). We published study books covering every book in the Bible. Circulation for that became easy since authors were writing them all over Africa.

By that time, we needed to import a professional editor. I wrote a six-page impassioned plea for our mission office in Canada to send me an editor. To my total surprise and delight, they sent Rev. Cal Ratz, who just happened to be married to my sister Ruth. He hung a sign on his door, "Word Merchant," and trained several African editors and eventual writers. One of the high school teachers at Nyang'ori, Arnold Labrentz, also transferred into the publishing house and became a lifelong friend and a very efficient editor.

At the same time, we became the official distributor for The Bible Society of Kenya for western Kenya. One highlight of that was receiving ten thousand copies of the newly translated Luhya New Testament. We sold them all in one day at a subsidized price at the official "launch" of the translation. What a time of rejoicing among the Abaluhya people!

Evangel began growing fast! We needed to develop more Africa-wide distribution so that we could publish in large enough quantities to make the books viable and profitable. A move of the whole operation to Nairobi became a priority in my mind. There was some opposition. I moved with my family and set up an office in Nairobi. My office was in Church House in downtown Nairobi for several years. The time finally came when both the African leaders and the missionaries agreed that bringing the press and the publishing sides of Evangel together was essential. Where should we move?

Stan Webb, an African/American architect, was a member of the Christ Is the Answer church that I attended and that my father had built some years before. (See *A Man Worth Knowing* by Cal Bombay.) We conferred, and he began to design. Meanwhile, I began looking for a place to build.

Just outside Nairobi, in Ruaraka, was the former Lumumba Institute. It had been a communist training centre until the government closed it because the graduates had begun to foment upheaval throughout Kenya. American evangelist Morris Cerullo had purchased it. I walked around the perimeter of that large acreage and buildings and asked the Lord to give it to us.

I contacted Morris Cerillo's organization. They said they would sell it since it stood unused for 95 percent of the year. The price? Four hundred thousand dollars. Gulp! I took the matter to Rev. Bill Cornelius, who had stood strongly with me in this vision for the growth of Evangel. We sent off an appeal to our mission office in Canada. They agreed to buy the property *and* to pay the asking price, which was, in fact, a real deal for 23 acres with many buildings.

Stan Webb just happened to have created blueprints for a similar project that had been cancelled. He made some slight changes and stated that he was willing to oversee the building of the large new "H" shaped buildings. One side of the building would be for the press and publishing house offices. The other would be for warehousing and paper storage. But where would the money come from?

God!

I picked up the mail one day and opened a letter from the USA. It was from a preacher I had heard once in my life years before at Cobourg Camp in Ontario. I didn't know he even knew who or where I was. When I opened the letter, there was a cheque for ten thousand dollars, designated "for the project you are building soon." How did he know what I was doing?

That was the seed money that began the miracle that never stopped. Morris Cerullo sent back two hundred thousand dollars, half the original purchase price, as a donation toward the building of the new facility. When I left Africa to return to Canada, there was a debt of less than thirty-five thousand dollars.

Before I left Africa, I went on several (often both dangerous and exhilarating) sales trips throughout East and West Africa. We had published books in 43 languages, including several West African languages. Our major thrust was English, followed by Kiswahili. Our Theological Education by Extension (TEE) series was eventually published in 104 languages, literally around the world. We became the distributors in Africa for a large Christian publisher in England. Evangel Publishing House became the largest Christian book distributor in Africa, other than the combined Bible Societies.

When I left, I was confident that it was in good hands, both missionary and national staff. One of our editors, Elkanah Salamba, became the general superintendent of the Pentecostal Assemblies of God, in Kenya. Others became pastors. I became a TV teacher and occasional host. Life just has too many surprises.

All of this illustrates clearly that what often seems like a disappointment, a crisis, or a terrible personal disaster, God can turn into good.

Me, a publisher? Yeah, I guess so!

At the same time, I could not help but rejoice that so many Kenyan young people were turning to God and unashamedly giving witness to their new birth in Jesus Christ. There are situations in Christian ministry that are sheer exhilaration. This was one of them!

Wisdom Gained: Whatever God puts in your hands to do deserves obedience, energy, and vision. You may find yourself subject to someone else's decision. Just do it! You may realize that your own decision would have been a mistake.

28 DIRECT TRANSFUSION

A KALENJIN TRIBESMAN was sitting on the rise at the side of the road, leaning against the legs of another man, who held the man's head upright. The bloodied man was distraught and babbling. One arm looked awkwardly displaced.

I was driving a Volkswagen Variant station wagon because of my need to transport literature. I never had looked on my car as an ambulance. I pulled to a stop beside the two men. The victim was a blood-covered mess. His left arm was almost severed and was hanging by some flesh and skin, the bone completely chopped through. He was delirious, breathing heavily, singing, and mumbling one language and then another. Then he would whistle. His rambling was terribly disconcerting and disturbing. He was near death.

I lowered the back seats of my station wagon so that we could lay him down flat. I went to help lift the thin man into the car. At that point, I realized why the man behind him was holding his head upright. The back of his head had been viciously slashed with a *panga*. I could see brain matter. Blood was pouring from both his arm and his head. He continued his mumbling, singing, and whistling. We lifted him as gently as we could into the back of the station wagon, and his friend got in with him to hold him.

I drove like a mad man to the hospital some 10 miles away.

I had to go through the Banja market, past the Goibei mission station (home), and on to the hospital on the Friends African Mission (Quaker) compound. When we arrived at the hospital the doctor and several aides were there. They acted quickly, assessing the damage. I sat and waited as they took the injured man into the operating room. Moments later, the doctor came out and asked me what blood type I had. I had no idea. He took a sample, evaluated it, and asked if I would be willing to give some of my blood to the man, who would certainly die otherwise from blood loss.

Mission hospitals, especially back in the '60s, were not very well equipped. They had no such thing as a blood bank or even a constant supply of electricity to maintain a storage facility if they did have a supply. It took only a moment to say yes. I figured they would simply take a pint and then give the man a transfusion. But it was not to be so simple. The man needed blood now. They laid me down on a gurney, rolled me into the operating room, and did a direct transfusion from me to the man. I'm not sure how much blood I gave, but it seemed to drag on forever.

Even lying down, I began to feel woozy. Finally, the doctor pulled his mask from his face, looked at me, and said, "We lost him." Then he unhooked the tube from my hand. He looked defeated. I felt deflated. I had done all that I could, even to the point of giving my blood to a total stranger.

The man who had come with me was still sitting outside, waiting. I was given something sweet to drink by the doctor and wobbled over to sit with the man. His English was imperfect, but between English and Swahili he told me what had happened. The man who now lay dead in the operating room had had a dispute with his own brother over the boundary of the land they had inherited from their father. The dispute was over a strip of about one foot of land between their properties. Their vicious disagreement ended in death.

When the sweet drink the doctor had given me kicked in a little, I felt like perhaps I could drive. I took the friend of the dead man back where I had found him and then returned to Goibei, where all I wanted to do was sleep. And I did, after I ate a good meal and told Mary what had happened.

It took me several days to recover, both physically and emotionally. This was early in my first term as a missionary in Kenya. I had seen extraordinarily little of bloody violence up until that point. Sudan was many years in the future, and the war at Banja market was yet in the future.

Later, I thought about having given my blood in vain. But I had tried. I had done my best. My best, even with the best the doctor could do, was not good enough. Then I began to think about some other blood: the blood of Jesus Christ, the Son of God, whose blood washes sins away. It never fails.

Wisdom Gained: Christian giving can be done in several ways. Sometimes it will be at great sacrifice and show no immediate benefit. Leave that in the hands of God. Love is selfless and sometimes seems wasted. Never.

29 SAVED FROM A FIERY DEATH

EVANGEL PUBLISHING HOUSE became larger through sales. We hired a man named Javan Kavai to be the driver and salesman for the bookmobile. It started well, almost too well. A lot of money was passing through the driver/salesman's hands. It became a temptation to Javan. Sales were increasing, and a weekly accounting was set in place for both stock and sales.

Then things went awry. When we compared stock with sales, there was a shortage. Javan was pocketing some of the sales, a rather lot of the sales. The more he got away with it, the more he tried to get away with. Javan was also building a fine house for his wife and children. He said people were stealing the books. My warnings were disregarded, and finally I had to dismiss him. He was not happy. As if I was?

It should be noted that poverty is an awful thing. When opportunity comes to get any kind of income, there is always a temptation to try to "improve" the amount of income. Most of us in the Western world have never experienced extreme poverty such as exists throughout much of sub-Saharan Africa.

In Africa, a man thinks not only of his own needs but often of the needs of his extended family. The needs are so many. They are hard to disregard. They also see the material advantages of those who have higher incomes. Under those circumstances, it is tough to choose to be satisfied with what little you do have. Politicians often set examples that seem to publicly justify theft.

Javan declared his innocence with vehemence. The proof was positive, so he was firmly released from his job. We never heard from him for over a year. We hired another man, and sales went on well, even better.

One day Javan appeared unexpectedly in my office at Evangel Publishing House. There was a strange, quiet tension in the bookshop just outside my office as Javan passed through to my office.

I stood to welcome him and waited for what might happen. I had some apprehension since on an earlier occasion my life had been threatened when I dismissed an employee at the Goibei mission station where Mary and I lived. I had found that our watchman seldom did his duties, but the end came when I found him sleeping when he should have been working as a groundman for the mission. He said he was going to finish me with a spear.

The loss of a job was a serious blow. It was considered a great embarrassment and "loss of face," as well as a threat to the family's survival. That Goibei incident passed with the help and involvement of the Kenya Employment Bureau. When they heard the evidence, they stood solidly with our decision.

When he was dismissed, Javan had just walked out in a barely repressed rage. Now I looked at Javan's disheveled condition and a haunted look on his face. He stood silently for a while, and then he told me his story.

He had been on a bus on his way to Nairobi from Kisumu. As the bus sped down the narrow highway it collided head-on with a truck carrying barrels of aviation fuel. The bus and truck both burst into flames, and the explosion of aviation fuel roared through the bus from front to back. Javan was sitting in the back row of the bus, and he was literally blown right out the emergency exit. He landed on the road and, in terror, leaped to his feet and began running back down the road away from the blazing vehicles. He was the only survivor. Everyone else was incinerated, and a great hole was burned into the tarmac of the highway.

Javan had come straight to my office, stating, "God had mercy on me, and I came to confess that I was guilty of stealing from the bookmobile. Please forgive me!" I forgave him and, after commiserating and praying with him, let him go home to his family. The last thing I heard about him, he was serving the Lord faithfully.

Sometimes God allows us to go through terrifying experiences in His love for us and His desire that we walk in close fellowship and obedience to Him.

The very fact that Javan survived such an ordeal seemed to indicate that God still had a plan for his life. It augurs well for a person who humbles himself, confesses his sins, and then gets on with living the Christian life.

Wisdom Gained: Truth is based on veritable facts. Truth is not based on a point of view or the interpretation of facts. You and I do not have a personal truth as opposed to others. That's why Jesus was able to say, with absolute verity, "I am the Truth."

30 THE DEAF HEAR!

RAIN IS IMPORTANT in any country that depends almost solely on agriculture for survival. This is true in western Kenya, where the land, though very fertile, is highly overpopulated. Through generations, sons have inherited pieces of their father's land until their holdings are so small, they can barely survive. If rains fail, it becomes critical.

When a person arrives just as a rainstorm starts, the people claim that that person has brought a real blessing, as though his arrival had something to do with the rain. Where we lived, we knew when it was about four p.m. because that's when it rained every day in the rainy season. So, you are a blessing when you come with rain. Time your arrival right, and you immediately have a great reputation!

Within a few miles from Nyang'ori, where Evangel Publishing House was located at the time, there were many churches of the Pentecostal Assemblies of God (Kenya—PAG). There were also many other churches besides PAG churches, representing a wide variety of denominations. It was not uncommon to have a PAG church within a stone's throw of one of the other denominations in the area. The population was dense. A great deal of growth had taken place in the church in Western Kenya, and the PAG was not the smallest by any standards.

I was invited to preach at a youth convention during the rainy season at a place called Maseno. The church was not far from the denominational headquarters of another large fellowship. Although it was a youth convention, everyone came, from babies through to the very elderly.

I had preached for two days. Each day I was finished before the usual rain began. The third day the rain started early, while the singing was going on. Their singing was loud and enthusiastic. You couldn't hear an individual voice because of the pounding of the rain on the tin roof.

While it was raining heavily, they turned it over to me to preach. There was no public address system. I didn't know what to do, so through my friend Joash Okong'o, who was interpreting for me that day, I bellowed out that I was going to ask the Lord to hold back the rain until the service was over. They looked at me, understanding but somewhat puzzled.

I prayed, and even though it was unlikely to be heard, Joash beside me shouted out the interpretation. Within a few minutes after we prayed, the rain stopped completely, though the clouds were heavy. I preached. I had promised that on this day I would pray for the sick. When I asked for those needing prayer to come to the front, the whole mass of people tried to move forward. I asked them all to leave the church and asked the elders to form the people into two lines. I would pray for one line, and Joash would pray for the other. We were laying our hands on them as we prayed. I was tiring fast after praying for scores of people. The rain held off.

Two boys reached the head of the lines, with their mothers. They were about nine and ten years of age. They were both profoundly deaf. I paused and asked the congregation to pray with us for the two boys. As I laid my hand on the boy in front of me and began to pray, I felt his bushy little head abruptly sweep out from under my hand. He was gone when I opened my eyes. He had raced for a woman he recognized and tried to stuff her flowered dress into his ears. I found out later that he had been born deaf. I assume that the sudden noise may have frightened him. People pray loudly in Africa.

The boy for whom Joash was praying was healed as well. He had not been born deaf as had the other and was not frightened as much by the noise. When the people saw what had happened, they erupted in praise to God and shouts of joy. I was blessed myself by the sight of it all.

We finally prayed for everyone who wanted prayer, and the sun was about to set, three hours after the rain usually began. As we left the church, it started to rain heavily, and we were soaked before we got into my car. There's only one word that comes to mind as I remember that day: Hallelujah!

Wisdom Gained: Your hands can be instruments of healing if, in faith and with prayer, you use them for the glory of God. You are more apt to see a miracle if you expect it than if you don't. That may be the only difference between hope and faith.

31 APES IN KENYA?

NYANG'ORI MISSION STATION was a beehive of activity. Quite a few missionary families lived there, serving in the workshop, printing press, or publishing house or in the primary, secondary, or Bible schools. Located in the hills above Lake Victoria, this was the birthplace of the Pentecostal Assemblies of East Africa. A beautiful place!

Golden shower vines covered some of the outhouses (yes, the old half-moon-in-the-door traditional backhouses). Jacaranda trees with beautiful mauve flowers towered high. Gum trees, pine, and others unknown to me peppered the whole mission station. Moon flowers adorned the gardens, and poinsettia bushes were everywhere. The gardens were well tended and beautiful, particularly around the grave of Otto Keller, who founded the mission back in 1911.

The mission station was located within shouting distance of three tribal groups: Maragoli, Luo, and Kalenjin. Nyang'ori was the headquarters for the hundreds of Pentecostal churches for many years. Everyone came to Nyang'ori for help of many kinds. "Please take my wife to the hospital. She is having trouble." "Please pull out a tooth."

Often, people would come and simply "help themselves." That was why we had two nightguards who were supposed to patrol all night around the mission. Often, they slept better than we did.

I don't know if there was ever a night we went to sleep without the sound of drums. Perhaps a celebration, a dance, a death, a home-brew drinking party, a wedding. Drums were just there. After a time, they went unnoticed. There were others sounds too, sometimes the result of our own guns.

Once, after a successful hunt, I had hung a gazelle in my garage to cure. Rev. Albert Vaters, pastor of the Stone Church in Toronto, was visiting. He stayed with me for a while, which I appreciated, since Mary was in Canada for five months looking after the legal matters of adopting our daughter. I was glad for the company.

We knew hyenas and cheetahs lived just over the hills going down to Kisumu and Lake Victoria, but I had only heard of one hyena getting into a scrap with an Alsatian guard dog one night. The dog survived. The hyena went home. One of the hyena's relatives came back one night when Albert was staying with me. The smell of blood from the gazelle, which was by then in my freezer, must have attracted it to my garage. We heard it snorting and grunting outside the house. This was not a good thing. They do eat dogs.

Albert and I were both awakened. I got partially dressed and headed out the front door quietly with my shotgun. I was able to pepper the south end of the hyena as it was lumbering away from me. I didn't know they could run that fast! No lead in his feet, but perhaps in his butt. The sound of the gun caused the whole mission to wake up, but by the time anyone was able to start looking and asking what had happened, my little house was in darkness and quiet. Our African friends knew we had guns.

Across the highway and down toward the west was one of the Pentecostal Kalenjin tribal churches. The population was dense in the whole area, except on the steep hill down to Lake Victoria and in the deep ravine behind the church and school. Not too many people went down into that ravine. Though there was a path through the thick jungle-like trees and underbrush, no people lived down there.

The pastor came to ask a favour of me. Would I please shoot the baboon that kept stealing their small goats and chicken? I told him that, because of the dense human population above the ravine, I'd had to have a letter of authority from the district commissioner before I could shoot his marauding baboon. In due course, he returned with a letter stating clearly that I had permission to shoot the "ape." It was duly signed and stamped by the district commissioner.

Ape?

No one had ever heard of apes being in this part of Africa. Nevertheless, I met the pastor at his church, and after he showed me evidence of the death of a little goat and some chicken feathers, we slowly descended into the ravine by a seldom-used path. We quietly stalked our prey through tunnels in the thick bush where the sun seemed never to reach. It was damp and dank.

At one point, we smelt a terribly pungent odour. It could have been a hyena, it smelt so bad. As we passed under the limb of a large tree with me in the lead, the smell was almost overpowering. Hearing a slight sound, I looked back at the tree we had just passed under, just in time to see a leopard slink off the big limb over the path and silently disappear. I wanted out of there.

We headed back toward the top of the ravine, but a quick escape was not to be. The pastor had sighted the "ape." I raised my 30.07 and was just about to shoot when it disappeared. A moment later, it jumped up into the crotch of a tree with its back to us, turning its head to look at us. It was a big male baboon. I aimed for the red patch on its buttocks, a perfect target in all that green. The sound of the shot was loud but almost swallowed by the thick foliage. The baboon was either scared so badly that it left forever or was ushered into the great beyond. The scream seemed to support the latter. We never went to check, not with a leopard nearby.

Wisdom Gained: Ask yourself if it is fun and fulfilling to be a Christian. I find it to be both fulfilling and fun. If your Christian living does not give you both fun and fulfillment, step it up a notch!

32 HUNTING FOR OUR FOOD

FOR ABOUT EIGHT years, almost all the meat we ate was a result of going out to the Loita plains with legal hunting licenses and bringing back a six-month supply of meat. I bought a 20 cubic foot freezer, in Canada, electrically equipped for the 220-volt, 50 cycle system of Kenya. It made a great packing case when we packed our stuff for Africa.

I was one of the few who had a freezer in that area. Mr. Virani owned the butcher shop in town. He had a cooler where he displayed his meat for sale. Occasionally, we got massive T-bone steaks quite cheaply, but the plains were our main source. Our most often visited hunting place was a hot spring at the foot of some hills out in the vast plains in Kenya. It was called Maji Moto, meaning "hot water." We set up tents and made camp. We were "the guys" bringing home the bacon.

The plains were crowded with game grazing on the rich grasses of the Rift Valley. Almost every animal of East Africa could be seen on any given day. The least seen were lions, leopards, and cheetahs. Vast herds of zebras and wildebeests mixed with other herds of hartebeests, and Thompson's and Grant's gazelles were common. Slightly less common were groups of impalas, the bucks with startlingly long horns. The biggest and the smallest animals were less common, such as elephants, rhino, giraffes, and elands. Dik-diks and duikers were as scarce as warthogs, bushbucks, and some kinds of monkeys. Not all were game, but all were fascinating.

I shot a warthog. When we brought the van to the animal, I got out of the sliding side door to bleed it properly. Suddenly it leaped up and charged me. Warthogs have vicious tusks that can tear holes in you and shred you. I established a new world record in running backward as it charged me. My feet had just left the ground as I leaped backward in through the side door of the van when the warthog reached me. I was fortunate. It collapsed in the act of climbing into the open Volkswagen, its tusk clanging on the lower door frame. Its heart had stopped beating, but mine was making up for its loss.

We needed another pig. Arn Bowler was walking in front of me as we were trying to flush a warthog out of a little ravine into which it had run when it saw the van. We had driven toward it, keeping our eyes peeled for the warthog rather than the terrain. The right front wheel abruptly dropped into a warthog hole, bending the wraparound bumper up so high that it prevented our opening the front doors. We all scrambled out the sliding side door.

Virgil Gingrich, with a camera and no gun, was chosen to go down into the little ravine and scare the pig out. Arn Bowler, rifle in hand, was in front on the left of the ravine with me behind. I had a skinning knife in my hand. Wilbur Morrison was in front on the right side with a rifle. His cousin Keith followed with nothing in his hands.

Suddenly, from our left, a black-maned lion leaped out of the bush, headed straight for Arn Bowler. I yelled, "LION!" Virgil came flying out of that little ravine, tearing both his skin and his clothes on a bush covered with thorns that grew backward down the stem. That bush had earned its name with most of us. It's called *ngoja kidogo* (wait a bit). Virgil didn't wait, and his light meter is still down there in the ravine somewhere.

The lion appeared to leap over Arn Bowler; then it sped off into a thicket of bushes and disappeared. So did Keith Morrison—disappear, that is! We called for him, often. No answer. Worrisome, that! We eventually headed back to the listing Volkswagen van, which was stuck in the warthog hole. We found Keith right about then. We heard him first. He had crawled into the back of the van and over the front seat and was sitting, trembling and white, with a hammer in his hand, saying repeatedly, "You guys are crazy. You guys are crazy!" Well, maybe we were, but we had a lot of fun.

One of the boring hunts occurred while I was hunting with Jack Lynn, a senior PAOC missionary. At evening, we went randomly off the road and set up camp near a few small fever trees. We parked my pop-up camping trailer a few hundred yards from the track on which we had driven. We had our supper cooked over an open campfire. Ah! Such luxury!

The heavens were beautiful, undiminished by any city lights. The blackness was pierced by the clear twinkle of a zillion stars. We left our camp chairs in front of the zippered entrance and went to bed thinking we'd go hunting for *kongoni* (hartebeest) the next morning. The meat is every bit as good as beef.

In the morning when we stepped out of the tent, we were totally dumbfounded. A herd of hartebeests surrounded us. They paid us no attention whatsoever. We loaded our guns, sat in our camp chairs, and said, "Let's choose our beasts, and on the count of three, we fire." Moments later the herd was gone, except for our two downed animals. We cleaned them and hung them in a nearby tree, and then we got bored. We had come for three days! We had finished our hunting, cleaning, skinning, and breakfasting within two hours or so. Jack began to wonder out loud how many bullets it would take to fell a tree about 100 feet away.

The trunk was about six inches in diameter. It was a question that really begged an answer. We started guessing. Three shots later the tree fell. We concluded that, had we been better shots, it would have been two bullets.

The most shocking experience happened while we (and I forget who all the "we" were on that hunt) were camped again at the hot spring on the Loita plains. We had hunted the day before and had our game hanging in the trees around our camp, all of it to become future roasts, steaks, and ground meat. Some we hung to dry as biltong.

Paul Twigg went for a walk and came back with an ashen look on his face. He said, "I found a head!"

"What do you mean?" we asked.

"A head!" he said. "A human head!"

We ran for our guns and followed Paul to where he saw it. Sure enough, there lay a human head. Perfect skin, no marks, but we were unable to determine the gender. The age couldn't have more than 20 to 25.

It was late in the evening, and the sun was setting; otherwise we would have taken the head to the police station in Narok about 25 miles away. Instead, we placed it carefully high up in a bush, away from the reach of hyenas, with the intent of reporting to the police in the morning. In the morning, it was gone.

That is still a mystery to us, and a gruesome one, at that! We did know that when someone died among the Maasai, particularly of old age, the body was often taken out on the plains and left for the hyenas. That was against the law by then, but the law didn't always reach those remote areas. It could have been a murder; it being at that age, that seemed probable to us. We'll never know. But I doubt we'll ever forget.

Often, when we camped, we had visitors. People from the Wandorobo tribe would wander into our camp and stay for a while, sleeping right on the ground near the fire at night. Little or no conversation. It was their way.

We had shot a warthog on the day a Mwandorobo man came in late in the day. We had butchered and salted the warthog meat, and the rib cage was basically all that was left. The man asked if he could have it. He found a few sticks and propped the rib cage over the dying embers of our fire. He didn't leave it there long, basically restoring the body temperature but certainly not cooking it. Then he broke it up with his hands, contentedly chewed away on the shreds of meat between the ribs, still red and fresh. Ugh! It was their way.

At night, he lay near where he had been sitting and pulled a part of the blanket he had over his shoulder around his body and went to sleep. He obviously had a very contented and unmoving sleep. The only sign he had moved at all was a wet spot where he had lifted his blanket a bit, right where he was, and relieved himself. It was their way.

Then, he took a few bones with flesh on them, said neither a thank you nor a goodbye, and left. It was simply their way.

I am not a crack shot, but I will admit that after taking a slab off a tree in Canada way above ground, I practiced and became quite an accurate rifleman.

On their way home from Thailand, my father and mother stopped by in Kenya to visit us. They had founded the "Christ Is the Answer Church" in Nairobi years before. Even years before that, Dad familiarized me with rifles. Here was an opportunity to show him the fruit of that teaching!

I took him hunting with me. I had never shot an eland, the largest of all African antelopes. That was my goal for this hunt. It would bring home about five hundred pounds of good meat. Dad happily came along. Stephen, who was our eagle-eyed housekeeper/cook, sighted the horns of an eland in the distance just over a rise of land. We stopped the car, and I walked to a massive anthill that was the legal distance from the car. I steadied my aim, leaning on the anthill. With an Enfield rifle from the Second World War, with only a peep-sight, I put the bead about a foot above his neck to allow for distance, pulled the trigger, and dropped him.

My dad, of whom I wrote in my book *A Man Worth Knowing*, could not believe it. That distance? He paced it out twice. It was 340 paces. One problem: the eland had been shot before, and one horn was shot off. I had not seen that, since he (which turned out to be a pregnant she) was standing perfectly broadside to me. Since the beast was pregnant, the meat was useless to us, as it infused with a strange taste. I paid the required fee for having killed an eland.

Once, unintentionally, I bagged some game with my car. Driving up over a rise in the dusty road at a good speed, I saw a large flock of guinea fowl right on the road. I had no chance to avoid them. They couldn't get off the road or into the air fast enough. We picked up 23 of them from the road. That night in camp we had a feast. We salted down a lot of good white meat for the future. Some of my best hunting was accidental.

After hunting for impala all day without success, I was driving out of the area through tall grass. As I swung around a corner in the track, a duiker jumped right into the front of my car. It dressed out nicely and had no hidden bullet to break a tooth while eating the meat.

I had an unscheduled race with a rhino once while I was stalking an impala back into the bush. The impala got away in an area with thin brush. I was walking back toward the car when I heard a loud and increasingly insistent thumping on the ground. I turned and saw a rhino charging straight at me. Had it not been for a steep bank leading up to the road where my car was parked, I would have been on the "horns of a dilemma." The rhino stopped at the base of the rise and sniffed and turned his or her head (I didn't take time to check) and slowly meandered off. Rhino don't see very well, but their sense of smell is marvellous, or perhaps my stink was.

Hunting brought some relaxation and was productive.

Wisdom Gained: Time spent in God's creation of the natural world can be a place of peace, provision, and providence and a place for pleasant prayer. Take time to talk or trek alone through trees and terrain, taking delight in God's great out-of-doors.

33 THE MAASAI TRIBE

THE MAASAI TRIBE of Kenya are an intriguing people. Their culture is both complicated and simple. They herd their thousands of cattle on the plains, building new *bomas* whenever they are finished in one area and have moved to better grass. Though they are traditionally nomadic herders, many have attended university.

While I was general manager of the Evangel Publishing House, I had an association with two Maasai men who exhibited the intelligence and compassion of their people. They were both named John.

The older of the two was John Mpaaiyei. He was head of the Bible Society in Nairobi. He was a brilliant scholar and wrote a most fascinating book. It put into written form much of the oral history of the Maasai people. Although the following is only one of many oral traditions of a similar nature, it reveals significant historical accuracy.

It involved the history of the Maasai when a great flood covered the earth. Eight people alone were saved from death by building a great "raft," on which they survived for a long period of time. It so closely resembled the biblical account of Noah and the flood that it could have had no other source. There were many such oral histories of the Maasai that were clear parallels of the Bible accounts. This oral tradition was retold long before any white people came to interrupt the lives of the Maasai.

The other John for whom I had great appreciation was John Swaakei. He was a student in the Pentecostal Bible College at Nyang'ori Mission, where I taught part-time while I was developing Evangel Publishing House. It was the practice of missionaries at Nyang'ori to go out on weekends to preach or teach in churches, even though their principal ministries were in the schools, the printing plant, or the publishing house. Weekends were not wasted.

John Swaakei had invited me to go into Maasai country to his uncle's *boma* to share the gospel. His uncle, a chief, gathered his wives as well as some elders with all the inhabitants of his *boma*.

A *boma* is a group of houses, surrounded by a thorny fence to keep the animals safe at night. The Maasai traditionally built their houses with roofs so low that it was impossible to stand up inside. The entrance to the house has several sharp turns, which make it most difficult to enter with a spear in hand. In those days, the beds were made of sticks on a slightly raised platform under which their goats and chickens slept. Walls and floor were smeared with a soupy mixture made of cow dung and mud to keep bugs and creepy-crawlies away. They were totally dark and lit only by a small flickering fire in the centre.

We pitched our tent outside the *boma*. The ground inside the *boma* was un-inviting—it was covered with cow dung. "We" consisted of Paul Twigg, a printer who worked with Evangel Press, and Arnie Labrentz, a teacher at Nyang'ori Secondary School, and me.

I've never been in quite the same kind of "church meeting" before or since. It started with their own protocol of introductions. Through John Swaakei as our interpreter, we were invited to speak. Paul Twigg gave his testimony of what Jesus had done in his life, though I'm not too sure how many of the Western concepts they understood. Then Arnie Labrentz spoke for a while, explaining who Jesus is. Everything was fine up until then.

Then I began to teach about the purpose of Jesus's coming, and everything seemed to fall apart. I had spoken for only a few minutes at most when the chief, John's uncle, raised his hand to stop me. I thought it was rude! John and the rest of the group began a discussion that went on for some time.

Finally, I was told I could continue, so I did, for another very few minutes. They repeated the same round of discussions. Then "Uncle" indicated that I should continue. I can't remember how many times I was interrupted. It was many, and it all took a long time, especially considering that I was trying to stand under a four-foot-high ceiling. My back and legs began to cramp.

I was interrupted one final time. "Uncle" made a speech representing the whole village; John interpreted. The speech of thanks went on for some time. Then the elder made an amazing statement that finally explained all the interruptions. He said, "We have heard what you have said. We have talked about it. We have decided we can believe in your Jesus as our God and Saviour. Thank you."

I was stunned! There had been no invitation, no altar call!

I didn't know how to respond. So, I did what I often do when I'm taken by surprise and don't know what to do. I prayed. John translated my prayer for them. I dedicated them to the Lord and asked God to lead them into a full understanding of their decision as a group. When we got out into the crisp fresh air again, John Swaakei was jubilant. So were we!

It was not until I read a book by Dr. Ralph Winters of Fuller Theological Seminary many years later that I heard a designation given to that kind of incident. Dr. Winters referred to it as "a people movement." It seems to have been happening in other parts of the world as well. Groups made a joint decision to follow Jesus. Anyone who disagreed was the odd one out.

That is quite a different process than what I was used to in the West. One person in a large family might become a Christian in the West, and suddenly that one person becomes the odd one out. Perhaps we need to take a closer look at how we win people to Jesus. A family discussion can bring a family to a decision. Perhaps in the West, fewer homes would become divided.

"Believe in the Lord Jesus, and you will be saved—you and your household" (Acts 16:31).

Wisdom Gained: There are values and principles in every culture. It is for us to understand that we are the foreigners when we are among them. *Foreign* applies to all of us, not just to "them." We were all foreign to God until Jesus bridged the gap.

34 WE SAW JESUS!

SOME OF THE most astounding things happen when you are least aware of it.

As was customary, missionaries living at Nyang'ori were often asked to go out and preach in local churches among the three different tribal groups within driving distance around the compound. There were the Maragoli, the Kalenjin, and, down the hill around Lake Victoria, the Luo. Often there was tension between them.

West of Nyang'ori was a town called Kakamega. I had been there before and was asked to come back and preach for a special occasion. As we drove into the church compound, there seemed to be a slight sense of tension, though this was well within the boundaries of the Maragoli subtribe. The very tall, thin pastor was a Maragoli.

When the meeting began, the church was packed. There were about eight large drums made from five-inch sections of 44-gallon drums, with dried cowhide stretched over both sides. Drummers were loudly thumping out the rhythm as the people sang with gusto and sincerity. I was getting a bad headache.

The people were worshipping loud and long! Finally, to get the attention of the people so that we could get on with the meeting, an elder ran a big stick back and forth on the corrugated tin roof from the inside. When things quieted down, I was asked to preach. I stood and read my main Scripture. Then I prayed. I don't remember exactly what I prayed, but I often pray that people will know and understand who Jesus really is.

Stones began to hit the tin roof. A few elders went out to try to stop the interference. There was a small group of rowdy young men who had caused some problems for the church before. They had fire in their eyes. The elders came back in quickly. The noise continued. It was really distracting, both for me as the preacher and for the people, whose gazes cast about in annoyance and apprehension of something worse than stones landing on the roof. After a few minutes, the commotion stopped, and the roof was silent.

As I was preaching, I noticed several young men appear outside the entrance. They stared at me with a strange look. Some of them stepped through the door and hunkered down against the back mud wall of the church. I continued to preach. I use a lot of Scripture when I preach. After all, God has promised that His word "will not return to me empty, but will accomplish what I desire" (Isaiah 55:11).

Other than the new quietness, I was unaware of anything else happening. At the end of my sermon, through an interpreter, I gave an open invitation for people to receive Jesus as Lord and Saviour.

About a dozen came forward, including several of the young men who had sat on the floor against the wall, the stone throwers. I prayed for each one, and the service was eventually dismissed.

I had put together a bookmobile, a pickup truck that was stocked with books we published. The back door swung out as a display rack for various titles and Bibles. I saw that Eleazer Chisanya, our driver, was doing a brisk business. I was invited to have dinner with the pastor. It consisted of *ugali* with chicken, some vegetables, and gravy.

As I was walking back to my car after dinner with the pastor, I noticed that there were still many people hanging around the church, more than usual. Eleazar approached me with a strange look on his face. He was normally a cheerful and fun-filled fellow, with whom I had a great relationship. He asked, "Do you know what happened?" I had no idea what he was asking about and said so. He went on to explain. "When you were preaching, you disappeared, and we saw Jesus!" That brought me up short!

I asked him what he meant. He just repeated it, "When you were preaching, you disappeared, and we saw Jesus! Didn't you see? Didn't you know?" I explained that all I had noticed was the sudden quiet and the appearance at the door to the church of several young men who watched to the end.

Eleazar said, "I am not the only one who saw it happen." He called several people. They had seen and repeated the same thing. I was astounded. I had sensed nothing extraordinary. I always asked for God's anointing to rest on my preaching but had not sensed anything unusual other than the presence of the Lord, as is quite normal in many services.

Jesus was described in various ways, including a light or glow around him. No one doubted who it was. I was personally astounded. I can't explain it. I can only accept what many witnesses said they saw. God certainly has the power and the prerogative to do as He pleases. I was deeply humbled by that day's experience. I had never had it happen before or since. People left that afternoon in awe, as did I.

There was a good harvest of souls into the kingdom of God that day. That's why I was there! Obviously, Jesus was there too. I have no way of explaining such a phenomenon.

Wisdom Gained: As Christians we represent Jesus, even though unaware. Thus, we must be mindful that our every action, good and bad, will influence what people will think of Jesus. His life is in us.

1 - I was born in North Bay, where I lived until I was two (photo taken 1938).

2 - Mom, David, Dad, Ruth, and cute little me before Lois and Rick enlarged the family.

3 - I crossed the equator seven times daily each way between Goibei, where we lived, to Nyang'ori, where Evangel was developed.

4 - My parents with Mary and me at Cobourg Camp while Dad was district superintendent in the Eastern Ontario District of the PAOC.

5 - Dressed to a T on arrival in Kenya, but the heat changed our dressing habits.

6 - Our parents at our wedding,
January 17, 1959, Willowdale,
Ontario.

7 - Mary, John, and me on our
first furlough.

8 - Greeting a young Karamajong
warrior in Uganda. (Photo by
Jimmy Hooten.)

9 - My son John was trained in
gun safety and hunting at an
early age. I shot this Grant's
gazelle.

10 - In 1970, I was general
manager of Evangel Publishing
House in Kenya, and such
curly hair I had!

11 - The family: Rick, Ruth, Cal, Mom, Dad, Lois, and David (left to right). We were seldom all together, as one or another of us was on a mission field.

12 - Here is Evangel Publishing House as construction neared its end, in Ruaraka, the outskirts of Nairobi, Kenya.

13 - Mary and I enjoyed our life on our little country acreage with chickens, goats, cats, and dogs.

14 - At this point, four of us hosted 100 Huntley Street—David Mainse, Moira Brown, Jim Cantelon, and me.

15 - Here is our family after our permanent return to Canada.

16 - Always a joy to deliver the "charge" to graduates of the Geoffrey R. Conway School of Broadcasting.

17 - As VP of Crossroads Christians Communications, my signature was everywhere.

18 - I delivered 3,000 commentaries from my set on 100 Huntley Street over a period of about ten years.

19 - I was thrilled when Crossroads took on my vision for television worldwide. We built a mobile TV production unit which we sent to Europe.

20 - I am holding Saviour, who was renamed after we saved his family from starvation.

21 - *Manase Lomole Waya was used of God to involve me in South Sudan's humanitarian crisis.*

22 - *Iddris ("Rambo") Kamara committed atrocities and invaded the government headquarters in Sierra Leone. He subsequently committed his life to Jesus Christ.*

23 - *I was sitting with South Sudanese slaves while negotiating the price for their freedom.*

24 - *I was honoured to speak to the central government of South Sudan about integrity versus corruption in government. A DVD of the speech was distributed to the civil service and all parliamentarians.*

25 - *The Bori Farm Headquarters was at the height of its operation here. It has since been ransacked and destroyed by the South Sudanese soldiers.*

26 - *In 2012, I was named alumnus of the year by Masters College & Seminary, Peterborough, Ontario.*

27 - *After years of civil war in Sudan, unexploded ammunition littered the countryside. This pile was sitting unguarded beside the road.*

28 - *What an honour to receive the Queen Elizabeth II Golden Jubilee Medal.*

29 - *It was a thrill to speak at the church my father established fifty years earlier in Nairobi. My family and I attended this church for many years. It has 50,000 members in various cities in Kenya.*

30 - *Fishing is my favourite way to relax. If you cannot find me on land, I'll be found on the water—not walking!*

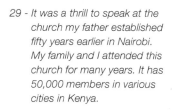
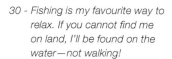

35 WE ADOPTED A FAMILY

MARY AND I are proud parents of two children, both adopted, and we consider them marvellous gifts from God. John became a Bombay at about three months of age after Mary and I had been married for nine years. We had endured several miscarriages. We adopted John while we were on furlough from East Africa. As life works out when serving the Lord, we could not have been happier.

Elaine was adopted while we were missionaries in Kenya. Mary went back to Canada with John for the adoption of Elaine, and we were separated for seven months. Had it not been for a change in the adoption laws in mid-adoption, the time would have been much shorter. After several telegrams and a phone call, progress was made. We had to book a specific time with the post office to make a call, and it cost 75 dollars for three minutes. Our monthly stipend as missionaries was 90 dollars each for Mary and me. Adoption involved a lot of faith. Elaine's adoption was finally complete, and a passport was eventually issued for her.

I met Elaine when she was eight months old on a Sunday when Mary and John flew back to Kenya with our beautiful daughter. Her first sight of me must have been frightening. A car had hit me a few days earlier. My head was bandaged up, and I walked with a heavy limp.

John was a constant joy to us. He was a beautiful baby, and we have the pictures to prove it. He went to a local very British kindergarten, where he learned to speak with an accent different to ours. For middle school, both kids rode the bus to the outskirts of Nairobi to attend a missionary school run by Southern Baptists and Mennonites. John was a knock-kneed hyperactive boy. Everyone around him was grateful for the Ritalin pill he took each morning.

In 1977, we had a short furlough in Ontario. The day before we returned to Kenya, we were guests on *100 Huntley Street*. Just before we went on air, Julia Madonik, the guest co-ordinator, asked if she could pray for John's healing. Mary watched in amazement as John's leg straightened out.

On the flight out of Toronto, John was admiring the CN Tower, where we had dined the day before. We asked him what it felt like when Julia prayed for him. John described a deep tickling tingle through his leg. Then his attention snapped back to the sight of the CN Tower getting smaller and left behind.

John is very skilled mechanically, and I cannot imagine a mechanical challenge that would defeat him. I performed the wedding for John and Karen. He is now a father of two and grandfather to our great grandson, Oliver.

John worked for years at *100 Huntley Street* as everything from cameraman to editor, sound technician, and lighting technician and became a director and producer. That was a dead end. He worked briefly in TV in Toronto before moving on to the Ford Motor Company.

Elaine grew up quiet but intensely intelligent and with a sparkling personality. She has been a delight since the time she became a Bombay. For twenty years, she worked with Wycliffe Bible Translators, living in Cameroon, Chad, and Kenya. While she was in Chad, Mary and I visited her. This is my journal for one day, slightly shortened.

Jan. 19, 2008—Saturday. It's a week since we left Canada. Seems longer in some ways. There seems nothing to see or do but read a lot. We had breakfast about 10:00 a.m. and then went to the Cameroon border, where Mary once again was enchanted with the people, the country, the sights, and sounds. We had lunch at the Pelican (restaurant). Mary had beef with a little curry. Elaine and I ordered fish with chips and got fish with canned peas—they had no potatoes. Came home and transferred PIX from Mary's camera. We ate leftovers for dinner, then read for a while. The sink is plugged badly. This house has a septic tank, but the streets look like I imagine the contents of a septic tank would look, with the appropriate smell. Black, unbelievably strong little plastic grocery bags litter the streets, in most cases mixed with the most amazing bits of garbage. On a still day, the black plastic shopping bags hang in leafless trees, looking like crows at perfect rest or over-sized bats. Locally, these bags are called the national flower ... The dun-coloured roads, walls, and paths have dust as fine as talcum, and puff into the air as easily, with a step or dirt devil or a breeze. Teeth feel slightly gritty if more than a few breaths are taken through the mouth. Goats, parents and kids, mix with Chadian parents and kids, often making approximately the same noise, depositing their own personal garbage near walls; one at least human-sized, from a dog that must have successfully scavenged some food somewhere sits in front of the locked door to this quarter of the concession. Dogs sleep in the middle of the streets curled as dogs will, never opening an eye when bicycle, motorcycle, or vehicle drives around them. They own the streets. It is unknown as to whom the dogs belong, and most of them look identical both in colour and size. They all have the same number of ribs—you can count them. A few ducks wallow in the gutters, which are green edged and wet, the sludge slowly festering the soil of the edges. Inside the compound, the leaf of every bush and tree is coated with the same dun dust as the streets and haze in the air. In the evening, little fires line the potholed streets with human faces detached from the muttering and cackles of laughter making the atmosphere slightly more bearable. A few electric signs pepper a long street, and flickering lamps cast long shadows for as far as the eye can see—about forty feet. Snippets of noisy music drift from the nightclubs. A siren squeals in the distance, and all the doors and gates are locked for the night. Elaine is a prisoner of her own calling to N'Djaména—sequestered unless accompanied by a friend and two good headlights. The mew of a cat falters near a window. A double locked door screen within a steel door denies entry to mosquitoes awaiting their dinner from whomever they may jab.

While there, we visited a holiday lodge that housed the French military, smartly uniformed in noticeably short shorts. We spent time meeting her co-workers in their offices, a quite mixed lot from Chad and around the world. The country around N'Djaména, capital of Chad, is flat, dusty, and dun coloured as far as the eye can see. It was a pleasant and lazy holiday for Mary and me. So different from the rich lushness of East Africa where we had lived and worked for 17 years.

One week after we left Chad, Elaine and her colleagues had to evacuate to Cameroon because of an attempted coup.

Elaine finished her African life in Kenya in 2015—where it had begun so many years earlier. She moved back to Canada to live with us (in our assumed declining years).

She was appointed by the board of directors of Cal Bombay Ministries as media specialist and understudy to me as CEO of Cal Bombay Ministries. She moved in with us in our country property. In April 2020, the board of directors appointed her to be executive director of Cal Bombay Ministries Inc. She's probably overqualified. I had been trying to retire for a while by then. I still cannot say that I have quite achieved that.

We are still a remarkably close family and try to eat together once a week or so. Those precious family meals were interrupted when our governments, both national and provincial, put us all unwillingly into self-isolation. This too shall pass.

Wisdom Gained: Raise your children in such a way that each one thinks they are the favourite.

36 ADULT DIAPER RASH

STRANGE THINGS TAKE place in aircraft, really strange. In 1968, Mary and I were returning to Africa for our second term as missionaries. John was nine months old. He was in a cot suspended on the bulkhead between first class and economy. We were in seats A and B, port side, economy.

It all seems funny now, but I sure didn't laugh at the time.

In first class, there were two Texans who were drinking all the beverages they were offered and probably asking for more. Their loud conversation was about what they would be doing when they got to Scandinavia. It was lewd and morally contemptible. Many passengers were annoyed and embarrassed.

The shorter one came back, stuck his head through the curtain, and offered a nip for us to give John, who was lustily crying. We felt the offer was inappropriate, and he left us with a drunken laugh.

In those days we were so new to travelling that we thought it suave to dress to the nines. I was in a black three-piece pinstriped suit. Mary was in a nice dress. John was in diapers. The perfect family! Finally, John ran out of energy to cry, and everyone happily fell sleep.

At about two a.m., I awakened to a hot, wet sensation on my right leg. I looked up bleary-eyed and then jerked back in my seat. The short Texan thought he was in the toilet and was relieving himself accordingly. On me! He missed the top of John's head by a few inches. I tried pushing him away, but he held on to the bulkhead doggedly. I punched him. The commotion woke up a French woman across the aisle, and she began to screech in a loud voice, "Zee peeg! Zee peeg!"

The yelling brought a steward, who scuffled with the fellow and knocked him down. He dragged the drunk to his first-class seat. It was quite a spectacle. It was quite nauseating!

The procedure of trying to wash my leg and trousers (in first class, of course) began. They stuffed my pant leg with small towels, and I finally went back to my seat. The steward later came with a notepad to get details about me. When I naughtily squeezed in the "reverend" part, he almost groaned. I slept again until about an hour before landing in Copenhagen. At that point, the steward wanted to introduce me to the now almost sober Texan. I became his morning-after headache.

This became comical almost to the extreme. The steward said to the man, "I'd like to introduce you to *Reverend* [emphasis by the steward] Calvin Bombay. He is the man you abused when you were drunk!" At this point I stood up.

The short Texan looked up at me and began to stammer, "If I did what they say I did ... I ... well ..." I interrupted him at this most uncomfortable moment and said, "You did!" and I lifted my right leg and began to shake all the little towels out of my pant-leg. The whole of first class was getting some first-class entertainment. His seat companion just looked down at his feet. The Texan mumbled, "If there's anything I can do ..." I wanted to suggest he step out onto the wing of the plane, but I refrained. Instead, I suggested it might be right for him to offer to have my suit cleaned when I got to Copenhagen. He had a US five-dollar bill in his hand so fast you'd have almost thought he had planned it. It should have been a ten-dollar bill, since the cost of cleaning, even in 1968, was nine dollars in Copenhagen! Years later, when I told my sister what had happened, she said, "You should have suggested a thousand-dollar donation to missions!"

As far as I know, I am probably the only adult male who has had diaper rash from thigh to foot at 37,000 feet. It would have been sad enough if that were the end of the story. But it was not!

In 1968, you could make lengthy stopovers on flights and change them, even to different airlines, without any cost or hassle. Since Copenhagen was so expensive, we cancelled our several days' stay there and went onward to Italy for a few days.

In the airport in Italy, Mary and I were walking down the concourse on a big wide red carpet. Coming directly toward us were the same two Texans, again talking in offensively loud voices about what they were planning to do "with the girls here in Italy."

The taller of the two suddenly recognized me, now in my clean three-piece pinstriped suit. He made an abrupt turn to his right. His shorter companion didn't notice and kept talking and walking. He would have missed me, but I stepped into his path. I can be a mischief myself when I want to. When he looked up to apologize, he looked puzzled, recognized me, then looked for his friend. I pointed to my left and said, "He went that-a-way!" The short man shrunk another inch or two and slunk off without a word.

Pleasantly, the story did not end there. Months later, I received a letter from SAS airlines, with an apology that started with the words "We apologize for the unfortunate incident on our flight ..." There was also a cheque for 67 dollars and 50 cents to buy a new suit. I'm not the litigious type, and I didn't need a new suit, so I bought Mary a nice Hoover vacuum cleaner, probably the first one on our mission station.

After that I thought it might be a good idea whenever I travel at night by plane to sleep with my feet in the aisle. Who knows? Perhaps I could furnish the whole house!

Wisdom Gained: Every experience, obnoxious or seemingly negative, has an upside, though you may not see it immediately.

37 NAKED TRUTH

IN ABOUT 1965 or 1966, Mary and I took a holiday from our work up-country at Nyang'ori, Kenya. We drove to Mombasa, then north up the coast about 70 miles to a campsite called Silver Sands, close to Malindi town. There were few campers when we arrived. We pitched our tent on the sandy beach, near some small bushes about forty yards from the Indian Ocean's high tide mark. There was a rough track behind our tent, with bush on either side, where cars could go farther down the beach.

Mary and I enjoyed several days of relaxing, swimming, and eating at the local restaurant.

I went fishing with the local African fishermen. First, we sailed farther down the beach, where we picked green sea lettuce to be used as bait. Then we loaded the outrigger with baited fish traps and stones to hold them in place on the ocean floor. We headed for a sandbar about a half mile out, where the traps were to be set.

We had to dive down about twenty feet, with flippers, simply holding our breath to place the traps. It was exhilarating. We brought up the traps from the previous day, filled with such prizes as red snapper, parrot fish, and sea bass.

As we were setting the new traps, I felt a poke in my ribs. One of the fishermen pointed away into the slightly murky waters.

Sharks! Five of them! We were twenty feet down. My African companion pointed straight up. I didn't hesitate! I thrashed my flippers and went straight up so fast that as I approached the outrigger I grabbed the edge of the boat and was into it in one flailing leap. Everyone else was already in the boat.

We fished several more times after that without incident. I did catch a blowfish, which I have to this day. When I approached it, it inflated itself with seawater until it was as round as a soccer ball with hundreds of sharp spikes sticking straight out from its bulbous body. In that condition, with such a load of water on board, it could hardly swim. I simply held the tail fin and dragged it to shore. Abbas, a local bodybuilder who hung around the campsite, cleaned it out and stuffed it with newspaper. It dried in the sun in its most threatening, bloated form.

It turned out that the biggest threat of the holiday was on land.

Mary had gotten up at dawn and gone down to the water. It was a sweltering day, and the rising sun was heating up the tent, where I lazed in a semi-stupor on an air mattress. I became aware of a strange ripping sound. By the time I realized what it was, a black arm was reaching through a knife slit made in the back of the tent. The hand grabbed Mary's purse and disappeared. I was suddenly wide awake.

In a flash, I was out of the tent and chasing the thief as he headed across the car track behind our tent and into the bushes. I shouted at him. He turned around to see how close I was to him. What he saw made him drop Mary's purse and flee into the bush. It was only then that I realized I was running around on a public beach, yelling and stark naked. It was probably a shock to anyone's system, poor guy! I grabbed Mary's purse and made a hasty retreat to the tent. I think every square inch of my skin was blushing. Certainly, it was not sunburn!

We went to the camp's open cabana area and reported the attempted theft (after I was clothed, of course). They contacted the police, who came with a tracking dog. Off they went into the bush, taking Mary's purse as evidence. The next day the police called us to pick out the thief from a lineup.

I had no trouble identifying him; he was wearing the same clothes as the day before. (I was grateful that I wasn't the one in the lineup with someone trying to identify me based on how I had been dressed the day before!) I asked that he turn around, just to be sure. The little bald spot on the back of his head confirmed that it was the right man.

The police explained that they had been looking for a thief who had been active at the campsite for a while. The tracker dog led them to his home, where they found cameras, binoculars, radios, and all kinds of small valuable goods. They had their man. He got two years for his efforts, and Mary got her purse back with all contents intact.

And I got a great tan—over most of my body. I slept either in my shorts or a bathing suit thereafter. Some things you just must learn by experience. It was a great holiday!

And that's the naked truth!

Wisdom Gained: When you turn back and see the wrong you've done, it's a good time to drop to your knees and repent.

38 TOO CLOSE TO DEATH

RETURNING FROM NAIROBI to the mission station at Nyang'ori was never dull. The trip took four to five hours and passed through some of the most beautiful scenery you'll ever see.

While it was a beautiful trip, it was never an easy trip. The pavement's main purpose seemed to be to connect the potholes. It was a hilly, winding road teeming with reckless drivers in overloaded vehicles, going too fast and overtaking on blind curves. It was almost a game to them to see how long they could wait before ducking back into their lane when passing. The sides of the road were littered with the wrecks of the losers.

By the time we'd reached home, we'd be filthy from the black clouds of exhaust spewing out of poorly maintained diesel engines. Buses and trucks were piled high with boxes, suitcases, bananas, other things destined for market, goats, and chickens. Inside the cabins, people were packed in so tight they could barely move. It wasn't unusual to see vehicles so overladen that their bumpers literally bumped down the road.

It was often impossible to pass these buses and trucks simply because you would be blinded by the cloud of exhaust as they laboured up a hill. Then they would hurtle down the other side at breakneck speed on questionable brakes.

So, you either took your chances and tried to pass, or you resigned yourself to choking on exhaust fumes while trying to focus on the scenery.

And what scenery it was!

It was common to drive through a series of extremely heavy rainfalls along the way. You could see individual rainstorms in all directions, punctuating the otherwise sunny skies. It was not uncommon to have to pull over and wait out a heavy barrage of blinding rain. Moments later, it would pass, and the sky would be bright blue and sunny again.

Descending from the highlands around Nairobi into the Great Rift Valley, the slopes and plains were alive with wildlife: giraffes, zebras, wildebeests, hartebeests, and Thompson's and Grant's gazelles! Beautiful! We once saw an exceedingly rare black leopard on that thickly forested descent. It stopped in the lights of our car, and we tried to outstare each other. It finally melted into the forest on our right. It was not far from the Rift Valley Academy, where hundreds of missionary kids got their education. I found out later that we had a rare privilege.

Kenya is a beautiful country, and the Rift Valley in particular. Books have been written about its lakes full of flamingos. Mount Margaret, Hell's Gate, and hillsides speckled with grass-thatched villages and gardens!

Mary and I were returning to Nyang'ori from one of our occasional trips to Nairobi for supplies. We were in the hills overlooking Lake Naivasha, just a few miles before the halfway point at Nakuru. It was a pleasant drive. We drove up a hill where we were able to look from the height across the plains from the cliff on our left and see the distinct pink of thousands of flamingos on the edges of Lake Elmenteita. It was a glorious view.

As we crested the hill, we met two buses. They were racing each other up the narrow road, taking up both lanes. Neither driver was willing (or perhaps able) to slow down. On our left was a three-foot shoulder and then a very steep 500-foot drop. On our right was the rock cliff wall.

With my heart in my mouth, I squeezed left to avoid the oncoming bus in my lane (we drive on the left in Kenya). Three feet is not enough room for a Peugeot 404 station wagon to get by, but it was either that or a head-on collision, and perhaps death. Strange how many thoughts rush through the mind when you're about to die.

We felt and heard the left wheels hit and bounce on the stones at the rim of the cliff. Then we felt the wheels go over the edge. I was sure we would plummet down cliff. The buses were now speeding past our right windows, almost brushing us. In the seconds it took for the buses to pass, I was keenly aware that our left tires were riding on air. I pulled right and felt the tires contact the ground again.

I regained control of the car and brought it to a stop about a quarter mile down the road. It took longer to regain control of ourselves. My heart was pounding. Both Mary and I were shaking uncontrollably. I have no explanation for what held our car suspended over air for those frightening moments, other than an angel of God held our car up. There was simply no room for all three vehicles on that width of road.

In times like that, verses such as Psalm 55:22 become exceptionally meaningful: "Cast your cares on the LORD and he will sustain you; he will never let the righteous be shaken."

As Mary and I sat recovering our composure at the side of the road, we could only bless God for His help and protection. We do not find it hard to believe in angels!

The closest we ever came to anything similar was when a bus insisted on entering a long single-lane bridge on which we were already driving. It smashed my driver's side rear-view mirror in onto my lap. No other damage, except that my gizzard was in my throat. Everyone in the car let out a collective breath.

Where would any of us be without the grace of God?

Wisdom Gained: Take time to remember situations that seemed impossible, and consider how close God's protective angels hovered nearby. Believe it. Angels are real, though most often invisible.

39 DEATH CAME KNOCKING

PEOPLE HAVE WANTED to kill me from time to time.

For a period, we lived at and managed the Goibei mission station in western Kenya. This was located miles from any main road and high in the hills on the border between the Maragoli and the Kalenjin tribes.

We had an employee on the mission station who preferred sleeping to working. Time and time again, we would try to find him when he was supposed to be cutting grass or trimming a hedge around the houses. We'd call, successively more loudly. Eventually he would turn up looking tired, as though he were overworked. It became exasperating since we could not see any work he'd done.

One day I decided that, rather than call, I would search for him. I searched the whole mission station. I was about to give up when I saw a ripe custard apple on the tree among our banana plants. This was unusual. This delicious fruit would usually disappear just as it was getting ripe. This time I was going to help that custard apple disappear.

As I was walking toward the tree, I tripped over what appeared to be a stack of trimmed banana leaves. Under it was Kip, our missing grounds man. He awoke with a start. I picked myself up, and because he had been warned repeatedly, I dismissed him on the spot (followed by a letter of termination of employment). We squared off. He objected to being dismissed for such an insignificant thing. I objected to his non-productivity. I sent him home, paying him his full wages up until that day.

A few days later, word spread through the villages nearby that Kip was preparing to kill me with a spear. Since I object to being dead unnecessarily, I asked the local church leaders what I should do. They advised me to write a letter explaining Kip's history of shirking his duty and the fact that I had finally dismissed him. I handed it in to the local ministry of labour office, with a copy to be sent to Kip. The ministry of labour wrote me a reassuring letter, with a copy to Kip.

I lived with some apprehension for a time. The loss of a job is taken as a serious offense, not the act of the dismissal but the "robbing" a man of his income. This brings hardship on his family. It was a serious matter, yet he brought it on himself. As you may have noticed, I lived to tell about it.

Kip's successor was a much more energetic worker. He knew what would happen if he didn't do his job. Sometimes an example is all that's needed.

But then there were other incidents.

It was my custom to take a little stove with me on my book distribution trips, along with a supply of eggs from my own chickens. I knew that these eggs had no semi-formed chicks inside the shell.

My intended trip was out of Nairobi, east to Mombasa, visiting towns and missions all the way. Then I would continue south along the coast through Dar es Salaam, Tanzania, and back inland to towns such as Dodoma, Moshi, and Arusha, and thus back to Kisumu via Nairobi.

Accommodations were rarely available, and I didn't have the money to pay for lodgings every night anyway. I slept on the mattress laid out over the load of books I carried. It was comfortable but had little headroom. Late into the night I pulled off the Nairobi/Mombasa road looking for an out-of-sight spot near that dusty washboard road. I backed the car into a space between some bushes, cooked my supper, crawled into the back, pulled the curtains Mary had sewn, and went to sleep.

On one trip I almost killed a woman beside another railway track in Tanzania. I was travelling along what might be described as an inadequate service road that paralleled the tracks. Up ahead I saw a man and a woman, both with sacks of flour on their heads, going in the same direction. The man was on the right side of the road, and the woman on the left. I pressed the horn to warn them I was coming and slowed down, not that any real speed was even possible on such a road.

There seems to be a prevailing conviction in the bush country in Africa that the other side of the road is always safer. Suddenly the woman ran up the slight bank to cross the road and join the man. I slammed on the brakes, but it was too late. The woman bounced off my left fender, and the sack of corn flour on her head burst on my windshield, blinding me temporarily as I lurched to a stop. When I looked back, the woman was lying on the ground. My heart sank. I dislike the idea of killing other people even more than I dislike the idea of getting killed.

Now what should I do? Go back to try to tend to her or take off as fast as I could? The common advice in such a situation, even by the police, was *not* to stop but quickly leave the scene and get help. People can appear out of the bush and exact "justice" by beating the driver to death. An eye for an eye! All very biblical of course! I headed for the first little town. I stopped at the police post, where the captain heard me out. We then went back to the scene of the accident. As we sped back, I explained who I was and why I was distributing Christian books. He surprised me by saying he had read one of the books I had written. His father was a bishop in the Anglican church in Tanzania.

At the scene, the old woman was sitting up and the man was squatting down beside her. She seemed to have no broken bones. It turned out, she was totally blind and was running across the road toward the sound of the man's voice. The captain, whose name I have long forgotten, took us all back to town to a clinic, where we dropped off the woman. She was well able to walk and went into the clinic with the old man. The policeman took me back to my car and sent me on my way, saying, "I know it was not your fault. It happens often."

Once was too often for me. Several of our missionaries had less happy endings in such incidents. Several of them were fatal to the child or adult who tried to dart across a road.

I had a close call in Nairobi as a pedestrian. My office was in Church House on Haile Selassie Avenue. I had gone for a quick fish and chip lunch, which cost me the equivalent of about 75 cents at the Hilton Hotel in those days. I was on my way back to my office.

Stepping off the sidewalk to cross a street in Nairobi is a little risky at the best of times, even at designated crosswalks. After looking both ways, I stepped onto the road. I remember it with remarkably clarity, up to a point. Just as I stepped into the road, I had to step backwards up onto the curb again to allow a cyclist to pass. Then, looking both ways again and seeing it was clear, I stepped out to cross the street. The screeching and screaming of tires came from my right. So did a beige Mercedes, through a stop sign and at a high speed making a tight, fast left turn to avoid trees in the median ahead of him. Now he was bearing down on me.

A remarkable thing had happened just two days before. I had been translating *Who Is This Jesus?*, a little booklet I had written, into Kiswahili. I knew Kiswahili well, but it took a lot of concentration and a dictionary. In the middle of this intense thinking, a question popped into my mind: "What should you do when a car is coming at you so fast you can't get out of the way?" Whoa! Where did that come from?

I thought about it for a while. I could just stand there and get hit, but that would hurt. I could throw myself down to the street, but that could crush and mangle me. I could leap as high as I could and try to jump over the car. Yeh, sure, like I was Superman! I concluded that was the best option. I went back to translating.

So, when I saw the car coming at me, my brain and body literally leapt into action. I jumped with all the strength of my then younger legs. My lower legs bounced off the hood. My head and shoulder whacked up against the windshield. I went over the top of the car and landed on my face and knees. That's all I could remember for a while.

When I came back to consciousness, people were bending over me. The driver had stopped. They bundled me into the Mercedes. The driver was shaking and apologetic. He drove me to the hospital. Fortunately, it was the Agha Khan hospital, the best in Nairobi at that time. To say I was groggy would be an understatement. The driver did mention that his uncle was the president of Kenya, the Honourable Jomo Kenyatta. It turned out later that he did not even have a driver's license. One does not seek reparations from the president's nephew in an African state. Oh! Did I mention this happened on Friday the 13th?

When I emerged from the hospital I was wrapped up like a mummy. I think they doped me a bit. But I wasn't too dopey to notice that the right leg of my pants had burst its seam right from my belt down to my pant cuff. I must have been some sight as I entered a public bus to find my way back to my office, where my car was parked.

I was as dizzy as a whirling dervish, but I got into my car anyway and started driving home. At a round-about on Kenyatta Highway, I felt I was about to pass out when I noticed that Art Rosenau, a fellow missionary, was on the same round-about. I yelled through the traffic, asking him to follow me. He was quite startled-eyed to see my head wrapped in white bandages. By the time I got near the home of Bill Cornelius, I couldn't take it anymore and pulled in. Art helped me into Bill's house, where I lay down. I have little memory of what followed.

The next day a doctor drained off a mass of ugly fluids that had developed over my right kneecap like a miniature Tower of Babel. I was told by doctors in Canada later that I would certainly have trouble walking by the time I was about sixty. I consulted the Great Physician of higher authority. At 83, I'm still walking fine. I don't think I could beat my grandchildren in a foot race, but what grandfather could?

Mary had gone to Canada to adopt our daughter Elaine and was arriving with both our adopted children on the 15th, two days after the event. My son recognized me at the airport and rushed and jumped into my arms. It hurt. When Mary saw me, she asked what had happened. I yelled back at her from my mummy uniform that I had been in an accident. Then she asked, "How's the car?" *Car*? What about me? That hurt too! When she found out what had really happened, she treated me with tender, loving care.

And at least it was a Mercedes Benz, not a cheap car!

Wisdom Gained: For Christians, danger is always near at hand, since both Satan and his agents will try to do us harm. But God is our shield and defender. Faith is simple. It is simply believing God!

40 FRIENDSHIPS IN AFRICA

WHILE IN AFRICA, I had several singular Kenyan friends, two about my own age, one who was a little older. Three of them happened to be from the Luo tribe: Joash Okong'o, Richard Ondeng', and Odhiambo Okite. I write of Odhiambo Okite in the next chapter.

Joash Okong'o taught at the Pentecostal Bible College (PBC) at Nyang'ori, as I did. Joash also was often my interpreter, both in the college and when I went into the Luo tribal area to preach and teach. Spending many hours driving and sharing the gospel together drew us into a close friendship. Joash later became a leader in the Luo Pentecostal Assemblies of God in Kenya.

Our friendship was noticed by some of the older missionaries, and on one occasion I was warned, "You don't want to be get too friendly and close with the Africans. We just can't do that!" I asked why. The answer was, "They will take advantage of you."

I had a great deal of internal turmoil over that! It didn't fit my theology. I believed that the Bible teaches the equality of all men under God. Perhaps those missionaries who had been there for many years might know something I had yet to learn! I agonized over that for weeks whenever it came to mind. *Do the missionaries think Africans are lower on the social scale, or is it worse than that?*

I wondered. Is it possible to want to preach the gospel to black people and not consider them as equals? Or did the older missionaries not trust my discretion? I finally decided to live outside the boxes some might have preferred.

I had heard some stories about African pastors, workers, and leaders that made them look bad, and I had no reason to doubt that the stories were true. I heard about moral lapses among the pastors, but then I remembered we had had to send a missionary back to North America because of a moral lapse. It seemed to me that all people are equal, though not all have the same education, cultural background, or access to the same resources as we from the Western world. I finally decided I would practice what the Bible taught, rather than the cautions that some missionaries gave, and I was criticized for it. My consistent answer to those who objected was "I came here to be taken advantage of!"

Joash and I were walking across the mission station together one day, and we were discussing our two sons, who were about the same age. It was during this conversation that suddenly I had what I thought was going to be a bad experience. Joash took my right hand in his as we walked. I knew from experience that holding hands with a girl was a not too subtle sign to everyone around that there was some form of budding romance. But to hold hands with a man! That was a sign of something I was not prepared to live with.

Joash must have noticed the uncomfortable reaction from me, and he burst out laughing! At first, I wasn't sure why he laughed. Then he said, "I know what this means in Canada, but here in Africa it means an entirely different thing." I asked him to explain, with my hand still in his. He said, "Men hold hands here in Africa when there is total trust and true friendship. There are no sexual overtones whatsoever." He grinned at my discomfort, and I relaxed a bit. I accepted his explanation and grinned myself, though I was still hoping that none of the other missionaries on the station would see me. As time went on, I became more comfortable with the gesture.

Richard Ondeng' was another man who became both a friend and a valued counsellor to me. I got to know Rose, his wife, before I met Richard. Rose worked for me in Evangel's bookshop on Nyang'ori Mission Station.

Richard was studying in America. I shall never forget the sad duty I had to tell him of an incident that would have devastated most Christian men. I will embarrass no one and keep the matter confidential. Yet his reaction and attitude through the whole situation demonstrated such Christian faith, grace, and gentility. Richard was a man I knew I could trust, and I would have been at peace if he had my life in his hands.

When I was developing Evangel Publishing House, I felt it needed a board of directors or, at the very least, a board of advisors. After all, we missionaries were the foreigners, even though some missionaries I knew seemed to think they were working among foreigners.

I asked Richard to become the chairman of a board that had both African and missionary leaders from around East Africa. Richard worked full time for the Kenya Churches Alliance as director of the Kenya Churches Educational Association. Through his influence, much of the content of the educational system in Kenya contained solid biblical teaching. Evangel Publishing House published some of the first indigenously produced textbooks for secondary schools in East Africa. Encounter with Christ was the first. Richard was the prompter behind that endeavour.

I suspect he was behind the fact that Evangel also published *The Kenya Churches Handbook,* compiled and written by Dr. David Barrett, who became the leading church research scientist in the world. Richard's office, Dr. Barrett's office, and my office were all located in Church House in Nairobi at that time.

Richard and I travelled to the USA to try to raise funds for the expansion of Evangel Publishing House. In America, we got tickets for 99 dollars each, which allowed us to travel anywhere in the USA within a 30-day period. I'm not sure how many miles we covered, but we had to come back to Atlanta, Georgia, to make all our connecting flights. Every time we came back, we hoped we'd get the same taxi driver we'd had the first time in Atlanta. He was a scream!

He always greeted us with, "*Wayyalwanago*?" It was around the fifth trip when we realized he was saying, "Where do you all want to go?" We laughed ourselves almost silly in the back seat of the taxi. We flew to Chicago, Detroit, Los Angeles, and a few other places, visiting The Kellogg Foundation as well as major Christian ministries, such as the Crystal Cathedral.

Dr. Schuller was kind enough to show us around that great facility. We were to present our needs to him after the tour. But I will never forget that moment when he realized we were Pentecostal. He turned on his heel and simply walked away. We never got to present our vision and needs. Richard and I were quietly led back the way we had come. It was a rather disconcerting experience.

Thirty odd years later, I sat with Dr. Schuller in the green room when he was a guest on *100 Huntley Street*. I'm certain he did not recall who I was, even though I reminded him of our visit. And I'm also quite certain he had shed any negative feelings he may have had about us as Pentecostals. Many things had changed in the previous thirty years. I also refrained from telling him that Evangel Publishing House had grown to become the largest Christian publishing house in Africa, although we got no help from the Crystal Cathedral.

Many years later, I was the director of the Geoffrey R. Conway School of Broadcasting and Communications, which was part of Crossroads Christian Communications. It was an absolute joy to me when Richard's son Philip, whom I had dandled on my knee as a child in Kenya, came to study with us.

Friends, true Christian friends, last forever.

Wisdom Gained: Choose your source of friends first, then bond with individuals from the heart. Source of friends? The family of God. True and total friendships are few. Stay true to yourself.

41 MY CLOSEST AFRICAN FRIEND

ODHIAMBO OKITE WAS tortured and eventually died of the terrible treatment he received at the hands of his own government in Kenya. He was a most remarkable man and one of my best friends.

Odhiambo was a man of great strength of character, integrity, and boldness. He was a journalist and a stringer for *Time* magazine. He was editor of *Target*, a Christian newspaper published out of Nairobi, together with *Lengo*, the Kiswahili counterpart. He became head of Voice of Kenya, the official government television and radio broadcasting authority in Kenya.

He had been educated in the USA and had married a lovely American blonde, Carol Ann. They had the most handsome of children. We had all become close friends in Kenya.

At one point I was president and Odhiambo was vice-president of the Evangelical Literature Fellowship of East Africa (ELFEA). This was a fellowship of Christian printers, publishers, bookshop owners, and writers in Kenya, Uganda, and Tanzania. These three countries shared a currency called the East African shilling, along with a colonial (British) administration. That was about to break down as each country gained its own independence from Britain.

It was probably at one of the earliest meetings of ELFEA that I met Odhiambo. Once we met, it seemed like we had been friends forever.

It was because of my friendship with Odhiambo that I was sometimes invited into situations and places where most non-Kenyans were excluded. We drove to a place on the shores of Lake Victoria not far from Rusinga Island, which was Odhiambo's home. It was also the home of Tom Mboya, a cabinet minister in the Kenyan government. Tom Mboya was a brilliant leader and a key figure in Kenya's fight for independence.

As we crossed the channel to Rusinga Island, I was entranced by the beauty and peace surrounding the island. On shore, Odhiambo introduced me to his mother, who was the women's leader in the local Pentecostal church. I met his father, who was not a believer. We were taken to their house. It was a simple but functional mud-walled hut. As we sat outside under the trees, some of the sisters/cousins brought us peeled and diced papaya, probably the best I have ever had. In that heat, it was better than a glass of water.

There was some excitement that weekend. We had gone for a dual purpose. We intended to rest, and I was to speak in the local church. We had taken our bathing suits just in case we had some time to swim in beautiful Lake Victoria.

On Saturday, we walked a short distance to the shore, which had big rocks sitting in almost pure black volcanic sand. Each of us sat on a rock and began to change, taking off our shoes and wiggling our toes in the sand. Odhiambo sat on a rock with his back to a bush growing at the base of a large tree. As he leaned down to untie his second shoe, I was startled to see a large cobra sticking out of the bush just behind and above Odhiambo's head and shoulders. The cobra's head was flattened, its body coiled in preparation for striking. I saw the tongue darting. I was chilled.

I spoke with urgency in my voice, "Odhiambo, don't move!" His eyes met mine, and he saw my seriousness. I told him, "Stay bent down and slowly take your one shoe and sock in your hand and very, very slowly move in a crouched position away from the bush and snake." He did so and made his way toward me. My eyes were on the snake. When Odhiambo saw me relax, he looked behind him just in time to see the snake slither off into the bush and disappear.

We both decided the swim was off. With shoes back on, we went a long way around that bush to get to the house. It's probable that I saved his life. The strike of a cobra that close to the neck would have killed him in moments as the venom would have reached his nerves and vital organs almost instantly. Most of the rest of the day was filled with snake stories, one of which took place on his first day in primary school on Rusinga Island.

He was leading a goat on a rope, his "school fees" for the teacher, when he felt a weight on the rope. As he turned to see what it was, he was so shocked that he dropped onto his bottom on the path. A python had wrapped itself around Odhiambo's "school fee." The snake was in the process of anchoring its tail to begin squeezing the goat to death.

Odhiambo ran screaming to his uncle's house, which was nearby. His uncle came running with a knife, grabbed the snake, and began to stab it, finally killing it. The goat was already beyond saving. There are very many pythons on that island.

On Sunday, we walked through light brush and flowering shrubs down a dirt path to the mud-and-wattle church. Odhiambo's father had contributed the land for the church. We ducked under the grass roof, which hung low over the doorless entrance, and entered the dimly lit church. Small windows were sculpted into the walls at regular intervals, but they let in little light since the grass thatch roof hung low over each of them. It was hard to read my Bible in the gloom.

The "pews" inside were just large branches supported at each end by a crotched branch sunk into the floor. They were not large, perhaps four inches wide, and were most uncomfortable to sit on for a two- to three-hour meeting! Like any other church service throughout the world, the elements were much the same: singing, announcements, offerings, and the preaching of the Word. I had the privilege that day of preaching.

The place was full, and the glow on the faces of the people as they praised and worshipped God made up for the otherwise gloomy interior. The experience of an African worship service with its rhythm, clapping, and dance is unforgettable. Though poor in possessions, they had riches beyond imagining in their spirits. Nothing in North America can quite duplicate the genuine joy of an African church service. When they worship, they forget all else but God's glory!

It was a thrilling weekend for Odhiambo, his mother, and family. Odhiambo's father had been kind to the church but had never become a Christian. That Sunday, he committed his life to Jesus.

The friendship between Odhiambo and me deepened as we spent more time together. At one point, our family lived in their house while they visited America for some months (one of the 17 houses we lived in during our 17 years in East Africa).

One day, he called me to pick him up at the police station. I drove to the station and went to the desk sergeant to ask about Odhiambo. After some time, I was taken into the room where Odhiambo sat. To this day I have no idea why they had arrested him, and neither did Odhiambo. I did suspect that it was a bit of tribal harassment. The Kikuyu tribe was politically powerful, and Odhiambo was a Luo journalist.

After I turned up, it seemed there was no longer a problem. I simply vouched for him and was able to drive him home. Perhaps it was the appearance of a "European," and they did not want a witness to what might have happened otherwise. I'll never know. But that was not the end of Odhiambo's problems.

While he was head of the Voice of Kenya, policemen suddenly appeared at his office door, seized him, and led him away. Robert Ouko, a minister in the government, was also arrested at the same time. Both were taken to prison, tortured, and interrogated.

Robert Ouko was murdered, and his body was found out in the bush. But where was Odhiambo? He was being accused of being a spy for the CIA. It was not altogether implausible since he was educated in the USA and married to a beautiful blue-eyed blonde American.

Years later, Odhiambo told me of his experiences. He was forced stand in a tank of water that reached up to his lower lip. He was just able to touch the edges of the tank with his fingertips. He was left there for at least 36 hours. If he went under, he would drown. If he slept, he would awaken choking for air and lurch back to his tiptoes in the middle of the tank where he was secured.

Eventually, they took him out of the tank of water. They injected him with sodium pentothal (known as "truth serum") and finally became convinced after two weeks of torture and interrogation that he was not an agent for the CIA. They held him for a further week, during which they "reoriented" Odhiambo to be able to re-enter society. But it was the beginning of the end for Odhiambo.

While he was being tortured, he simply trusted in the Lord. He told Mary and me about a vision he had during those hours, and I was able to share it with Carol Ann, his wife, after his death. I had not known that he had never told Carol Ann of this vision. He saw heaven from within. As he tried to describe it, he was lost for words, even though as a journalist he was more than capable with words. He saw rolling green hills filled with sheep at complete rest. In the end, his attempts at description failed, and he conveyed only that a great and assuring peace filled his soul and mind.

After his release, Odhiambo began working for the United Nations. On a return trip to Nairobi, he stopped at the Kericho Tea Hotel for lunch. As he began to walk up the granite steps into the hotel, he went completely blind: sheer blackness! The chemicals that had been used on him during his days of torture and inquisition had finally taken their toll. His spleen was severely damaged. His health deteriorated terribly.

He moved to Wausau, Wisconsin, where he lived with his family. His contact with the world was a special computer that digitally voiced his email and the articles he wrote. He continued as a journalist until his untimely death in 2006.

The last article he wrote was the story of my involvement with the people of Sudan in the establishing of farms under the Savannah Farmers Cooperative. I had just answered his last two questions about it by email several days before I was informed of his death. The passing of a very dear friend under such circumstances can break one's heart, but he is with the Lord, a sheep at peace in green pastures.

Odhiambo was buried on Rusinga Island in Lake Victoria, his birthplace.

Wisdom Gained: Stand with your true friends through the good times and the bad, through strengths and weaknesses. Adversity binds true friends.

42 FRUSTRATIONS —REAL AND IMAGINED

NO NON-AFRICAN can live in Africa, even for a short time, without running into all kinds of frustrations, usually culturally based. My work in Evangel Publishing House took me away from our home at Goibei, and later Nyang'ori, for nights, weeks, and once even months at a time. Often, the frustrations take a greater toll on missionary wives than on the husbands who escape from some of the domestic challenges by their deep involvement and perhaps overcommitment to their work and ministry.

I was often away when things went wrong.

Like the day our old washing machine refused to work. It ran on a small gas engine. Mary had learned to clean and change the spark plug, but even at its best it was hard to start. After a long time and a sore arm for Mary, the machine sat motionless, filled with hot water, soap, and dirty clothes. A coffee break was in order. Mary went into the kitchen. A pall of smoke hung up near the ceiling. The kerosene refrigerator had run out fuel, and Mary had run out of fuel too.

Mary tried trimming the wick and lighting it again, and all it did was produce little parachutes of carbon, which settled throughout the kitchen. The stove ran out of propane at the same time. That was hard on Mary. No coffee to soothe the soul, no way to cook dinner or to wash the clothes, now sitting in cool water.

Missionary wives face things that most North Americans would find cause for murder or, at the very least, divorce.

I came home to a very frustrated wife. I think I was probably a source of some frustration for Mary even when I was at home too. Mary was very patient, both with me and with circumstances.

Someone told us that what the refrigerator needed was a good roll in the yard. They claimed that the coolant would collect and plug up part of the system, and it simply needed to be "joggled" into activity again. Yeah, right! We figured we had nothing to lose, so we emptied the offending appliance of both food and kerosene. With Luka's help (our house servant) we dragged the fridge out onto the grass beside the house. We rolled it around the yard. Luka must have thought us to be out of our minds. As I thought about it, I realized it wasn't past the fellow who advised us to do so as a joke. Well, wonder of wonders, when I filled the kerosene tank, trimmed the wick, and lit it, it worked with better efficiency than ever.

Before Mary could consider offering me clean clothes to wear, I was going to have to fix the washing machine. All it needed was a spark plug. I drove to Kisumu town and found one that was close to the right size. I bought propane to re-energize our stove. I was back in Mary's good graces.

I like root beer. My dad used to make it when I was a kid, and it was always good. So, I brought some essence of Hires Root Beer from Canada so that I could make my own soda pop. I never realized the fallout of such a simple desire. It was almost my undoing!

I carefully followed the recipe, using fresh, filtered, and boiled well water. The process was not complicated. I made a large batch, put it in bottles, forced corks into the necks of the bottles, and began to let it age in the kitchen pantry on some top shelves.

How was I to know that the heat, both from the dry-season weather and the cooking in the kitchen, would cause fermentation? We suddenly had corks popping, foam spouting to the ceiling, and a kitchen that smelled like a brewery. When Luka came in, his eyes popped wide open, and he concluded we had been brewing real beer. After all, it was called root beer!

Word got around, and it took a long time for Mary and me to live down the reputation of preaching against the dangers and evils of alcohol while at the same time running our own brewery.

There were many hiccups and tensions as the church transitioned from missionary leadership to national leadership. Twenty-three new churches were established the year that Mary and I lived in Uganda. It was exhilarating. It was also draining to be on the road, staying in villages, and suffering from amoebic dysentery.

Often there were even more silly frustrations. They had little or nothing to do with Africa or its people, yet we were in that context and, like most missionaries, at first blamed everything but ourselves. It took some years to understand that we are ourselves no matter where we happen to be. We had to start dealing with our own weaknesses, biases, and attitudes.

That is precisely the hump that some new missionary recruits seem never to get past. Over the 17 years we lived in Africa, it became apparent to me that after about two years, all new missionaries had their own crisis. "I want to go home! I can't take this any longer. Why is everything and everyone so slow in Africa? I don't think the Africans like me. I can't stand the heat! Everyone is asking for a handout! The local church leaders are corrupt!"

There is one simple yet comprehensive answer: culture shock. In most cases, Western missionaries come from relative affluence, with up-to-date technology at their fingertips. They come from a society with everything, into a society with little or nothing. There are language barriers (over 45 of them in Kenya alone). There are cultural sensibilities that vary from tribe to tribe. It is quite easy to insult someone by a gesture or a motion, a misunderstood word. Westerners often come with the mindset of "My way is the best way."

When Mary and I went to Kenya, we were committed for our whole lives. Despite occasional blips and dumb attitudes, ours and others, things were going well. But housing became a major problem. In the 17 years we were there, we moved to a new house 17 times. We were sometimes in a guest house or another missionary's home for a few months. The Missionary Aviation Fellowship rented us a house for a while, and as mentioned earlier, once we stayed in the home of an African friend who spent time in the USA.

Finally, Mary, with my support, talked to our mission's leadership and said, "Get us a permanent house, or we're going back to Canada." Often we had no time or even inclination to unpack our goods, we moved so often. At one stage in Nairobi, we were living out of suitcases with two children, frustrated to the extreme. I began to lobby for something that I thought made a great deal of sense.

I asked the question, "Why are we spending so much rent on so many city houses when for the same monthly cost, or even less, we could be buying those houses?" The idea caught on eventually, and we finally moved into a house the mission bought. We unpacked and stayed there until we retired from the field a few years later. Soon the mission was buying more houses and renting less. They had equity suddenly.

Of course, when you own a house, the roof leaks. In our case, right over the dining room table, with water running down the electrical wires on the light above it. Why couldn't the mission afford to have it fixed? I didn't know how to do it.

Bill Cornelius, the field secretary for the PAOC, was at our house discussing the future of Evangel Publishing House with me. There were numerous snags and frustrations we were trying to solve, and we sat up quite late. Mary was in a bit of a state when our Dalmatian, close to birthing pups, was hit on the road in front of the house and died that same evening. Some days just don't work out too well.

It was finally decided that we should turn the Evangel Publishing House over to national leadership. Our family was going to return to Canada, and Bob Skinner would take over the leadership during the transition. We had worked ourselves out of a job. We were going home to a totally unknown future.

That meant liquidating what we could, packing what we could, and leaving Africa behind. Hard to do.

We had two unique possessions. One was a collapsible camper we had packed full of our goods to ship to Africa. We had cut off the tongue in Canada and had it welded back on in Kenya. It served us well when holidaying as a family or I went hunting for our meat. For eight years running we ate almost no other meat than what I hunted: hartebeests, wildebeests, impala, Grant's and Thompson's gazelles, warthogs, and such. We had paid about 450 dollars for the camper.

The other unique possession was a 20 cubic foot freezer made in Canada for the 220-volt 50-cycle electrical system in Kenya. That cost us just over 200 dollars back then. We also packed it full of our goods to take to Africa. It served us well for many years.

Now get this. When we left Kenya, we sold the camper for 1,000 dollars and the freezer for another 1,000 dollars. Judging by the interest when we sold them, we could have asked and got more. I was tempted to start a bidding war, but my conscience would not permit it. Real estate always goes up in value, but a camper and a freezer?

We at least had a bit of coin to start life over again somewhere in Canada.

Wisdom Gained: When facing an unknown future, know with certainty that God, who brought you this far, will take you with both surprise and delight into the future He has planned for you. I believe I sleep well when I know I walked with God that day.

43 LIVING IN NAIROBI

LIVING IN AN African capital city is much the same as living in any large city anywhere in the world. Modern amenities (sometimes), well-dressed people (most of them), modern homes with hot and cold running water (some of them), and large shops to buy almost anything. There are some beautiful four-star hotels, paved and crowded roads, and close neighbours of every nationality.

Nairobi's airport seemed to be the crossroads of air travel in eastern Africa. It was busy and beautiful. In our earliest days, we could see zebras and other wildlife as we landed.

Nairobi was a great city, but it had its little quirks. Like diplomats. I had one embassy car drive me right off my motorcycle and the road while going home from my office in Church House. I ended up in a thornbush hedge. I got back on the motorcycle and chased the woman home, kicking her car door. When she finally stopped, I told her quite firmly that she may be a diplomat, but she needed to learn how to drive a car, and I would report her to the police. I didn't but just let her stew about it for whatever time it took her to find her own peace. Very unmissionary of me, I know. But I was bleeding.

It wasn't long after we moved into a slate-roofed stone house with a leaky roof that we came to own a Dalmatian dog that someone from the American

Embassy needed to leave behind when they returned to America. His name had been Spot, which we thought was just too common, so we called him Sport. He leaked too. Later, there was a female Dalmatian on auction at the school our children attended in the middle of a coffee plantation. She didn't serve as a watchdog too well, so we bought her cheap. She was called Chips. The two had a litter of pups.

Someone saw me with the dog one day and invited me to attend a meeting of the Dalmatian Club. I was curious enough about the English and their obsession with dogs to accept the invitation. Once.

Every person was white. I assumed their dogs were left at home. We sat around an outdoor kidney-shaped swimming pool, and I listened with a mixture of awe and suppressed laughter as these fine folks found foolish stuff to discuss, all about Dalmatians. Occasionally a spastic cat (honestly!) came out of the house and in fits and starts threw itself wildly around the people and pool. Its legs seemed to have no central control but threw the cat in unpredictable directions, once on its back. It skidded to a stop just before flipping into the pool.

I heard remarks about the cat such as "Oh, isn't he cute!" and "He must give you such comfort." Comfort? I'd be in a panic it would drown itself. After finger food and what must have passed as "business," we disbanded. I went home to the safety and sanity of my own wife and home. A few months later, I received a letter stating that in the next meeting, in my absence, I had been elected the new president of the Dalmatian Club. I declined by letter.

We lived on Gitanga Road, which led to a poor slum, Kawangwari, just a few blocks away. Our son, John, had a bike and made friends in Kawangwari, mainly through a kind fellow who repaired bikes. John ate with his friends and played with their children. Occasionally I would load both John and Elaine on my motorcycle and pass slowly through the area. John introduced me to everyone. Everyone seemed to know John. They couldn't seem to do enough for him.

I've often wondered if that was the reason that, of all the houses on our street, ours was the only one that wasn't broken into and robbed. Ours was the only house that had no guard. We did have a sign on the gate that said "*Chui kali.*" That meant "fierce leopard." Our spotted dogs patrolled the hedge, so maybe that helped too.

An unfortunate fact is that in Nairobi, as in all African capitals, there are obvious class and tribal distinctions. There are some churches that are exclusive to one tribe only, made up of those who have moved from rural areas. There are other churches where the tribes are totally integrated.

One tribe usually had the ascendancy in politics and, it naturally followed, in business. No matter how brilliant you were, if there was the slightest suspicion by the tribe that held the presidency, you were watched closely and often harassed.

Risks exist where you least expect them. There were gas shortages. Most of us had filled jerrycans set aside for such emergencies. Getting gas into the car was a simple matter. Set the jerry can on the roof of the car, use a siphon hose to suck it downward, then whip the end of the siphon hose into the gas tank without losing too much in the process. It worked well, except when your young son has walked unnoticed up beside you and catches a stream of gasoline full in the face.

He lost his breath, and I panicked. In minutes, my much calmer wife washed his face, and his breathing became less frantic gasps. We did warn him of the dangers of cigarettes and suggest he never smoke until he's at least 104 years old. Fortunately, he does not have an explosive personality.

John ran into some other problems in Nairobi, or rather, problems ran into him. He was just about six when our house servant, Stephen Mbiti, took him by the hand as he went down Gitanga Road to buy some fresh vegetables. Stephen held his hand firmly, as instructed. A truck came careening down the road, and even with Stephen jerking John out of the way, the truck tires left tread marks on the side of our son's running shoe. Stephen was ashen when he told us the story.

Bus service was not reliable. Mary had to get to a doctor's appointment. She stood for a good length of time waiting for a bus at a bus stop. A Singh offered her a ride. She thought him kind and accepted the ride. He said he was an architect and offered to take her to a hotel. In full daylight he "flashed" her as he was driving the car. Mary pretended not to see what he was obviously doing and suddenly had a revised destination, much closer to home, where she went into our dentist's office. The Seventh Day Adventist dentist prayed with her and calmed her down. She recovered quite well considering what might have happened had that Singh been more aggressive and farther from our home.

Mary often saw the same red car with the same driver cruising, apparently to offer helpful rides for people. Expatriates often offered each other rides into town. Mary did accept rides from Brits, Americans, and Swedes, but never again in that red car!

Another Singh attended our church and was a fine Christian friend of ours. When the time for our departure permanently from Kenya came, he organized a farewell dinner for us at an Indian buffet in the historic Norfolk Hotel (where some early settlers used to ride into the bar on horseback). The meal was marvellous. Mary and I both had so many curried dishes that day that our perspiration carried that odour for a week after the feast. Sodi Swaran Singh and I remain friends to this day.

We had our favourite restaurants of course. Every nation's capital in the world seems to have a very representative variety of ethnic restaurants. But my favourite was our own dining room at home. Always has been, always will be. Nairobi or Canada!

Wisdom Gained: Wherever you go, live, or work, you take your true self with you. Live true to yourself, recognize your own weaknesses, and never fault others for your own shortcomings. Be willing to be corrected.

44
ASSASSINATION

WHILE I WAS walking across Nyang'ori mission station in Kenya with my friend Joash Okong'o, a distraught-looking man breathlessly ran up to us and gasped out in Dholuo (the language of the Luo tribe) something I did not understand at all. Joash blanched, and his face was as sober as I had ever seen it. He turned to me with a stricken look. "Tom Mboya has been shot!" They were from the same tribe. Tom Mboya had been a vital part of Kenya's journey to independence. He had served in President Kenyatta's cabinet for the six years since then.

The memory of that moment is so etched in my mind that I could take you to the very spot where we stood as we digested the news. Tom had been in a chemist's shop (pharmacy) in the middle of Nairobi when a car pulled up beside him. Seconds later, shots rang out and Tom lay dead at the door of the shop.

Tom was an outstanding Kenyan politician, a man of integrity and world-wide esteem. He was also a friend. Tom was on the "short list" to be considered as the next secretary general of the United Nations at the time. Had he been chosen, he would have been the first from the continent of Africa to hold the position. He also was perceived by many to be the heir apparent to the presidency of Kenya, following Jomo Kenyatta. I was good friends with Tom's cousin Odhiambo Okite. Odhiambo wrote speeches for Tom.

It was a defining moment for Kenya. Had he become president, it is probable that Kenya would have been less corrupt than it became later on. Tom was from the Luo tribe, which was the second largest tribe in Kenya. Jomo Kenyatta, still alive at that time, was from the Kikuyu tribe, the largest of the more than 40 tribes in Kenya.

Life became tense for a few days. Tribal animosities that had been quietly simmering suddenly surfaced. I happened to be in town in Kisumu when Tom's body was brought through the city on the way to be buried at his family home on Rusinga Island. When the crowds began to gather, I was able to reach the roof of the post office and watch safely from three storeys up.

The mourning was mixed with great anger. I could hear shouts of hatred for the assumed assassins. The Luo people simply "knew" that the Kikuyu were responsible. After the crowds had followed the cavalcade down Kisumu's main street toward Lake Victoria, I felt it was safe to go down and finish my shopping. That was not to be.

I ended up on the floor of a butcher's shop behind the meat counter as the riot rerouted itself all through the centre of town again, this time with guns blazing. The window was shot out of the butcher's shop. The burly shop owner and I shared the floor in relative safety behind the meat display cooler. As soon as it seemed safe, I went to my car, which had escaped damage. I fled for the hills and home at Nyang'ori.

A few days later, I accepted an invitation from Odhiambo Okite to the relatively small funeral and interment. I saw only one other white person, a woman, at the funeral. It was a sad day for Kenya. It may well have been the beginning of the turning point in Kenya's stability. As far as I am aware, no one was ever brought to justice for Tom's murder.

Assassinations in Africa are not uncommon. Coups d'état were not uncommon. But for a man who was not yet in the primary office to be killed seemed to set the tone for some awful things to happen in Kenya's future. Though I spent 17 years in Kenya and Uganda, tribalism is something I still don't fully comprehend. It is probably the base cause for most of Africa's instability. Tribalism, power, greed, and corruption mixed with power and money!

Often, we missionaries were unwittingly caught in the middle when tribal animosities bubbled over. Since we lived near the borders where several major tribal groups bordered within Kenya, there were often tense moments. Despite the acceptance of the Christian faith, tribalism was occasionally a stronger loyalty than to the peace that Jesus taught.

The sheep and the goats will eventually be revealed.

Wisdom Gained: Tragic things occur in everyone's life. Christians can be assured that through it all we have the immediate presence of God with comfort, resolutions, and often healing. Walking with God is much more than just talk.

45 JAIL AND A GHANAIAN ANGEL

I TRAVELLED EXTENSIVELY throughout Africa on behalf of Evangel Publishing House. I promoted the sale and distribution of our books in English and several other languages. Some of these trips I took by car, throughout Kenya, Tanzania, and Uganda. Some of my trips were by air.

One such trip took me up and down the West African coast. I got all the necessary visas and documents to travel and set out. It was an awful trip in many ways. I flew into the airport in Lagos, Nigeria. It took nine hours to drive to central Lagos, where I was to meet with Samuel Olusigon Odunaike, the author of one of the books I was distributing. He was an executive of Shell Oil in Nigeria, as well as a powerful lay preacher with the Foursquare Gospel Church in Nigeria.

I cannot tell you how terrible it was to import the one box of sample books I had shipped to Nigeria in advance. Customs was crazy. Sam asked a local pastor, Joe, to go through it with me. I had papers signed and stamped in 26 offices before we suddenly realized that we had been in same ones several times. It dawned on me, finally, that they wanted a bribe to release my books. At the twenty-seventh office visit, I shook the papers in the official's face and said, "I'll walk around these offices forever before I give you any *dash* [as it was called in Nigeria]." I got my books, but I was totally frazzled.

Sam told me later that corruption had reached new levels in Nigeria. He knew of people who had had to pay a bit of *dash* to the teller to get their own money out of the bank.

I got on the plane in Lagos, and that too was an experience I'd like to forget. The plane was fully booked, and we all had assigned seats. When they opened the doors to let us walk across the tarmac to the DC-10 on the apron, a mad rush took place. Flight attendants were roughly pushed aside. A big crowd gathered at the ramp leading up into the plane, scrambling to get aboard. They pressed so hard that the bottom of the ramp was plugged. I stood back in awe. It was awful. Finally, I got on. My seat was empty, so I sat down. I still wonder why there was such a mad rush when we all had assigned seating.

I went on to Ghana, Senegal, and then Ivory Coast. I speak no French, the inherited language much of West Africa. The people I was to meet ran a Christian bookstore in Abidjan, Ivory Coast. They were from Britain, so I knew I'd be all right.

When I presented my passport for stamping, the immigration official looked at me with a hard glare. "Where is your visa?" he asked. I answered that I had been told by the travel agent that I did not need to obtain a visa in advance, because Canada was a bilingual country, speaking both French and English. He looked at me sternly, saying, "You are trying to sneak into our country!"

I said that was not so and went on to explain why I was travelling and whom I would see. He was having none of it. He confiscated my passport and put me in a locked windowless jail cell. I didn't know what to do. One chair, one locked door, and no window. No one came or went. I prayed that I could get out, thinking I'd offer to leave the country, and good riddance!

I pulled out my pocket Bible and read until something did finally happen. A key rattled in the lock, and a little lady in a uniform came in and began to wash the floor with a mop. The door was locked again behind her. She looked at me out of the corner of her eye several times, then asked me, in the most delightful English, "Are you a Christian?" I answered that I was. She asked why I was there. I explained as much as I knew and that I had to see the people from the Christian bookshop. She said she knew them.

She stopped washing the floor, knocked on the door, and said, "Wait here," as though I had a choice. After she left the door was locked again. Half an hour later she was back. "Don't worry," she said, "you will be all right." She went on washing the floor as she explained that she was from Ghana, where English is the official language, that she was a Christian, and that many Ghanaians worked in Ivory Coast.

Finally, an immigration officer came and gave me a pass to enter Abidjan but kept my passport. He turned me over to a missionary lady from the bookstore, who had come to pick me up. It's easy to get out of jail if you're a Christian, under the right circumstances, when God sends a little Ghanaian angel to open the doors!

That's not the end of the story in Abidjan. You never can tell what a visit to a Christian bookshop will lead to. I was at the Christian bookshop the next morning after getting out of jail at the airport. This shop in Ivory Coast was run by two British ladies who were fluent in the French spoken there, as well as a very cultured form of English. Although we had few books in French, they did have a large English-speaking clientele. We finished our discussions, and I took their order. One of the ladies asked, "What are you doing this evening?"

My answer was simple, "Sleeping at the guest house."

She asked, "Would you be willing to speak at a weekly prayer meeting, which happens to be tonight?"

"Sure!" I answered.

"All the people who come are English speaking, so there's no need for a translator. There will be local Ivorian people, as well as quite a few expatriates. It's held in our apartment."

They gave me directions as to address and the apartment number. Then they gave me instructions on what *not* to speak about. They knew I was a Pentecostal missionary and told me it would not be appropriate for me to talk about Pentecostalism. They asked me specifically to talk about the work I was doing in Evangel Publishing House in Kenya.

No problem. I'm not backward about my Pentecostal experience and position, but I am not ready to cause unnecessary waves or disputes. I agreed to their wishes.

When I turned up at their apartment, I was amazed at how many people were there. Black and white were chatting and enjoying a little buffet of finger foods and cold drinks. Most of them were professionals. There was a clear sense of camaraderie in the room. Everyone seemed to know everyone. I joined in the finger-foods feed.

Several choruses were sung, one in French. One of the ladies introduced me and told them that I was general manager of Evangel Publishing House in Kenya and that their bookshop had placed an order. Then I was asked to speak. The crowd was so large that I spoke with my back against the entrance door. Everyone sat on the few chairs available or on the floor, and one squatted uncomfortably on a windowsill. When I had read a few relevant Scriptures, I explained as much as I felt was appropriate about Evangel and then was ready to sit down.

The resident lady asked if I would be willing to answer any questions. I said of course I would.

Something remarkable began to happen. A black lady began gasping, and finally burst out what was not a question: "Tell us about the baptism in the Holy Spirit!" I glanced at the woman who had told me to avoid the subject. She looked nonplussed for an instant, then nodded her head in affirmative resignation. What could she do? She wouldn't want to quell a citizen of the Ivory Coast.

From that moment, I had totally undivided attention. I didn't preach a sermon but simply began to give my own testimony, backing up what I said with quotations from the Scriptures. As I was speaking, suddenly someone burst out loudly, speaking in other tongues. Someone led her into the kitchen, where she continued, not too quietly, speaking in tongues as the Spirit gave her utterance. I picked up at the point of interruption.

Then someone else began speaking in tongues with his hands raised above his head. He was led into one of the bedrooms. Then another went into the other bedroom! Then more began to praise and worship God in tongues, including the man sitting on the windowsill.

I concluded by simply backing up against the door and watching in amazement. I could not help but think of the Scripture where Peter was preaching and "while Peter was still speaking these words, the Holy Spirit came on all who heard the message ... For they heard them speaking in tongues and praising God" (Acts 10:44–46). The meeting was out of my control, and no one else tried to control it. Eventually quiet settled on the folk, and they were invited to finish up the finger food and to talk.

Neither of the two ladies made any comment to me for or against what had happened, but two people came to me with their stories. One was a teacher who told me he had been out of a job for two years in England and had become quite discouraged. This apparently affected his Christian walk. He told me that he had attended Kensington Temple in London, England. He saw an advertisement for teachers needed in Ivory Coast, and now here he was teaching English in an Abidjan school.

He went on to say, "I think, therefore, God brought me to Ivory Coast. What you said tonight and what happened has convinced me that I must rededicate my life to Christ." I prayed with him for a moment, and he went his way—or, should I say, God's way?

An African man came to me and told me a most remarkable story. He was from the Republic of Niger. He had been seeking God in his home in Niger. He just wanted "more" of God. He said the Lord spoke to him clearly to go to Abidjan. He took a train from the capital, Niamey, through Burkina Faso and on through the interior of Ivory Coast to Abidjan. He didn't know where to go or what to do. He prayed for guidance.

He then related the most remarkable events. "God told me to walk up a certain street, then make several turns onto other streets. God was showing me all the way." He was then led to an apartment building and instructed to go inside, climb the stairs, and knock on a certain door. It was the apartment in which we were meeting that very night. One could hardly call that a coincidence!

God had filled him with the Holy Spirit, and he was speaking with other tongues among total strangers. As he told me his story, his face and eyes shone with the glory of God. I have never heard from or about him since that evening, but as I went to sleep that night I could only marvel at the ways of God. I can't explain them all, but I accept them.

Wisdom Gained: God's ways are past finding out. He moves in mysterious and startling ways. Always keep your heart open to God's guidance and intervention, even to what otherwise may seem unreasonable. Expect His sovereign interruptions. They can be glorious in their results.

46 SOME INCIDENTAL MEETINGS

THERE WE WERE, grown men, three ministers of the gospel, sitting or crawling across the floor of Mary's once-tidy living room in Nairobi. We were sorting through white papers, speeches, scrawled notes, and pictures: Michael Cassidy, evangelist and president of African Enterprise of South Africa; Cal Ratz, my brother-in-law and chief editor at Evangel Publishing House; and me, the general manager—all on the floor. It was quite undignified!

We were preparing to publish all the material and reports resulting from the Pan Africa Christian Leadership Assembly (PACLA). I had been invited to help organize the event. Michael Cassidy, from South Africa, an Anglican minister who had a vision for *all* of Africa, was the energetic driving force behind the conference.

PACLA was a conference of massive proportions. Speakers from every country in Africa, as well as overseas, came together to confer, listen, pray, preach, sing, and worship. Billy Graham came from the USA, Dr. John Stott came from England, and others came from non-African nations. Most of the 73 speakers came from African countries.

There is far too much to tell, but I had the joy of publishing two large books that came out of PACLA. *Together in One Place!* was the story of how PACLA came about, and the other contained the papers presented by delegates and speakers.

Two weeks later, Archbishop Janani Luwum, a delegate to the conference, was murdered by Idi Amin in Uganda. His body was not made available to the Church of Uganda for burial. There were persistent reports that Idi Amin had eaten parts of his body. In some cultures, it was once believed that if you ate the heart of your enemy, you gained all his strength and power. Current practices of witchcraft in 1973 bolstered that belief. No conclusive proof of these rumours surfaced.

I stepped off of the elevator on the wrong floor in Church House. Walking to what I thought was my office, I was distracted by a loud clattering noise. I glanced into the office, the source of this strange noise.

I saw a slight but not gaunt man sitting in the centre of piles of paper. Nearby a printer was churning out large pages, which were piling up accordion-style on the floor beside him. He sensed my presence and my fascination with the clutter and clatter. He stood and introduced himself. "Hello, I'm David Barrett." I glanced at his door inscription as I introduced myself. It was Dr. David B. Barrett, the well-known church research scientist. He explained that he was putting together the statistics of every denomination in Kenya. This was to include every church and entity of every possible category, together with information he had gleaned over several years of research. His co-editors were George K. Mambo, Janice McLaughlin, and Malcolm J. McVeigh.

As it turned out, he knew more about my own denomination in Kenya than I did. He mentioned that he was going to publish the statistics as a book entitled *The Kenya Churches Handbook*. If you wanted to know what, where, how, when, why, and who about any Christian entity in Kenya, he had it all over his floor.

I introduced myself a little more, since he was considering where he might have his book published. He knew about us, more than I would have thought. It was part of what was on the floor in his office. He was just going through his final checks to be certain that his manuscript accurately represented his research.

Evangel Publishing House subsequently published *The Kenya Churches Handbook*, a 350-page perfect bound and hard-covered book, the largest project of Evangel up to that time. It covers the development of Kenyan Christianity from 1498 to 1973. I have in my possession what may be the only copy of the book signed by Dr. Barrett and all the editors, and the publisher — me. Dr. Barrett went on to publish *The World Churches Handbook* many years later.

At Evangel Publishing House, we received orders to print literature published by various international ministries, some of them based in North America. Rev. Rex Humbard was planning a mass evangelism meeting in Nairobi. He wanted 50,000 copies of the Gospel of John printed for distribution while he was in Kenya. That became the responsibility of Evangel Press. It was done according to his instructions, and we delivered it to Nairobi. I was a little put off by the requirement that there be a full-page picture of Rex at the end of the booklet, but since he was paying the bill, and there was an extra blank page, it was done.

Somehow, I was designated to pick up the Humbard family from their hotel and take them to the large park where the outdoor evangelistic meetings were taking place. After several days of this, I began to wonder if I had gotten tangled up with a slightly dysfunctional family! I would never have talked to my parents the way their two sons spoke to their parents. Their daughter seemed much more respectful and genuine.

Maud Amy Humbard, the featured singer at the meetings, had reached a stage where she could not always remember the words to her songs. Large cue cards were placed in order in front of her on the platform. When she was about to sing, one of the sons deliberately mixed up her cue cards to confuse her further. Looking at the floor where the disordered cue cards lay caused her great consternation. All this happened in front of thousands of people!

It was also during this event that I began to wonder just how the statistics were compiled by some evangelists regarding how many people came to faith in Jesus Christ. It seemed to me, sitting on the platform, that the number "saved" was strangely related to how many copies of the Gospel of John were distributed to all who were invited to come forward to the platform to get one. How many of the same people came forward every evening?

I wondered who did the follow-up to bring them into a church fellowship. I didn't see much evidence of it. When we had evangelistic meetings, 50,000 people attended the meetings in South Sudan, over two weeks. Only 3,023 filled out the "decision cards" filled out, expressing a new faith in Jesus. Every single one was followed up by the local churches in Juba. On the other hand, the Holy Spirit is also quite capable of follow-up when humans fall short!

The tensions of Mau Mau were still hanging over Kenya when Mary and I went there as missionaries. Many people were killed, including some white farmers and many, many Africans who refused to join in the atrocities of Mau Mau. There was still great apprehension in the air.

The first elections were about to take place, and several political parties were vying for the leadership of the government. Jomo Kenyatta had been released from prison, where the British had held him as leader of the Mau Mau movement and the bush gangs who raided at night throughout central Kenya. Many Europeans were ready to flee.

Jomo Kenyatta became the leader of the Kenya African National Union (KANU). His party won the election, and Kenyatta became president. Unlike many African nations, the transition was exceptionally smooth, and Kenyatta led the nation into independence and through the rough times and decisions of those days, which led to national prosperity. He became a folk hero and is considered the founding father of Kenya.

When President Kenyatta died, Daniel Arap Moi succeeded him. Many expected a tense transition, but it was peaceful. Moi had been educated in Christians schools and had often mentioned Christian principles in his speeches. My good friend Odhiambo Okite and I prepared some of the speeches for President Moi while some traces of the Christian faith yet remained in his mind. Then things changed.

It was under the rule of President Moi that the beginning of the end for my friend Odhiambo was touched off.

Wisdom Gained: Meet new people. It always leads to something more, something interesting, sometimes significant, and often an incredible event. Be interested in others. In humility, consider others more important than yourself.

47 THERE'S NEVER A CAMERA WHEN YOU NEED ONE

WHILE LIVING IN western Kenya, Mary and I were asked to drive a car most unsuited for Kenyan roads at the time, a 1956 Chevrolet, to Nairobi. Mary and I lived at Nyang'ori, just up in the hills west of the town of Kisumu on Lake Victoria. We had to make the 350-kilometre trip to Nairobi in any case to pick up our new Volkswagen Beetle, which had finally arrived from Germany.

There were no paved roads across the Luo plains in 1963, so the very dusty and well-used dirt road was the only way to go. That narrow road led up into some hills behind and above our Muhuroni mission station. Lake Victoria was visible off in the distance to our right. The car we were driving was a very unusual car in Kenya in those days. Land Rovers, Volkswagens, Peugeots, and Mercedes seemed to be the most popular. Large cars from North America were as rare as hen's teeth.

As we drove upward on an extremely dusty part of the road, we were startled to see what appeared to be a large crocodile lying in the sun, stretching from one side of the road to the other. As we drove closer, we realized it was not a crocodile; nor was it anything we had ever seen.

Its head was like that of a large snake, or a monitor lizard, but bigger, complete with darting tongue. Its dust-covered sides seemed to be somewhere between scaly and plated, but the most startling of all was the row of triangular plates standing up on its spine, from head to tail. They were large in the middle and became smaller near both the tail and the head. It was about 15 feet long.

We stopped the car and watched it for about ten minutes. It was just about 30 to 35 feet ahead of us on the road. There was no movement, except the occasional darting of a thin tongue from its mouth. I did not yet own a camera; otherwise I'd have had a prize picture. Smart phones were in the distant future. Years later I came to realize just how prized a picture it would have been.

When I gunned the engine, it became alert. We didn't realize that it was an unusual sighting since we had been in Africa only a few months. We simply concluded it was some regular African creature about which we had not yet heard. I drove slowly toward it. When we got closer, it suddenly trundled off into the sparse brush and was gone. We told a few folks about it, but no one seemed to think much about it. We let it pass. We never saw anything like it again.

Many years later, Dr. Kent Hovind was a guest on *100 Huntley Street*. We were both in the green room preparing to go on-air. I had no idea that he was a scholar who believed that many of the so-called extinct species, such as some forms of dinosaurs and ancient water monsters, still existed. He had a book with him, illustrating some of these ancient creatures. I told him about what Mary and I had seen. Dr. Hovind got quite excited.

He grabbed one of the thick books he had with him and began to show me illustrations that had been reconstructed from bones of ancient creatures. After dismissing many of the drawings and describing a bit more detail, I was shocked to see an illustration that almost exactly resembled the creature Mary and I had seen. I have forgotten the official Latin name for it. Dr. Hovind was delighted at what I had described, quoting it as proof of his beliefs that such creatures still existed.

I personally had no doubt that what Mary and I had seen existed. I just had no idea at the time that it was anything unusual. It was some sort of dinosaur. Later, Bill Gibbons, a cryptozoologist, contacted me to interview me about the incident. It was included in a book he was writing on the present-day sightings of supposedly extinct creatures that most evolutionary theorists have written off as having existed multi-millions of years ago. Over the years, people have called me to ask if I had truly seen the creature. I affirmed that I had.

I bought a camera later and am still almost anguished that I had been unable photograph it.

Mary and I lived at the mission station called Goibei, located almost on the equator, and on the border between two tribes, Maragoli and Kalenjin. One night, we heard loud ululations and cries from the villages surrounding the mission station. Not knowing what was happening (we had recently lived through a tribal war around the station), we cautiously went to the back door of our house. No one was in sight, so we stepped out into our back yard in the compound. We saw nothing at first, because we were looking at ground level, from where the cries were coming. Then we saw it!

Up in the sky, not too high but certainly large and seemingly close, we saw it. It was perhaps two or three hills beyond the hilltop on which we lived. It looked like a massive light bulb in shape but with a radiant glow in its centre. It cast no light outward or downward. The stem of the light-bulb-like "thing" was dark but discernible against the starlit sky. It was rough in shape like a pear-shaped hot air balloon commonly seen over our communities now. It was opaque but unmarked in any way. We stood and looked at it for a long time. The cries of the people gradually diminished to an eerie silence. We watched and wondered. I have no idea for how long. Then, suddenly, it was gone.

We mentioned it to several people from Nyang'ori, about 13 miles away, the next day, but they had no explanation. Some suggested it was a satellite, which was a new manmade phenomenon back then in 1964 and 1965. If so, why was it so close, and why did it stay in almost the same place? Others suggested it was smoke or some strange gas.

We were ready to dismiss it as some strange natural phenomenon, but again the next night and yet again the third, we saw it. It hovered again in the same area, looked the same, and disappeared as suddenly as the first night. The people in the villages around were spooked, and the ululations of the women pierced the night air again. Three nights of the same weird phenomenon! And then nothing, nothing but a lot of questions, still without answers! It never happened again, and life went on as normally as before. I have no idea what it was. I'm just reporting.

Years later, when several staff members from *100 Huntley Street* and I were caught between Sudan and Uganda after both borders were closed for the night, we had to find a place to stay just inside Sudan. We finally did, at about two dollars a night each. The accommodations were not worth even the few dollars we paid, cramped mud huts with audible insect sounds coming from the floor.

It was a bright clear night, and several of us, including David Shelley, Byron Winsor, Tim Whitehead, and me, went out onto the road and looked at the sky. Inside, the huts were repulsive. The night sky was pure and clear. Beautiful! It was undiminished by the intensity of large city lights. There were a few kerosene lamps in sight at ground level, but the sky was vivid and remarkably clear. You felt you could almost reach up and touch the stars.

One of us noticed a particularly bright "star" and asked which one it might be. No one had an answer. As we watched it, we noticed movement. Ah, we thought! A satellite! The longer we looked at it, the less convinced we were. Since it was positioned at about a 45-degree angle, just over and beyond a large tree, we could not trace a straight track across the sky. There was no breeze. The "thing" just made small movements, left, right, up, and down. We stood in the road and puzzled for quite some time. We checked with each other. Did it just move left? Everyone said yes. Now up? Again yes.

It was impossible to judge its distance, or even its possible size, except that it seemed closer than any of the myriad stars in sight. We went to our separate huts, still quite puzzled. It was not ordinary. I have no idea what it was. I am just reporting.

The Bible does talk about signs in the heavens, but I am personally not too sure what those signs might be.

Wisdom Gained: Inexplicable phenomena happen often. Human science cannot explain most of them. Yet the Bible indicates that strange things will happen, especially preceding the return of Jesus for His church. Be waiting, watching, and looking for His soon return.

48 SNAKES I HAVE MET

AS STRANGE AS it may sound, we saw very few snakes in the 17 years we lived in Africa. There were plenty of them there, but most often, they sensed us first and slithered for cover, disappearing into the grass and bushes. Normally, snakes leave you alone if you leave them alone. It's when they feel cornered or threatened that they can become aggressive.

When teaching in the Bible college at Nyang'ori, I walked down the path toward the original house occupied by Otto Keller, who founded the mission in 1911. Then I would take a shortcut through the beautiful mission garden on a narrow dirt path, past Otto's grave, and turn right to our little one-bedroom mud-walled house.

After we got used to the house, we liked it. The mud walls were more than a foot thick, plastered over with lime and/or cement, then painted white. The door trim was painted a dark green. I leaned against it at shoulder height one day, and it crushed inward. The wood in the door frame had been eaten entirely by termites. Multiple layers and colours of paint held everything together. It was not too bad an arrangement.

One day, we were rather disturbed to see army ants, a stream about six inches wide, crawling right through the house. It looked like a little river of ants, flowing in perfect order under the front door, across the concrete living room floor, down the two steps into the kitchen, and out under the back door. We sometimes protected the wooden legs of our furniture by setting them in little tins of kerosene to block the termites from dining out on the furniture in our house.

I was returning to this exciting little house after teaching a class at noon. On the garden path, under my right foot, I felt a mushy rolling sensation. I looked down quickly, and my foot was on two green mambas, deadly snakes, that had been crossing the path. Tails and heads were whipping around my foot. I felt like I was treading air in a fury before I hit solid ground and took off. I came back with a rifle, rather a stupid weapon against snakes. They were long gone, of course.

Another time, Dr. Charles Ratz, from Eastern Pentecostal Bible College in Canada, was visiting Nyang'ori. Dr. Ratz and I had gone over to the evening chapel service early, since he would be speaking to the students. Mary was to follow later. "Later" became too much later. I began to be concerned, since she was seldom late. I went back to the house. Mary was outside the woodshed holding a torch (flashlight) beamed into the shed. It was shining into the beady eyes of a spitting cobra. If it stayed in the woodpile, it would be dangerous to whoever came for wood. We didn't need fires to heat the houses, but to heat water. The fire was under a 44-gallon drum built into the wall and attached to the outside. Its heated water was piped into the house.

Dilemma! I took the torch from Mary and told her to back away from the woodshed door. I did the same. Finally, it came out and slithered very slowly through the grass toward the back of the house. I gave the torch to Mary and picked up a rather heavy beam of teak planking we used as a little bridge over a drainage ditch. I'm not sure where I got the strength, but I carried it toward the retreating cobra, then threw it onto the snake. It pinned the snake to the ground but did not kill it. Snakes do not die willingly or easily.

I raced into the house and got a Maasai spear I had. When I got back, the tail and head were thrashing about. Only about eight inches of the head end was sticking out from under the plank. The long tail, perhaps another two or three feet, thrashed wildly out from under the other side. I stood on the plank, and with the spear, after many jabs, thrust it through near the head. We left it there, put the spear away, and went back to the chapel, both of us pretending we were not in the least afraid. I have no idea what Dr. Ratz spoke about that night.

Another encounter with a snake was on a hunting trip for meat for the freezer. I solved that problem with a shotgun, more effective than a rifle. It was a python, perhaps 12 feet long. It had wound itself around a dik-dik (the smallest gazelle in Africa, about the size of a rabbit). It had squeezed the dik-dik to death in preparation for swallowing it. I shot the snake in the head, leaving most of the pellet-pierced head, the skin, and the length of the snake intact.

There's a sad ending here. I had skinned and salted the snake for tanning. This was a fine specimen, so I took it to the commercial tannery in Nairobi to be preserved. That was the last I saw of it. Several of my best animal hides seemed to disappear from that tannery. We did save the soft little pelt of the small dik-dik, which had died a rather horrible death.

Of course, the most frightening was when I almost certainly saved the life of a good friend, Odhiambo Okite. But you've read that story already. Only a few snake experiences in 17 years? That's not too bad!

Wisdom Gained: A serpent appeared to Eve in the garden of Eden. Beware, he also comes like a wolf in sheep's clothing, or an individual disguised as a friend. Con artists are friends of the serpent. Trust only those who prove their trustworthiness. Deception is now popularly accepted in some places. Be wise.

49 DAVID MAINSE INTERRUPTED MY LIFE

MARY AND I returned to Canada from Africa in 1979, with our 11-year-old son John and our nine-year-old daughter Elaine. We settled into a rented apartment on the 32nd floor of a high-rise in Willowdale, in the north end of Toronto, just beside a large mall on the corner of Yonge Street and Steeles Avenue. It was a rather restricted place, especially when it came to storing bicycles. That meant taking them up the elevator, through the apartment, and onto the balcony.

Within a week or so, I had received 13 offers of ministry opportunities. This included several senior pastorates, the vice presidency of a large ministry in the United States, and several other less attractive offers. The least attractive offer was to work with David Mainse at *100 Huntley Street*. How could I possibly be involved in such a big and public ministry?

Meanwhile, I travelled across Canada promoting missions for the PAOC for some months as was required. For six weeks, I struggled in prayer over which position might be the right choice and God's will. Nothing became clear. I wasn't interested in TV. I had done some TV in Kenya as the "last voice" on *The Voice of Kenya* every night. I was doing this Christ-centred epilogue just before the station shut down for the night.

Doing the epilogue on Kenyan television was a weird experience. I came prepared. They turned the broadcast signal off and went to a black screen, which was the way they ended their broadcast day. A few minutes later they turned the signal on again, for my epilogue. I walked into the station, after the last news of the day, neither met nor saw anyone, and simply entered a small studio. I sat on a stool in front of a very strange and ancient TV camera that looked more like a torpedo than a camera. I did my epilogue, prayed, and walked out of the station again, never seeing a soul. I really was not very interested in a career in TV.

I had known David Mainse, both as a classmate in college and as a neighbour in our first pastorates. I had also been a guest with David on his *Crossroads* program before *100 Huntley Street* had been born. "Sorry, David, I'm not really interested." It hardly figured in my praying about the future. Missions was in my heart.

Finally, after six weeks, I changed my prayer tactics. I asked the Lord to close every door except the one that was in His will. Within a week, 12 offers were either withdrawn or the positions filled. The only one left was David's invitation to join him at 100 Huntley Street.

I hesitated for several days. Since I had visited the studios once, I knew the lay of the land. I put in some conditions before calling David. First, I would call on the following Saturday morning when the place was closed. Second, if David himself answered the phone at the receptionist's desk, I would take it that perhaps that's what God wanted. I'm not one for laying out fleeces, but I really needed a clear sign on this.

I called. David answered. Although I was still very frightened by the prospect, I agreed to meet him for lunch at Cap's Bar and Grill across Jarvis Street from 100 Huntley Street. As we ate lunch, I said to David, "I think God might want me to work with you. Is that job still open?"

As soon as the question was out of my mouth, the answer was in my heart. David did not really need to answer, but he did anyway. "I knew that God had spoken to me that you should come. You're hired! How much salary do you need?"

I was flabbergasted. No one had ever asked me that question before. I told him I had no idea how much I needed to survive in Canada with two children. I had lived in Africa for 17 years. I knew nothing about salaries and the cost of living in Canada. If I'd had my wits about me, I'd have asked for a lot more than I eventually got. We lived "thin" for some years.

I started as a volunteer at 100 Huntley Street in July 1979, since I was still travelling and raising funds for the missions department of the PAOC. It was not until September 18, 1979, that I became a full-time employee with Crossroads Christian Communications Inc. I can't say the salary was any better than what I was getting from the missions department of my denomination. In any case, neither was quite adequate. But God was!

One thing I have avoided throughout my life. I have never asked for either a position or a raise in pay. Certainly it was difficult at times, but I stuck to it on principle.

Wisdom Gained: Money is merely a tool to use wisely, never to become a main goal in life. The lust for money can lead to compromise and can lead to a weakening of our trust in and devotion to God.

50 TV OPENS INTERESTING DOORS

DAVID INTRODUCED ME to Lindsay Stevenson, who was producing programs in several languages, basically all by himself. He was a workhorse but was working himself half to death. I joined him as director of Christian multilingual programming to help organize and look after the financing of the programs. They were many: French, German, Greek, Portuguese, Spanish, Italian, Chinese, and Korean. The list eventually grew to more than twenty languages.

One of the first activities was to raise funds to support the many languages. We had a telethon, and I was faced for the first time with having to go live on camera. I was unprepared, though it went well. Suddenly, I had a large budget to control, divided into a sub-budget for each language.

The French program, *Au Centuple*, became by far the most effective. In Quebec, it garnered many hundreds of phone calls from viewers. At one point, 23 per cent of all calls into *Au Centuple* were people seeking to know Jesus Christ as their personal Saviour. The harvest was clearly ready.

We expanded many of the Christian Multilingual Programs (CMP) to reach to the lands of the origins of the languages in which we broadcast. That went well. I was asked with some regularity to host the *100 Huntley Street* program when David Mainse was away. It always made me nervous, but I did my best.

CAL BOMBAY

More and more responsibilities were given to me until at one stage I became senior vice president. *100 Huntley Street* kept growing and reaching into new areas of ministry. Reorganizations took place. I held so many different responsible positions, I can hardly remember them all.

I was co-founder and director of The Geoffrey R. Conway School of Broadcasting. This had been initiated with help and guidance from Lorne Shepherd and other vital production staff. I created the WHEAT Fund (World Harvest Evangelism and Television) to help graduates of the School of Broadcasting to get established in their own countries.

The 28 telephone counselling centres across Canada were under my supervision for some years after Rev. Don Osborne, who had established them, resigned and began pastoring in British Columbia. This brought on the duty of regular visits to these centres right across Canada, from St. John's, Newfoundland, to Victoria, British Columbia. Some of the finest people I met in all my years of ministry were serving as volunteer telephone prayer partners.

It was in connection with these prayer centres that I often travelled for a week of local television fundraising productions designed to cover the expenses of airtime in those areas, as well as the costs related to the prayer centres. I didn't travel alone, of course. There was most often a group, but I had the main hosting responsibilities. At various times I went to the local stations with either Reynold or Glen Rutledge or Norma-Jean Mainse and others to provide the music. Occasionally local musical talent volunteered. We took along an administrator to care for the organizational aspects and to train and supervise volunteer telephone personnel to take calls, prayer requests, and pledges. A member of the *100 Huntley Street* production staff was also there as a producer/director.

These trips were often very wearing on the flesh. Ending a Monday through Wednesday telethon, we would quickly break down our equipment to be set up in another city for a Thursday and Friday telethon. We often travelled through the night. These telethons invariably included a "partners rally" on one of the evenings we were in town, at which I would preach. Many people came to know the Lord and Saviour in those rallies. There were other teams doing the same thing, of course, led by Don Osborne, Gordon Williams, and Father Bob MacDougal. Sometimes we led these telethons as a team.

I led several telethons in the USA as well. In Canton, Ohio, the studio was in the basement of a house, with the lights almost touching our heads. One of the studio lights exploded right over my head, showering me with very fine hot slivers of glass. We carried on in the semi-dark. That was live TV.

In Los Angeles, we were scheduled to interview Pastor Jack Hayford. He had not been adequately informed of what was expected of him by those who organized these forays into the USA. When Rev. Hayford arrived at the studio, he gave me a well-deserved lecture on proper preparation. He wanted a list of questions I would ask him live on air. I made as good a quick fix as I could, and Dr. Hayford was very gracious on air. I really felt quite out of my element with men of such stature.

There were often dangers attached to Christian television. In Sudbury, one of the local station's staff came in to inform me that they had received a bomb threat and that we should vacate the studio. An unknown man in a trench coat had been seen wandering in the building, so the threat was taken seriously by the station. I decided to go ahead live to air despite the threat. Although there was tension among some of our volunteers, the program went ahead as scheduled with no incident. Television can be interesting!

One day, the receptionist at the front desk received a telephone call from an irate man who claimed I had insulted his mother on television that day. He announced that he was coming with a gun to shoot me. I was told about it, of course, but my office was on the top floor. I reviewed my commentary of that day, and there wasn't any reference to any mother, let alone the mother of this unknown man. I carried on work at my desk, not under it.

We contacted the Toronto Police, who just happened to be headquartered behind the 100 Huntley Street office, on Jarvis Street. A few of the officers would join us in prayer from time to time. On this day, two big, burly uniformed officers responded. The man did arrive with a level of rage that identified him. The two big and burly "good guys," with an arm under each of his, waltzed him right back out the door. It turned out he was not armed.

Because of *100 Huntley Street*'s involvement in Sudan and my comments on air about the vicious abuses of slavery and human rights, we stirred up some wrath. We had bricks thrown through our front windows, rather shocking a few people working in those offices.

There were other threats because of our Sudan involvement. Several newspaper articles, written by a journalist who accompanied us to Sudan, stirred up the ire of some Muslim extremists (Islamists). They wrote from Montreal to President al-Bashir of Sudan, calling for the elimination of Baroness Caroline

Cox, a member of the House of Lords in England; John Eibner, a human rights investigator from Switzerland; Pierre Richard, a journalist from Montreal; and me. The "International Brotherhood" was to carry out this call for our elimination.

Five of us from *100 Huntley Street* travelled to Prince Rupert, BC, for a telethon. All went well. On our departure for Toronto, to get to the local airport, we had to wait for a bus in a small shopping mall. As we stood around chatting, a mother with a 13-year-old daughter recognized both Norma-Jean Mainse and me, since we were the on-air persons. She was obviously troubled. She asked us if we would pray for her daughter, who had a very serious and suspicious growth in her abdomen. Of course, we agreed. As we prayed in the small concourse of that mall, there came a hush. Storekeepers came to their entrances and watched with a degree of astonishment. We laid hands on the young lady as the Bible instructs and prayed for her, some of our team with hands raised in appeal to God.

The mother thanked us, and the bus arrived. We all boarded and headed for the airport. Sitting behind me on the bus was a shy but determined Salvation Army believer. He wanted prayer as well. I turned around and held his hand as I prayed for his physical ailment. We heard from both later. The girl had no lump when she got to the hospital in Vancouver. The Salvation Army gentleman was healed as well. God can work His power in a mall or a bus as well as in a church. And yes, Jesus still heals on the Sabbath.

Mary and I were shopping in a mall at the corner of Steeles and Yonge Street in Willowdale. I'm not much of a shopper, so I just meandered around. I noticed a woman sitting on a bench, who had obviously recognized me from TV. She hesitantly looked at me and seemed somewhat distraught. I went and sat down beside her. Weeping, she told me that her husband had been given three weeks to live. His liver was ruined by heavy drinking, and he was not a Christian. "Would you pray for him?" she asked.

I prayed very specifically that he would first surrender his life to God and receive Jesus as Lord. I then prayed that God would spare his life and heal him. Three weeks later, I received a letter stating that the following Sunday he had accompanied her to church and given his life to God. A few months later, I received another letter reporting that her husband's condition had reversed, and he was getting healthier by the week.

Do we praise God enough for His wonderful works?

Wisdom Gained: Take every opportunity to share the truth about Jesus. Go through open doors rather than trying to force doors that are closed. If you keep aware, there are many opportunities to demonstrate God's love and power. God has a purpose for you everywhere.

51 THE CHICKEN MAN

FOR SOME TIME, Rev. Gordon Williams did what we called a "scriptural overview" (an audit) on each *100 Huntley Street* program, summarizing and only very occasionally correcting wrong impressions of doctrine made on the program, according to Scripture. When Gordon left to go into full-time evangelistic ministry in 1980, I was asked to take over that function by David Mainse.

It was a tough assignment. I was to listen to the discussions with the guests, assess them for doctrinal/biblical accuracy, then summarize my observations into just a couple of minutes. It is hard to describe the pressure that put on me. I worked with a *Strong's Concordance* next to me, my Bible, and a notepad to jot down my thoughts. Computerized Bible programs were not yet available.

When someone did make a statement or remark that was biblically questionable, the pressure of trying to make a correction as kindly as I could without offending our guest increased. I took it seriously, but it was a solid hour of intense concentration, and I was expected to come up with an intelligent summary of all that was said on the 90-minute program. I was given about two minutes or less. Fortunately, it was a rare occasion when I had to point out an unbiblical statement. In any case, David Mainse would normally have made a kindly correction or comment right away.

One day, I suggested to David that I simply do a commentary. I had an idea for one, based on some research some scientist had done on the origin of the human species. The scientist had concluded, through gene research and several other sources, that humankind had a common mother whom he chose to call Eve. I figured I could better him.

David agreed with the idea, and I did my first commentary, entitled, "Why didn't they ask me?" I then proceeded, with a slightly acerbic tone, to point out that the biblical account of creation had made that same claim for the past six thousand years. So what's with science? Why must someone waste my tax dollars to ascertain what was already very well documented, and in much more detail?

Another study came out regarding prayer for the sick. One group knew they were being prayed for, a second group had no idea they were being prayed for, and a third group was not prayed for at all. The scientific research showed better and faster recovery was indeed a fact, even among those who had no idea they were being prayed for. The biblical statement proved true from James 5:15, where it can be read by anyone who wants to: "The prayer of faith will save the sick, and the Lord will raise him up" (NKJV).

This turned into a daily commentary called "Cal's Commentary" that continued for years.

In about 1987, we learned that the building belonging to Confederation Life, which *100 Huntley Street* occupied in downtown Toronto, was to be demolished to make room for an expansion of the insurance company. Crossroads moved. So did Mary and I.

My love for animals and nature naturally took its course. We were given some "used" chickens by a farmer from our church, Clarence Persall. We got a bitch (now don't get all excited; *bitch* is the proper English word for a female canine) called Henry, short for Henrietta, from the pound. Eventually we had four dogs, three cats, fifty chickens, three goats, and of course those lovable little rodents in the barn that helped feed the cats.

One thing led to another, and another led to my observations of nature on TV, quite often of my chickens. People began to telephone my office or write in, asking for copies of certain commentaries. They were printed in various magazines and church bulletins. This eventually led to *100 Huntley Street* publishing seven books of my commentaries. I have written a total of about three thousand different commentaries, which resulted in books published under the titles: *The Right Stuff—Vols. 1, 2, and 3*, *The Wisdom of Nature* (also published in Russian), *Practical Thoughts from the Book of Romans*, *A View from the Barn*, and *God Down to Earth*.

These commentaries were well received by the viewing audience, and I was told repeatedly that the Nielsen Ratings on the *100 Huntley Street* program peaked during my commentaries. I wondered at first why that would be. Slowly I began to realise that the method of Bible teaching I was using through these commentaries was precisely the method Jesus used in teaching both His disciples and the crowds that followed Him: parables. I can't imagine a more excellent method of getting truth across than the way Jesus did.

I used my chickens so often as illustrations for my daily biblical teaching that I began to pick up the nickname "The Chicken Man." Yet I'm no expert on chickens, other than putting food in one end of a chicken so that eggs come out the other end.

Some people supposed I was a well-versed theologian as well. I am not, although I studied in a theological college. I just apply the practical teachings of God's Word to everyday living. I try to be practical in my faith and in the simple way I feel we should live as Christians.

Our grandson Joshua, about three years old at the time, was terrified one day when he saw an advertisement in which a truckload of chickens broke loose, and one chicken smashed against the windshield of a car, as seen from inside the car. Every time that ad came on TV, he would run, crying in terror. I had to fix this. I told Joshua that chickens were "chicken," afraid of almost everything. I explained that was why people would call a person a chicken when they showed fear. Then I took him to the barn, holding his hand for security, and opened the door to the chicken coop. Joshua recoiled in terror. I then asked him to watch me. I left him outside and stepped through the door, and the chickens milled around my feet. Joshua was riveted with fear, his eyes wide. Then I said, "Watch this!"

I made a sudden jump, and the chickens fled, squawking and flapping in fear. In a little time, I finally got him in and asked him to jump at the chickens. He hesitated at first. Then he jumped at them and they scattered. He was so delighted that he overdid it. He now was ruler of the "chicken" chickens. His fears fled as fast as the chickens fled.

That's probably a lesson most of us could learn. Face our fears head on. In 2 Timothy 1:7 we can all have confidence: "God has not given us a spirit of fear, but of power and of love and of a sound mind" (NKJV). As Christians, we can also face down satanic forces on the basis that Jesus already has won the victory, and we stand secure in Him.

My chickens were not a good investment when it came to dollars. Eventually, even selling some of my eggs cheaply to our staff at the office, I lost badly. We had eggs in abundance, but I worked it out that one dozen eggs cost me about six times as much as I was selling them for at $1.50 a dozen, nice brown free-range eggs, delicious. But they provided me with no end of insights into human nature and material for my commentaries.

I came by my interest in chickens honestly. My father kept chickens in the backyard in a rather middle-class area of Oshawa, and the neighbours never complained. Wherever we lived, we had chickens. My paternal grandfather developed a feed mixture back in 1908 which, according to a letter I have in my possession, brought one Mr. Bailey's chickens back to good health and better laying. People on my mother's side of the family were chicken farmers as well, way back before my mother was married.

Wherever I went to preach across Canada, someone would inevitably ask, "How are your chickens?" One day on TV, I finally said, "Everywhere I go, people ask me about my chickens but never ask about my wife, Mary!"

A few months later, I was in New Brunswick preaching over a weekend. A very nice lady came up to me after the service and asked, "How is your wife?"

I answered: "Fine, she is doing well. Thank you for asking!"

She then went on to say, "Now that that's out of the way, how are your chickens?"

Sometimes you can't win!

Wisdom Gained: Never let your understanding of God's creation, nature, and the world around you go beyond the simplicity intrinsic in life. In this modern age, science has become a god to many. Science is good, but the final and only anchor in life is a real relationship with God through Jesus Christ.

52 THE MAKING OF BOOKS

AFTER MY FIRST term in Kenya/Uganda as a missionary, I took a course in journalism and basic writing at Moody Bible Institute in Chicago. At the time, it only improved my letter writing.

In Africa, I was trying to run a publishing house without authors. I knew the subjects and even contents of books I needed to publish, but few people were willing to even consider writing them. Who was left? Me.

My first efforts were little booklets on little subjects. They seemed to be acceptable to readers and my associates. I then graduated to some booklets of a more usual size in inches but not too many pages. They too seemed to succeed and met needs of pastors and people in East Africa. I wrote under pressure. The course at Moody was finally making sense to me. I was writing.

When I joined the staff at *100 Huntley Street*, my first writing experience was job descriptions. There were none when I joined David Mainse in his work. Verbal instructions seemed to be the way of the day. Hence, from verbal instructions, I created my own job description, which was approved; then I went on to the job descriptions of people working under my leadership. I had used them in Africa, so why not here?

Eventually I began to write my daily commentaries. Every day, either early in the morning before the *100 Huntley Street* program went to air, or at home the evening before, I would take two hours to prepare a four-minute segment. I worked on it, honed it down, made it more understandable, and ended up with 700 words I felt were worth saying.

David suggested that my commentaries be compiled into book form and be offered to our viewers. This of course required a rewrite. Writing to be heard in speech where you can make emphasis with voice inflections, tones, and gestures is one thing. Writing to be read on the page must take a different form, including descriptive language and appropriate written emphasis. I had to rewrite my commentaries. From this came seven full books. I had begun to improve my craft as a writer. There were many pamphlets and small series of teaching papers that also came through my heart, head, and fingers into print.

Then Sudan happened to me. After my third covert trip into Sudan to free slaves, I had come down with a fever and a few issues that prevented me from going to the office. I was in bed all week. I don't take kindly to being inactive. I got my diary of those first three trips into Sudan, and with a laptop on my knees in bed, I began to rewrite from the highlights I had recorded. I filled in details from memory that I had had no time then to record but that came back to me in vivid detail. By the end of the week, I had a manuscript.

I don't even remember who read it, but they suggested, "This would make a great book!" I was convinced to go through it and clean up some grammar and paragraphs. I submitted it to three different publishers in the USA, and within three days I had a positive response from Multnomah Publishers in Sister, Oregon. They published it as a current affairs book, 23,000 copies. I could hardly believe it. It was entitled *Let My People Go!*

Several years after my father's death, I came across his notes and accounts of various events in his life and ministry. The material looked to me like the sort of stuff that people should know about, how God can take a little nobody from the backwoods of Muskoka and use him as an effective evangelist, pastor, missionary, and denominational leader. I interviewed some of his peers and received added material. Then it too was published by Essence Publishers and later by Bay Ridge Books in the second edition. It is titled *A Man Worth Knowing*, for the very good reason he was just such a man.

When I was a young father, with two young children in Kenya, we had no such luxuries such as television or internet. In the evening, while putting my children to bed, I concocted a story that began to stretch into many, many evenings. It was about a North American aboriginal boy, a slave taken from Africa to be sold in America, and a young English preacher's kid, set in about 1812. I would just pick up the story where John and Elaine reminded me I had ended the evening before, and continue the fiction. They enjoyed it those many years ago.

Then, when I had grandchildren, my son asked me to retell the saga to his two children, Joshua and Victoria. One evening, my daughter-in-law Karen told me to stop. She went and got a little tape recorder and said, "Start over again." Karen then transcribed the recording into one long single paragraph and handed me the transcript. I wrote and rewrote.

I sent it to Multnomah, but they did not do children's books. One of the brothers in Multnomah had started another publishing company called Loyal Publishing. He contacted me, saying he wanted to come to meet me in Canada, and at the same time contact a Canadian lady he later contracted to edit the book. The decision to publish was made, and Margaret Sharpe became the editor. She did a fantastic job, and the book would never have been what it became without her. Some sections she rewrote almost entirely. It was titled *Slave, Brave and Free*.

I was then informed that Loyal Publishing wanted it to become a series of ten volumes, and they were setting aside $1,600,000 to make a film out of the first volume. I was flabbergasted. My first fiction to become a film! They had already begun the process of choosing screenwriters and actors. I didn't know what to think. I was advised to start writing volume two. I began. Then I got word that Loyal was not going to publish books any longer but become a writer's representative or book broker. That was that! Oh well, I was already too busy doing what God called me to do.

Through my years I had always kept in contact with my parents through mail and visits. Inevitably, we talked about some of my weird and wonderful experiences, both in Africa as a missionary and on my various trips to the many countries I had visited. Those letters became part of the biography I had written about my dad.

My mother nagged me for years to write a book about my own experiences. Well, here it is.

The Bible says, "Of the making of books there is no end." No kidding!

Wisdom Gained: Never start anything you are not committed to finish. Otherwise you will start running in ever-shrinking circles. You never want it said of you, "That person can never seem to keep a job."

53 BEING A PUBLIC FIGURE

TELEVISION SEEMS TO transform a person into someone who is not quite the real person. I cannot help but think of the former host of a children's TV program, who gave a final happy, jolly farewell to his young viewers. Not knowing that his microphone was still live, he added, "You little b——s," with a few other expletives. On air, he was a TV star and hero to the children who watched. Off air, he was a foul-tongued reprobate, who of course lost his job. And that's all it was with him, a job.

Having been in television, I've heard a lot of horror stories of certain "stars." With Christian television it is different in most cases. We don't swear at our audience after we go off air. What you see is much more reality than those just doing a secular job for money. And of course, there are many people in secular television who are as real and pleasant off air as they are on air.

But still there is a difference. The voice, smile, and appearance remain the same. What you believe and stand for is clearly recognized. But there are things unknown to a Christian audience about their Christians hosts. Most do not consider themselves stars. Though on television for much of 24 years, I never thought of myself as a star, and I never will. I am simply a person doing what God has opened doors for me to do. I just happened to get a lot more exposure than most pastors, evangelists, or teachers. I cannot say it is a particularly comfortable position to be in. The fact of the matter is, I personally get somewhat uncomfortable when someone fawns or gushes over me or refers to me as a TV star. I'm not. I don't know even after all these years how to react when someone gets gushy and fawns.

But television does do one thing for you. You are recognized everywhere you go. I've been recognized on the streets of almost every city in Canada, in airports throughout Europe and Africa, and sometimes even in my own home. The "recognition factor" does sometimes work in my favour, though it leaves me with less than normal public anonymity. One result is that I get preaching invitations from unexpected places.

I was invited to speak in Saskatchewan. The event was advertised widely. My subject was Sudan's living horrors and the slave trade. My presentation was followed by a book signing. That would be followed by a much more intense presentation of the horrors inflicted on the south of Sudan by its Islamist government up north in Khartoum.

As I was chatting with book buyers, signing books, and answering some general questions, I saw something out of the corner of my eye to the left that captured my attention. A woman in a burka was walking toward a large concrete pillar about thirty feet from me. She was carrying a large sports bag. She set it on the floor, unzipped it and, glancing at me, reached into the bag. Two of the four security people moved in on her. She grabbed the bag and fled.

The book I was signing had quotes from a Muslim leader in Montreal, addressed to President al-Bashir of Sudan, calling for my elimination. I was revealing many of the terrible violations of human rights in Sudan. I was "hurting Sudan's reputation."

Only God knows for certain what that was all about. I have since wished that someone had detained her, perhaps for probable cause, just to know what might have happened had we not had two uniformed policemen and two plain clothes security people on site. We went on with the second half of the program undeterred.

I was asked to speak at Lakeshore Pentecostal Camp in Cobourg, Ontario. An offering was to be taken, but not for my specific work. I spoke of Sudan a bit but gave a general appeal for support for Christian missions. A large offering was received.

.I had closed with an invitation for people to visit my book table at the back. Before I was finished that afternoon, over $6,000 had been handed to me for redeeming slaves in Sudan. I sold a few books, but the spontaneous offering was astounding to me.

I was often asked to speak at church anniversary services of various denominations. In one instance, it was a small United Church in southwestern Ontario. It should be noted that when people ask me to speak, they know that I am both evangelical and Pentecostal and not shy about either. At the same time, I don't go with the intent of upsetting any apple carts.

The pastor was a recent graduate of McMaster Theological College in Hamilton, Ontario. He had pastored the church as a student pastor for three years. It was the 150th anniversary of that congregation.

In its beginnings, it was a Methodist congregation. I introduced my sermon by saying I was going to preach a sermon after the same manner as a Methodist preacher would have preached it 150 years ago. I then gave a simple, solid, biblical sermon on salvation through faith in Jesus Christ. Then I gave an invitation for people to receive Jesus personally as Lord and Saviour and be "born again," using that same term Jesus Himself used in John 3:3.

About five people raised their hands to indicate that they wanted to be saved in the good old-fashioned Methodist tradition. I prayed with and for them. Afterward, they had a banquet downstairs as a celebration of the 150 years of the church's ministry in that town.

Before I had a chance to go downstairs, and after shaking hands at the door with those who could not stay for the banquet, the pastor pulled me aside. He sat me down in the back pew and asked me, "How did you do that?"

"Do what?" I asked.

"Five people decided to put their faith in Jesus as Saviour!" he said.

I interrupted, "Actually, six! Another older gentleman talked with me as he left, and I prayed with him. He too accepted Jesus as Lord."

He said, "I have been here three years, preaching and teaching, and not one person has accepted Jesus as Saviour in those three years. How did you do that?" he asked again.

Then people began to call us to come down to the banquet, but the pastor delayed and said we'd be down in a while. But they were insistent, saying they needed him to pray over the meal and that everyone was waiting. He again delayed and asked them to wait a bit longer and that we'd be down shortly. This seemed very important to the young pastor.

He then asked me what made the difference. I asked him, "Have you ever heard of the baptism in the Holy Spirit?" He said he had heard of it. I told him perhaps that is what makes the difference, referring to Acts 1:8, Acts 2:1, and other passages in Acts. I suggested he seek God for the infilling of the Holy Spirit.

He diverted for a moment and said, "One of those who accepted the Lord was the leading lady of our church. She is deeply involved in almost everything. I was shocked that she had never had a personal relationship with Jesus Christ." My comment in return was that many churches are filled with "Christians" who have never been born again. They may be committed to the church but not personally to Jesus Christ. Only the Holy Spirit can perform that work of grace and salvation in anyone's life.

We then went down and joined the festivities of 150 years as a church.

Several years later, that pastor wrote to me from Sherbrooke, Quebec, where he had been transferred, telling me he had received the fullness of the Holy Spirit, speaking with other tongues, and that his ministry had been revolutionized.

Walking in the Spirit makes the work of the ministry an act of God, not merely a function of formal ministry. Real power comes into the ministry.

I have spoken at summer camp meetings from Newfoundland to BC and with various denominations.

Nanoose Bay Camp is located on Vancouver Island, with a large bay just beside the camp. Mary and I picked so many wild blackberries just along the entrance lane that we almost made ourselves sick eating them.

We were there for seniors' camp. Most if not all the people knew me from television. My reputation as "the chicken man" had preceded me. We had good meetings and wonderful fellowship. Both Mary and I enjoyed it. Around the tables, we had great fun and conversations.

I was invited to fish on the Pacific Ocean on the western side of Vancouver Island. I love fishing but don't often get the chance. This was a real treat. There was a beautiful little fishing village tucked into the end of a small bay with quite a narrow passage out to the Pacific.

We headed out into the deep waters, and it was rough—seasick rough! Mary was with us, and she was terribly seasick. I came back with a good catch of Pacific salmon. Back at the camp, we set a few boards on some sawhorses, and I began to fillet the salmon. This seemed an amazing thing to some of the seniors. A preacher knew how to clean a fish!

We got a two-litre milk carton, waxed inside and out as they are, filled it with water, and stuffed most of my salmon into it and froze it. We carried it back to Ontario in our luggage. Just another bonus that I utterly enjoyed.

The last day of the camp, they made a presentation to me. Some of the camp leaders cooked up this hilarious little scheme. They presented me with a wrapped package. When I opened it, there was an extra-large box of Kellogg's Corn Flakes. At first this puzzled me, until I turned it around and saw the whole side of the box with its signature rooster printed on the side. "The Chicken Man" was being honoured for my many commentaries on television where I used chickens so often in my parable-like teachings from the Bible.

If Christian camp meetings can't be fun as well as serious Bible study and preaching, then we need to get a balance in our lives. No one in the world should be able to have more fun than Christians.

In a camp meeting outside Regina, Saskatchewan, I was invited back for a second time. Trossachs Gospel Camp was a family camp nestled on the edge of a beautiful lake and filled with wonderful people. Families with children of all ages were there. In the morning, I taught Bible for adults in a medium-sized auditorium, while there were special meetings for the youth. In the evenings I spoke in the tabernacle to the whole group.

A phenomenal thing happened in one of the morning sessions. A very old gentleman, in his early nineties, had been convinced to come to the camp. He was not a Christian. As I was teaching, suddenly there was a commotion in the centre of the crowd. The old man had fallen over in his seat. Norm, a retired doctor, rushed over to him, looking for vital signs. There were none. After a while, Norm pronounced him dead. It was a disturbing experience for some, but other people began to pray. After a while, the old man stirred a bit. The people around him set him upright. He looked up, more than dazed. That brought a rather abrupt end to that session.

They took him to his cottage where Norm, the doctor, explained to him what had happened. Then he explained the way of salvation, and the old man accepted Jesus as Lord and the resurrected Christ. Three years later, I was talking to Norm on the phone and he assured me the old man was still alive and serving God. God's mercy is astounding!

It was at that same camp that a young Muslim girl had been invited by friends to come and enjoy the week of camp with the youth group. It was interesting to watch her with her proper head cover having typical teenage fun with her Christian friends. In the youth meetings, she sat a bit aside, since she had been warned by her parents (one a short-term "exchange" university professor in Canada) not to listen to the religion of her Christian friends.

I noticed her first as I was entering the tabernacle to get ready to preach in the first evening service. I invited her to come in since she was sitting on a bench outside the tabernacle to wait for her friends to come out later. She replied by saying, "I can't." She sat patiently with her head covering in place. She was an attractive teen and had a friendly personality.

Every evening service she sat closer to the tabernacle, until one evening she sat inside, alone, at the back. On the second-to-last service, she was sitting about five rows from the front among her many friends. After the service was over, I had been praying with people at the altar and was about to leave. I saw that this lovely young lady was still sitting with her friends, her hair uncovered and looking radiant. Her face glowed with joy. I stopped by, and her friends told me she had accepted the Lord. I took her hand in mine and welcomed her to the family of God.

I was told that she and her parents and a sibling were going back home to the Middle East three weeks later. I have heard nothing since but commended her to the grace of God, knowing that God had a plan. I have prayed for her often. I can hardly wait for the knowledge when I get to heaven.

One last incident of many I could tell:

Rev. Mervin Switzer had invited me to preach in quite a large church in Regina, Saskatchewan. Thank God for my occasional ignorance in a situation. I knew very little about the church. I was just there to preach. Pastor Switzer was away, and the younger assistant pastor very capably led the service. There was a real sense of God's presence in the worship and all the preliminaries. When I was introduced, I announced my subject: obedience. I had no idea that this church's theological position was "eternal security" or as some describe it, "Once saved, always saved!" That may be a bit strong, but that's the way some look at it. It may be true occasionally that those who take that position use it as an occasion to do things that are quite unchristian, with the hope that everything will be okay in the end.

I'm not sure I said anything that trespassed on that theological position. I simply preached on the biblical imperative that we as Christians must obey the Lord we say we love. A genuine sense of the presence of God was palpable in that service. Not knowing the protocol in their services, I took it upon myself to give an invitation for Christians who were living in disobedience to God to stand to their feet, thus indicating they wanted to change their ways. Many did, including a man on one side of the church, and a woman on the other, both having been sitting with their spouses as it turned out.

I asked all those standing to come forward for prayer. There were many who came, including the man and woman from opposite sides of the church. They came to me at the altar and confessed that they had been committing adultery. In tears they repented and asked God and the congregation for their forgiveness. The Spirit of God overshadowed that meeting in a way that raised goosebumps on my arms. Our God forgives the truly repentant.

When the altar was cleared and the service dismissed, I noticed a very elderly man with a troubled look on his face still sitting by the aisle to the right of the pulpit, about halfway back in the church. He had sat unmoving through the whole service, standing only for a hymn or two. I walked back to him and engaged him in conversation. I asked him if he had ever been saved. He told me that this was the first time he had been in any meeting other than a Mormon service. He was 82 years of age. I asked him if he wanted to accept Jesus Christ as Lord and Saviour. He did! We prayed together, and he left the church a new man.

I met Pastor Switzer a year or so later at a function in Ottawa, and we became friends. Denominations mean less to God than they do to us.

Most of us still have a way to go to fit into the answer to the prayer of Jesus recorded in John 17:21, "that all of them may be one, Father, just as you are in me and I am in you. May they also be in us so that the world may believe that you have sent me."

Wisdom Gained: Never take yourself too seriously. That leads to pride, and then you're on your way to destruction. God is the centre of the universe, not you or me. Just walk straight in joy, and hop around a little if you like. Dancing before the Lord is not unbiblical!

54 EUROPEAN CHALLENGE

"TELEVISION IS OF the devil!" he told me with fire in his eyes.

This European Christian leader was adamant in his conviction. He told me that Christians should not have a television set in their houses under any circumstances. I was told this, strangely enough, at a conference I had organized in Switzerland to acquaint Christian leaders from across Europe with the potential for preaching the gospel over television.

I was vice president of Crossroads Christian Communications (CCCI) at the time. I also oversaw CCCI missions. I had gone to the president, David Mainse, and presented the idea for the conference. After listening to my proposal, David gave an enthusiastic "Go for it!" What I did not know at the time was that David Mainse had already been to Sweden at the invitation of church leaders and had challenged them with the potential for TV. Some of the groundwork had already been laid.

I told David of the European pastor's adamant stand and that we'd probably have an uphill battle to introduce the idea in some quarters. David felt much the same as I did. "It can and should be done."

My response to that fiery European Christian leader was that television was just controlled by the wrong people. "It's time we Christians take some initiatives and begin to get control of some of the airwaves." I was convinced Christian television could have a very positive and country-changing effect in any area of the world. Light always overrules darkness.

I wrote letters to everyone I had ever met from European Christian leadership while a missionary in Africa. We found the names of many leaders who had been guests on *100 Huntley Street* in its early years. We sent out invitations, reserved a place called Schloss Naumburg near Frankfurt in Germany, and prayed. Letters passed back and forth across the Atlantic, before the advent of email. Then we went to Europe.

People from 14 countries turned up at Schloss Naumburg. I had asked several *100 Huntley Street* staff who worked as directors, cameramen, producers, and technicians to come with me. My German secretary was married to one of them, so she came along to act as my mobile office and interpreter when necessary.

I'd like to say that a good time was had by all, but a few "Satan-sighters" had also come. They had nothing good to say about TV, even Christian TV. There were some very tense moments in that conference. Strangely, when the dust settled a few years later, the folk from some of those countries led the pack in introducing Christian TV production. Meanwhile, there was heated debate, and a few denominational antagonisms.

The idea of a school of broadcasting was born in the heat of that debate. Lorne Shepherd, the director of *100 Huntley Street*, was there and invited people to come to Canada and see how we did it. Zack Davidson, a producer at Crossroads, and others were also there. When we got back to Canada, I assigned the task of writing a full curriculum for establishing Crossroads School of Broadcast to Zack. He put together a six-month course.

One of the more immediate responses came from a small Danish contingent. They wanted to get started right away, asking us if they could come and see how *100 Huntley Street* operated. Three men came for three weeks to Canada. They looked over the shoulders of almost anyone who did any kind of job in the production and airing of *100 Huntley Street*. When they got back to Denmark, they jumped in with all their six feet and began developing the first Danish Christian television.

Europe had no private television stations in the early seventies. The governments of European countries had perhaps two national stations, and occasionally, a large city had a third. All of these were government controlled.

God's timing is so perfect! A groundswell was beginning throughout Europe for freedom of the airwaves. Agitation was in the air, and as it turned out, Christians were among the first ready to jump in when TV control was loosened.

Since we had been right there at the right time, interest began to swell. We formalized the School of Broadcasting and eventually began teaching students from all over the world. Our graduates came from more than 70 countries. Not all went into TV; some went into radio broadcasting. Many have had outstanding success.

Crossroads had already been producing programs in languages other than English when I arrived at 100 Huntley Street. We eventually produced 22 non-English programs in the Crossroads studios. I could list them all, but just for an example, consider the Italian program *Vivere al cento por cento* produced at Crossroads.

Onofrio (Ony) Micolis was producer and host of the Italian TV program. He had tried radio in Italy for some years but had little response. When he moved to Canada, he met David Mainse, who invited him to start an Italian television program. It was met with immediate success. People telephoned to the counselling centre and were led into wonderful personal relationships with Jesus Christ. When Ony thought of Italy with its vast millions, he wanted to release the program there. But it was not an easy start. There were three hurdles that had to be conquered.

Who in Italy would endorse the program since there seemed to be strong opposition from the Italian Pentecostal church leadership? Ony was Pentecostal. Second, where would he find people to undertake the massive task of setting up counselling centres for those who would call in? Third, and most difficult, what station in Italy would carry a strongly Evangelical program?

So Ony and I went to Rome to negotiate with the Dr. Francesco Topi, General Superintendent of the Pentecostal Assemblies of Italy. Dr. Topi had some very hard rules he laid down. The programs would have to have his personal approval, and most restricting, the programs would not begin in Italy without his personal go-ahead. Six months later, it was literally taken out of everyone's hands.

The Italian program was being produced by the expert production team at 100 Huntley Street. The quality and professionalism of the program were exceptional for any non-English or French language program in Canada.

And then the pirates took over.

Ony and I again went to Italy for a meeting with Dr. Topi. From the very beginning of that meeting, we knew there were problems. Just how big they were we never could have imagined. Dr. Topi looked at us with a stern face and said, "You have broken your word. You have begun airing your program without our knowledge or permission. That is not what we had agreed to!"

Both Ony and I were baffled. We asked, "What do you mean? We have not yet sent the program to Italy."

He retorted, "Well, it's on a station right here in Rome!"

Ony and I were flabbergasted. We knew nothing about this. Stunned, we listened to a litany of accusations that made us sound like liars, manipulators, and frauds. Finally, we asked Dr. Topi which station it was on and he told us. The station was still under construction but had begun to air programs from various Italian sources around the world. We were confused and pled our innocence and bafflement at the accusations.

Ony and I arranged to visit that station in Rome. When we walked into the partially finished building, we were led to the manager's office. We asked where he got *Vivere al cento por cento*. He simply said, "From a station in Toronto." He named the station. Again, we were stunned. It was the very station, Channel 47, owned by an Italian who had received a license from the CRTC in Canada to air programming in a multiplicity of languages. The footprint covered Toronto and miles around. It was the very station where we at Christian Multilingual Programming bought time for the Portuguese, Greek, German, French, and Italian programs.

Without our knowledge, Channel 47 had sent the programs to the station in Rome. They had been airing the program weekly for months before we found out about it. As Ony and I sat with the manager of the station in Rome, we exchanged glances, and we suddenly knew what to do. One of us would play the "bad guy" and the other would play the "good guy." We traded roles a few times during our "confrontation."

I started the ball rolling by asking a little brusquely, "Do you know you're breaking international copyright law?" He looked at me, troubled. I continued, "We can sue you! Have you never heard of the International Copyright Agreement signed and settled in Finland in 1937?" I continued. He looked even more troubled. Quite frankly, I knew about the Agreement myself only vaguely.

Then Ony started in. "It's a professionally produced program and costs a lot of money to produce. You've taken it and used it without our permission. Even though we want it to be released in Italy, we have to have control of our own product." The manager didn't know, but we would have been willing to pay for airtime in Rome, just as we did in Toronto, but there was no way we were telling him that. Yet!

By this time, the manager of the station was rather upset. We deliberately kept him that way for quite a while. We had him over a barrel, and there was little he could do about it. He was wrong and he knew it. Then it got interesting. He squirmed. We went on the attack, in love of course!

It took time, but we finally told him we would forgive him provided (a) that he allow us to put up a telephone number for people to call who were anxious to talk about their eternal salvation, (b) that he would continue to pay for the shipment of the programs from Canada to Italy, (c) that he would bear all the costs involved, including the cost of conversion from North America's NTSC format to the PAL format used in Europe, and (d) that he would air it at the same time every week at no cost to us. He agreed and began to breathe easy. He did admit the quality of the production was better than he could produce.

He then showed us through the studios under construction. There were massive revolving floors with various sets that would be turned for gala productions with large live audiences. We suddenly realized we had won more than the lottery. It was to become the largest, most modern TV station in Rome.

When Ony and I went returned to our lodgings in Villagio Betania, a Christian orphanage just outside Rome, we talked about it over and over, then tried to sleep. One or the other of us would break out in laughter. I'm not sure whether we had more delightful laughter or sleep that night.

Ony visited many unregulated TV stations throughout Italy and got free airtime on most of them, citing that "the big one in Rome" was giving us free airtime. At one point, 93 stations were carrying the Italian program, and many thousands of people were being saved because of it. With the full involvement and approval of Dr. Topi, counselling and prayer centres were opened all over Italy. The reach of that program in Italy had far more potential audience than that of the mother program in Canada, *100 Huntley Street*. Italy has a potential audience of more than one hundred million people. Crossroads in Canada had given birth to a *big* baby!

The Italian program, along with all the other non-English programs, grew to become independent of Crossroads Christian Communications. Ony was also involved in a very large and aggressive missionary outreach in India. A book could be written about that. At his death, Ony left a legacy for the kingdom of God.

Speaking of India:

Several young men from India graduated from what became known as the Geoffrey R. Conway School of Broadcasting at Crossroads. Two of them are broadcasting Christian programs in several languages, reaching most of India, and several countries surrounding India, with a potential audience of well over a billion people.

One young man began Christian television in Germany, which became so highly professional that it became a commercially supported success, as well as a spiritual success. In one country in South America, one of our graduates was able to replace three hours of pornography with Christian programming. Take *that*, devil!

I have always considered the School of Broadcasting to be the most effective evangelistic tool that ever came out of Crossroads Christian Communications, 100 Huntley Street. The success stories of the graduates are totally remarkable.

Wisdom Gained: Radio supplanted reading. Then television overshadowed radio. Now we have the internet. Too much of any of these can give you spiritual indigestion. Go back to reading, especially the book above all books—the Bible. That gives spiritual stability and growth.

55 THE HILL
OF THE LORD

ALTHOUGH AN INTERNATIONAL speaker, I don't consider myself as being any big deal. Occasionally, I receive an invitation, and if it fits into my schedule, I'll accept. Years before, I had promised the Lord that I would never say no to any opportunity to preach His Word.

There are times when these invitations are quite unique and become quite a memorable experience. One such was in Holland.

John and Auguste Koeslag were both telephone prayer partners at 100 Huntley Street. They approached me about my willingness to preach at a specific place in the eastern part of Holland. Their relative, Mr. Jan van Heek, owned several castles of great historical significance, which he had restored as tourist attractions. His family had made their money in the beginning of the industrial revolution and through the years textiles were their source of great wealth. Jan's father had bought several castles in the Netherlands, including Kasteel Huis Bergh in 's-Heerenberg in 1912.

The first castle on this site was built about the year 1100. It changed hands and construction materials over the years. The van Heeks had restored the castle to its medieval state.

I wondered at first how John would get this distant relative to agree to a Pentecostal preacher preaching in a castle that now belonged to a Roman

Catholic family. The castle had been under the control of the Roman Catholic church, and no one other than Catholic priests had preached in its small chapel since the castle had been relinquished in battle by the Protestant William of Orange hundreds of years before. Protestants were simply not allowed to preach in the pulpit of a Roman Catholic sanctuary. It just is not done! (More recently, these rules have been relaxed in some places.) No Protestant had preached from behind that pulpit for centuries.

Since I am rather given to doing things that just are not done, I agreed to go while I was in Europe on one of my regular trips during the late 1980s or early '90s. I doubted it would happen. I also underestimated the tenacity of John and Augusta.

John made all the arrangements. It was the most beautiful castle I had ever seen in such intimate detail. John introduced me to Jan van Heek. I was shown around the castle, the keep, the chapel, and the grounds. I was to spend the night in the castle before I preached. I slept in what had to be the main bedroom. It was huge.

It was also rather daunting. An ancient four-poster bed complete with ancient curtains stood almost in the middle of a stone-walled room about 14 metres long and 12 metres wide. The mattress was of a more modern vintage. Knights' armour stood, as if on guard, against the walls in at least six places, complete with swords and battleaxes. Fantastic antiques filled the room. This was a room where tourists stood in awe at genuine antiques from hundreds of years in the past. And I was to sleep in that antique setting surrounded by the reminders of knights, fights, and probably frights.

I put my small suitcase down on the floor by the bed. I felt like a mouse on the huge stone floor, surrounded by walls of rock. It was cold. It felt more like a dungeon than a bedroom. One modern concession was a single bare light bulb of perhaps 25 watts hanging from the ceiling. I went to bed and turned out the light. The room was reduced to shadows and moonlight reflections from my guardian knights. It felt as if I had stepped out of a time machine into the past. I'll admit to a deep sense of awe at the history in Europe.

My mind went almost wild with imagination. I had been told of various battles and how everyone would retreat to the keep if it there was a threat or breach in the walls. I imagined the calls and screams, the clatter of swords on chain mail and shields. In a way, it gave me the creeps. But what a privilege to sleep where ancients had slept, crept, and probably wept. I imagined the knights in shining armour, the frights experienced by those being attacked, and the fearful fights to defend their rights. I was experiencing a little of my own fright regarding what was to happen the next night. I prayed that God would make the meeting in the chapel the next day more than merely symbolic.

John and Auguste had arranged for a small group from Youth with a Mission to attend the service. A few others came from 's-Heerenberg, the local town of 17,500 people. John and Augusta sat with Jan. I preached the simple gospel sermon straight from the Bible, a little bit in awe that I was the first Protestant to preach in that chapel for many years. I gave an invitation for those who wanted to follow Christ as Lord and Saviour to raise their hands. A few responded, and I saw Jan's hand among them. Tears were running from his eyes.

Knowing John and Augusta, they probably "explained to him the way of God more adequately" (Acts 18:26).

It's difficult to remember the details of all that followed, but I did leave "my" castle in 's-Heerenberg with the knowledge that a better home awaits both Jan and me, and all others who trust in Jesus as Saviour.

Wisdom Gained: Study history. The past is what developed the present. The people back in history gave us what we have and made us what we are. History reveals both good and bad, right, and wrong. Choose the good and right.

56 CHRISTIAN TV WORLDWIDE

YOU RECALL THE conference I called in Germany? At the last session of the conference, we made the offer, "If you want to learn how to do Christian television, come to Canada, and we will teach you." Zack, Lorne, and the others who had come with me from 100 Huntley Street began to wonder how this was to come about. So Lorne and I decided.

I asked Zack Davidson to write a course to cover the whole spectrum of Christian television. He had graduated from Oral Roberts University and had been the producer at Crossroads of the "Creation Series" programs.

We started getting inquiries about training in television production from across Europe.

Our first students were from Scandinavia, then Israel, Switzerland, England, and Germany, and it kept growing from year to year. The six-month course was a long time for people to be away from their duties and families in Europe. We subsidized the course itself, but each student was required to pay their own airfare to Canada.

The course was eventually shortened to a very intense 15 weeks. The teachers on the staff had had years of TV experience, including Zack Davidson and Dennis Curley. We also used other staff at Crossroads to teach specialized areas of expertise, such as audio, lighting, make-up, etc. Karen Wiseman was my secretary and the registrar of the School of Broadcasting. She later became my daughter-in-law.

Ray Rodriguez later came to teach as well. He was a graduate student who came as a non-Christian but surrendered his life to the Lord during the duration of the course. After some experience in Christian television in various places, including the Canary Islands, Ray joined our staff, and was a brilliant addition to the full-time staff. Between Dennis, Zack, and Ray, I had the genuine dream team of teachers.

The course was subsidized for some years by the Geoffrey R. Conway Foundation, and was named The Geoffrey R. Conway School of Broadcasting and Communications in honour of a Christian statesman in TV in Canada. It became a division of the Missions Department of 100 Huntley Street, of which I was vice president until 2003.

By the time I retired from Crossroads, more than 1,750 students from 74 countries had taken either the full course or a specialized course. More than 1,200 had taken the full course. These courses had been held both in the facilities of *100 Huntley Street* in downtown Toronto and in the newer facilities in Burlington. Full courses have also been taught outside Canada in Austria, Sweden, Denmark, inland China, Costa Rica, India, and Russia. Books could be written about the impact many of the graduates are having in their own countries after graduation.

I was beginning to feel like I was suffering from permanent jet lag because of the many trips I took to Europe. I had a friend with CP Air at the time, Barry Greaves. He was able to bump me to first class occasionally, which left me feeling less like a wrung-out rag when I got home from these trips. Also, Eddie Levens of Schiphol Airport often recognized me and asked me for my ticket, bumping me up to first class once with Fr. Bob MacDougal.

Some of those trips stand out in my memory. I was invited by Rev. Gerhard Wessler to speak at the General Conference of the German Assemblies of God. He had warned me that many German pastors looked at TV as devilish and wanted no part of it. That set me slightly on edge. I was to have 45 minutes to present the challenge of Christian TV. I was nervous.

The conference was held in a small city that was just a little blip on the map of West Germany, intruding into East Germany. Every now and then we'd hear gunshots. I asked my friend and escort, Rev. Paul Waresch, what was happening. Paul calmly said that they shot at anyone who tried to escape from East Germany into West Germany.

At the conference, I made my case for TV being a wonderful tool for Christian evangelism. At first, I was met with a stony silence. I told of the thousands of telephone calls coming into the studios and how churches had begun for people who had come to faith in Jesus Christ through our programming. I was in a good position to relate these facts, since at the time I was also vice president over the Counselling and Follow-Up department of *100 Huntley Street*.

The stony silence prevailed.

I was nearing the end of my 45 minutes. Asking God for wisdom, I cast about in my mind for some parallel to illustrate that TV can be good if Christians reclaim it and use it for God's glory. Suddenly I had it.

I asked, "How many of you have a bread knife in your kitchen at home?" Perhaps a strange question to ask a conference of pastors. Many hands went up. Then I said, "That bread knife can be used for murder in the wrong hands. In the right hands, it does the job it was designed to do: cut bread and meat or chop vegetables. Television is the same. We have left it in the wrong hands, and it is murdering our populations. It's time we took it back into our hands and used it for the spread of the gospel and the truth of God's kingdom."

An awakening happened in that crowd of pastors. Light applause rippled through the 500 or so people there. I talked a while longer, a little past my 45 minutes, and turned the meeting back to the chairman of the conference. He asked, "Are there any questions?"

Immediately, they came pouring in, and I answered as best I could. Almost another hour passed with questions and answers. Finally, I excused myself and turned to sit down, very tired. Without warning, a loud clapping of hands erupted throughout the whole place. I turned, and they were all on their feet giving me a standing ovation. I was stunned. What a turnaround!

There are several very successful Christian TV ministries operating now in Germany, some run by our graduates, others run by those who just took on the challenge. How many, if any, were in that conference that day? I don't know. But I think it may have broken the ice.

Books could be written of the impact these various graduates have had after taking the course.

In the early '90s, the full course was taught in Klosterneuburg, just outside Vienna in Austria. I sent a team of teachers who worked closely with a newly formed organization called CMP, after our own Christian Multilingual Programming division in Canada. Although the equipment was not the best, the students were eager. Some of the students came from Eastern Europe.

One fellow came from State TV in Romania. Kristi Tepis had already had experience in TV, but, as a Christian, wanted to gain some knowledge of Christian TV and what the possibilities were to begin some form of evangelism through State TV in Romania. On his return from Austria to Romania, he presented his certificate to his superiors and asked if he could produce a Christian TV program. The answer was yes. He took it a step further. "Will you allow me to control the content of the program fully?" He was not sure how they would react to his request, but to his delight, they said yes again. He decided to push the envelope a bit further and asked, "May I put up a mailing address so that people can write in to respond to the program?" They affirmed that he could, and he did.

Did he ever!

After about 20 months of programs going to air, I received a letter from Dr. Paul Negrut. Dr. Negrut was president of the Evangelical Alliance of Romania. The president of Romania had asked him to be chancellor of the leading university in that country. He had declined the offer in order to continue in Christian ministry. As president of the Alliance, he represented more than 400,000 Christians, most of whom were Baptists and Pentecostals.

Dr. Negrut told me the impact of the Christian programming was being felt by the whole nation, and it began an awakening of the existing Christian church to be more overt in its life and evangelistic ministry to Romania. Almost unbelievable! A country that had been deprived of Christianity and denied God for over seventy years was awakening to the need for a personal relationship with God through Jesus Christ.

The Evangelical Alliance of Romania mobilized thousands of Christian volunteers to personally visit the address of every single one of the 1.6 million people who had contacted the program. They shared, taught, and invited people to commit their lives to Christ personally. In many cases, whole families turned to God.

I went to Moscow just before Christmas one year in the mid-'90s. I was to teach at the first short course in Christian television to be held there. It was quite an experience. The walls had come down slightly but not yet as much as they would. The KGB was still very much present.

My accommodations were in the most unique setting I have every experienced, other than sleeping on the ground in Sudan. My room was cold, small, and exceptionally uncomfortable. It was also cheap. The bed was a narrow shelf with a very thin foam mattress, kept in place by a raised edge on the side opposite the wall. There was nothing of any interest within walking distance, except a new little marketplace, like a North American flea market. The beginnings of capitalism? Some kiosks sold the famous Russian carved wooden nesting dolls. I bought several beautifully painted sets.

I visited Red Square with a cameraman. I had always thought that Red Square was the centre of Moscow. The longer I was there, the more it seemed that Moscow has no major commercial centre. It has scores of centres, none of which seemed to be either the commercial or historical centre of the city. Red Square was the political centre.

In Red Square, I wanted to interview people about their first opportunity to celebrate Christmas in over seventy years. I saw a highly decorated man in army uniform crossing Red Square in my direction. He was a general. I asked him if I could interview him. He spoke quite acceptable English, so I asked him, "What do you plan to do to celebrate Christmas this year?"

Judging by the dozen or more medals in rows across his chest; he must have done something right (or wrong, according to your political persuasion). He responded, "I am a Christian. I will go to church and think about Jesus Christ. I will thank God that Mother Russia is going to prosper."

I asked others. Some had no idea what Christmas was. Others secretly had heard a little about Christmas from their repressed and cautious parents. I came away thinking Communism had certainly done no favours for the millions of Russia. But changes were on the way.

Hannu Haukka, a Canadian missionary to Russia, had informed me that the "Creation Series" had been aired on the state television station in Leningrad. When I told David Mainse, who had hosted that series, I was met with disbelief. "That can't be!" I affirmed it was true. David said, "When I see a signed affidavit that it was seen on Leningrad television, I'll believe it." He believed in miracles, but how this could possibly have come about was unbelievable.

Within weeks I was able to show David signed documents. It was the first presentation of the biblical creation account to be seen in Russia, even before the failure of Communism. Since then, Christian television has been seen throughout Russia, much of it produced out of Finland and Moscow by Hannu Haukka and his teams.

Hannu's wife, who is Russian, also translated my first book into Russian in 1992. Twenty thousand copies were printed.

Some years later, Christian programs had become regular on several state television stations in various parts of Russia and Ukraine. I visited the compound where many volunteer Christians were responding to incoming letters. It was just metres away from the prison where political prisoners were incarcerated.

While I was there, looking at the operation to open, sort, and answer the thousands of letters being received, I was struck by several things. Every letter was in an envelope of the exact same size, colour, and proportions. The contents were almost all the same too, people seeking knowledge of life in Christ. A year or so previously, I had made the decision that the Missions Department of the Crossroads ministry would support these Christians who spent their days in these close quarters, answering cries from hearts.

It just happened that the daily mail was delivered while I was in Moscow. A government postal truck pulled up at the back door of the office. With a great deal of noise, racks with at least eighteen to twenty shelves were rolled in the back door. Every level held a tray about two feet square, packed with envelopes. They rolled in no less than twelve of these multilayered racks, full from top to bottom. I stood out of the way and watched.

I asked Hannu what this was all about. He grinned and said, "The post office brings *all* their mail here for us. Since most of the mail that comes into this post office is for us, they've asked us to sort it and return to them what is not for us. We don't have very much to return to them."

There had to be tens of thousands of letters in front of me. Hannu told me they had stopped keeping track of how many letters had come in after they surpassed two million. He said, "The same type of thing is happening down in Kiev."

Communism had left a spiritual vacuum that had to be filled.

Before we left Moscow, I had been invited to preach at a Baptist church in a place in Moscow I would never ever be able to find again. The place was packed. The platform was in a corner of the large room. The singing was magnificent. Before I was asked to speak, an invitation was given for anyone who wanted to "bend the knee." I pondered the term for a few moments, and finally asked the young lady who was giving me a running translation of the proceedings. "What does the pastor mean by 'bend the knee'?" I asked.

She looked at me with a slightly puzzled look, as though I should understand. After a pause, she said, "It means bending his knee before Christ to take Him as his Saviour." She was pointing at the uniformed man on his knees. "He was with the KBG." I was beginning to think almost everyone was KGB at one time or another. This all happened before I had even preached. When I did speak, I greeted them in the little Russian Christian greeting I had learned just before the service. Then I taught for a while from the Word of God. It seemed they were doing what the early church did: evangelism outside the church; fellowship, worship, and teaching inside the church. Works for me!

Meals consisted of cucumbers, potatoes, and borsch. Breakfast, lunch, and dinner were all the same. I cannot eat cucumbers. I had a little bit of ham once in the three days I was there, and this was a tourist hotel. When I asked for milk, they said they'd ask. They did not return. We never saw more than one other table occupied in the whole dark dining room. We saw very few people at all in the hotel, other than the sentries, for lack of a better word, at the end of each corridor.

From Moscow, we had to go by train to Kiev. It was exceptionally cheap, even though it was a very long trip: less than three dollars each, Moscow to Kiev. No wonder their economy was not working.

The train slowed down many times on the way to Kiev. At one point, we saw large, open-topped railway cars on a siding. We had almost stopped as we passed by them. The stink was horrible. We were able to see into them, and Hannu said: "They're full of rotting potatoes and cabbages. Their freight system is so inefficient, this sort of thing happens often." I thought back to a few hours previously, to people scattering from buses, looking for just one or two potatoes in harvested fields outside Moscow. It made me want to scream at the futility of it all, and it made me grateful to God for the abundance we have in Canada.

When we arrived in Kiev, there seemed to be a little more life on the streets, though there was also tension. I learned that Chernobyl was not far enough away for the comfort of the people of Kiev and that when the wind shifted to blow from Chernobyl, people felt a great deal of anxiety. Some walked with handkerchiefs held over their mouths and noses. The wind was from the "bad" direction that day. People were reluctant to leave their homes on those bad days. I found out later that one of our graduates from our School of Broadcasting, Paul, had died of cancer caused by the Chernobyl catastrophe.

The centre where incoming mail was dealt with was much the same as the one in Moscow, though not quite as overwhelming. I spoke to a large crowd of pastors and church leaders in what was formerly a communist headquarters.

Wisdom Gained: Spending time with Christians of another culture, whether internationally or from a local ethnic church, will bolster your understanding and appreciation of the power of the cross in a world of chaos and degeneracy.

57 PHNOM PENH, CAMBODIA

WE WERE ALREADY tired when we arrived in Phnom Penh, Cambodia. It's a long trip to the other side of the world. There were four of us: Reynold and Kathy Mainse, Reg Parks, and me. We were met by Setan Lee, Tara, and three others. They had survived the killing fields of Pol Pot.

We were there to set up a housing project for families with nothing and to introduce the "Seeds" program created by Rev. Keith Parks for use in schools.

After a quick shower and change of clothes and a lunch in the Goldiana Hotel, we headed for the "Torture School." It had been converted from a school to a torture centre under Pol Pot's vicious rule (April 1975 to 1979) and was now a museum of torture and death. I have rarely been as horrified.

In the entrance was a map of Cambodia made up of human skulls. School classrooms had been converted into torture chambers where the victims died. There were pictures of actual victims and the torture equipment on display. My stomach lurched.

Dried blood was still on the floors. There were electric chairs with harnesses that held victims as slowly the voltage was turned up. Mothers with babies in arms died anguishing deaths. What horrors! What inhumanity!

Then we were taken to the killing fields. There was a tall tower built of glass where 8,985 skulls were encased, bullet holes clearly seen in many skulls. Eighty-six pits had been dug up, leaving forty-nine pits left to excavate. About twenty thousand people had been slaughtered where we stood. Why?

We were told, "It was because Pol Pot failed his engineering exams in Paris." In a communist-backed revolution, Pol Pot took over the country. He set out to kill first all schoolteachers, then all intellectuals. Then it seemed, anyone within reach was attacked, including hundreds of fellow members of the Khmer Rouge. The total killed was about three million, almost half of Cambodia's population.

I cannot remember how I was able to do it, but I taped a segment for television, entitled "From Killing Fields to Harvest Fields." We were there to show the compassion of Jesus Christ by replacing housing in a slum that had gone up in fire like tinder. Another, more modern tragedy.

We were given accounts of the Khmer Rouge's despicable acts against innocent people. Muny, one of our guides, told us a story that was not untypical. He told of a man who had heard the gospel in 1973 but did not respond. From age 13 he became Khmer Rouge. He shot his own parents to prove his loyalty to Khmer and "Anka," as Pol Pot was known. He was elevated to command ten others and passed on orders to kill others. He later told of unspeakable atrocities he had been involved in. He was ordered to go as a spy to the Kampuchea for Christ Bible school. He heard the truth there, became a Christian, and survived. He became involved in the church, which eventually was burned out in the slums where we were going to rebuild houses.

We visited almost every official office in Phnom Penh for both information and license to do what needed to be done. We went to a former Catholic monastery that was now the city hall and met with the deputy governor of the municipality of Phnom Penh, Mr. Seng Tong. He was very cooperative and gave us permissions we needed, plus an interview for TV. His wife was a Christian.

Reynold Mainse was intent on going to the dump to interview kids who were picking through the garbage for anything of even the slightest value. We crossed the Mekong River to eat at a restaurant that had a form of entertainment I didn't understand at all. When entertainment was done, no one clapped or smiled. We asked our host, Setan, why. He said, "Since Pol Pot, no one smiles or claps hands."

At that time, about 200,000 Christians lived in Cambodia. We recorded a lot of TV footage and commentary on the situation all over the city, which amazingly remains very beautiful.

To illustrate some of the great needs in Phnom Penh, Setan Lee took us down what he called "prostitute street." He explained part of his ministry to these abused women and young girls whom they rescued. Most were young girls who had lost their virginity in order to entice men to buy beer at the bars where they hung out, for their pimps. Laws had finally been passed making prostitution illegal, yet about 50 percent of the police force had AIDS because of illicit sex offered to disregard the charges against a girl.

I interviewed Dr. Chhin Senya at the AIDS wing of the Phnom Penh General Hospital. Dr. Senya's story was most unusual. He had been thrown into a prison with about two hundred others. No one had ever come out alive. He was not a Christian then, but he cried out to God, "If you have something for me to do, let me out. If not, leave me here to die."

At seven o'clock that evening, two Khmer Rouge guards came with rifles and ordered him to go with them. He thought he was to be shot. He was taken to an office where he was told Pol Pot had made a mistake and that he was free to go. Later, he met some Christians and became an enthusiastic follower of Jesus. He volunteered to work in the AIDS ward of the hospital when the death toll from AIDS was still very high. In that hospital alone, about 25 people died every month from the disease.

Our last meal together in Phnom Penh with those who were to be involved in the housing project was in a private dining room. As I remember it, there were nine of us, with me placed at the head of the table. While we were eating, a young and very beautiful Cambodian waitress stood behind me and began to caress my shoulders and the back of my head lightly. I was startled. When the waitresses all left, I told the group what had happened. The five Cambodians began to laugh. When she came back, she continued caressing my back and shoulders with little light pinches. I was getting red in the face and quite flustered.

Finally, Setan told me that I was the oldest man there and had grey hair. It was a sign of very high respect, and that any Cambodian woman would do it, including his own wife after 20 years in America. Then I felt a light touch on top of my thigh. I was startled and further flustered. I glanced to my left, and Reynold Mainse was leaning down toward my leg. Young rascal! That dinner, in a private room, and for that many people cost only $56, along with some embarrassment. It was a dinner I would not quickly forget.

The last day I was able to squeeze in another interview with our Canadian ambassador to Cambodia. I left being grateful I didn't have his job. We never did air that interview.

When flying home to Canada, I thanked God for the privilege of being a Canadian.

I must admit, writing this out from my diary has been a tough emotional experience. Some things need to be forgotten. But then again, we should be aware that we live in a fallen world, and evil is a reality.

Wisdom Gained: Travel as widely as you may. See the world not just for pleasure but with the eyes of God. Never walk away from a great need. You can always afford to be loving and kind. It may also revolutionize prayer habits.

58 HEARTBREAKING HORRORS

MOST PEOPLE FACE moments, and even long periods, of heartbreak. Living the kind of life I live, and doing the kinds of things I do around the world, I was thrust into situations where the sheer magnitude of heartbreak becomes a potential emotional collapse.

Some of the following incidents could each take a chapter. I neither want to relive them nor impose the full horrors on you. But there is a real world out there that suffers to a depth no one can understand unless they see it with their own eyes. Television footage conveys a modicum of feeling, but seeing the reality nails it all to the psyche. There comes a time when you have the choice of two things: grow callous and unfeeling in the midst of horror, or learn to compartmentalize the realities so that they are stored in a closed area of the mind, available only by deliberate choice. When they are accessed, all the horror returns.

I find it impossible with mere words to convey the horror of mind and soul when faced with certain natural catastrophes, human depravity, evil at its worst, and the long-term results in the lives of those who are the victims. I just don't want to go there too much.

In 1980, a devastating earthquake hit Lioni, Italy. Onofrio Miccolis, who hosted the Italian Christian TV program, happened to be in Italy when the earthquake hit. He was standing in a church pulpit in Milan, and the church "wiggled like rubber," as he described it. A chunk of ceiling plaster fell from the ceiling onto the pulpit from which he was preaching. He rushed to Lioni, the epicenter of the quake. He was able to record the first video footage of the disaster, which was first shown to North America over the *100 Huntley Street* program.

The response from Canadians was immediate. Crossroads, together with some Swedish churches, were able to build 22 houses to replace homes destroyed by the earthquake. Those houses, built of fieldstone, had stood for centuries. The walls had been built by carefully placing the stones, using little if any mortar. When the quake broke loose right under them, the walls simply collapsed and slid down the mountain, taking many lives with them.

Later, when I arrived in Lioni on behalf of *100 Huntley Street*, I felt like I was in London or Berlin during the Second World War. Camera images couldn't really capture the breadth of the devastation. One multistorey building had crumbled and collapsed flat down, storey after storey on top of most of the youth of Lioni who were having a dance. Hundreds were crushed to death.

I walked down what used to be the main street. I watched an elderly man walk back and forth, up and down the street in a daze these months later. It was hard to imagine his state of mind. Was he still looking for survivors? Did he think he was still in that nightmare? Whom had he lost? He seemed condemned forever to gaze, wonder, and search to find what could never be recovered. Would he ever recover? Would I, even though I had really experienced only the aftermath?

It was the same in El Salvador. An earthquake had unleashed a landslide. Trees, rocks, houses, and other debris had thundered loose from the mountain above the town and swept away a wide swath of the city. Many houses were buried. Others were literally sliced in half at the edge of the slide. As I walked down the slide, looking at the remaining ruins, I was keenly aware of the people who had been buried alive under my feet.

As I approached the bottom of the rockslide, I gazed with amazement and horror at houses that were still half there. The interior of the rooms remained very much as they had been before. On the second floor of one house on my left was the end of a baby's crib with a disconcertingly lifelike doll hanging from its corner. One leg of the crib was suspended in air. The rest of crib was standing in its place in the still fully furnished room. On my right at almost ground level a rocking chair stood perched on the edge of a floor that had been torn away from the house. Again, what was left of the rest of the room was fully furnished. A whole block of houses was much the same.

I felt like a peeping Tom, looking into the private horror which had shattered these otherwise normal middle-class lives. I thought of their lives now, and their families that had been ripped apart viciously by that slide. There are many things emergency relief and development cannot replace!

Hurricane Mitch left devastation and ruin behind it in Central America. In Tegucigalpa, Honduras, I was awed at what floodwaters had done, sweeping a solid reinforced concrete bridge away like tissue paper. It left the rest of the structure dangling over a chasm with sewer pipes spewing sewage into the small river far below.

Further downriver, two whole towns had been swept into oblivion as the rush of billions of gallons of water and debris swept around a double curve in the original riverbed. The massive flash flood waters rose to snatch a whole town and its people into its grip. When it hit the second curve, it rebounded across the river in an S bend to reach up and snatch another town and smash it and its people to nothingness. Bodies were found far out to sea for weeks afterward.

Going into a village in southern Sudan after a raid by government-backed tribal militia called Janjaweed had a devastating effect on soul and mind. What they couldn't steal, they destroyed. They set fire to everything.

A few aged women were spared simply because they weren't worth a bullet. They sat quiet and unresponsive under the shelter of a reed mat to protect them from the roasting sun, their new enemy. They watched these white strangers come and then go after we'd seen and done all we could. That time we took no pictures. It was too much.

Some hastily buried bodies were just below the fresh earthen humps on the ground, haphazard, unplanned, and unmarked. Cattle carcasses were rotting nearby. The smouldering remains of small granaries and the single surviving leg of a table and some scorched black human remains in the circle of what used to be a grass-roofed hut told a potent story. Their fields were burned. Their men were dead. Their daughters and grandchildren had been taken north to become slaves.

The few people we did see were traumatized. Their eyes were empty, their dreams and lives dashed to pieces. They sat and just survived, but barely. You do what you can, then move on to the next village and see the same again. We were there to buy back slaves from their northern predators.

Some of the slave women we were able to rescue told us such horror stories that the mind almost refused to absorb what the ears were hearing. "They took my two-year-old son by the feet and swung his head against a tree to kill him." Another, "The Arabs took my neighbour's baby boy and threw him into a hut that was burning down. He died in there." Yet another, "The Arabs took my baby and drove a spike through his head into a tree. I watched him die as they took me away."

Others told of pregnant women having their bellies slashed open, to die in desperate pain and anguish. In Nyamlel, a village near the River Lol, I was told how the Arabs had taken 15 pastors and forced them to dig a pit in the centre of the village. The pastors were then pushed into the pit, doused with fuel, and burned to death. Some survivors swept that spot daily as an act of respect for their slaughtered pastors.

A few old women in Nyamlel lived in simple enclosures walled with papyrus reed matting and partly covered with a mat roof. They were living off the few fish in the ponds of the dried-up Lol River and foraged greens, including the boiled leaves of some trees. Their boiling pots were sections of former water jugs with which they had once carried water from the Lol to their homes, now all gone.

I saw it all. I still feel it all when these disturbing memories flash through my mind, memories I'd rather forget, and yet not! Memories that remind me of a simple verse in Scripture: "Religion that God our Father accepts as pure and faultless is this: to look after orphans and widows in their distress and to keep oneself from being polluted by the world" (James 1:27).

Wisdom Gained: Seeing is not only believing. It is feeling. It is heart-wrenching and life-changing. It is a challenge to sustained action, not merely the mewing of temporary concern. You may see some such horrors and find that you cannot just walk away from them. Christian love motivates action.

59 JESUS LOVES ME

STARVATION WAS RAMPANT in Ethiopia in the early 1980s. A communist regime had taken over the government after the assassination of Haile Selassie, the last king of one of the oldest kingdoms on earth. Haile Selassie claimed direct descent from King Solomon of the Bible. He was, from all I ever read or heard, a benevolent king. I saw him once in Addis Ababa leading two black-maned lions on leashes down a wide thoroughfare in the city. People gave him a wide berth.

Now, many years later, starvation had come. Addis Ababa appeared to be well fed, but everywhere outside Addis seemed to be without any resources whatever. Between floods and drought, and a communist political system which had been imposed on a 2,000-year-old kingdom, the whole traditional supply-and-demand system was out of whack. Centralization simply doesn't work with a multimillennial system so deeply entrenched.

As vice president of missions of *100 Huntley Street*, I had to squeeze the most out of about eight million dollars of donations from the viewing audience, combined with the Canadian Food Grains Bank and the Canadian International Development Agency. To ensure that we were running an effective operation, I went several times to monitor the use of the two helicopters we had leased to deliver the food.

Why helicopters? Trucks could simply not get to the valleys of so many hundreds of canyons, many of them equal to the Grand Canyon in the USA.

In Ethiopia, we had just inspected the installation of a solar-powered pump installed to bring water up a cliff from the Omo river 40 metres below. It pumped water into a network of small garden patches in an otherwise barren brown expanse of dry, red, cracked earth. The greenery of the vegetables was heartening. I saw money well spent, and these people were surviving.

The pilot, Don Wederford, said, "We still have to deliver the food on this crate [referring to his helicopter]. We'll go that way. People are starving over there," as he pointed at canyons somewhat north-east. It all looked as barren and lifeless.

Just before we landed, Don informed us that three relief workers had been violently killed by these people just about ten days before. I didn't think my thin shirt would be very effective body armour.

We got out, leaving our cameras behind lest we offend the people. I really didn't want to offend them. They did not look very welcoming as they stood off to the right of the helicopter beside a thorn fence around their village compound. We pushed several sacks of grain onto the ground. Don left the engine running with the rotors spinning very slowly, just in case. We got out and began to walk on a dirt path toward the men.

The warriors stood in typical fashion, one foot on the ground and the other foot braced on the opposite knee as they leaned on their spears. Their hair was packed with red ochre. They reminded me of the Maasai and Turkana of Kenya, and the Karamojong of Uganda. This group looked fiercer to me than the others I knew. Perhaps it was that my senses were put on high alert by what Don had told us. I was nervous.

All the tribes in this area of Africa lived by and for their cattle. Cattle raids were common. Cattle were the measure of their wealth. I saw none. They were hungry, but their faces were stoic. As we walked toward them—knowing that they were quite proficient in throwing spears and that if I had to run, their legs were much longer and faster than mine—I whispered to Don, who walked ahead of me, "Should we be doing this?"

He answered, "Don't look afraid, and don't worry."

I've always believed that God would look after me, but I also knew God expected me to use some common sense occasionally. I just figured this was an occasion when I really wasn't using too much common sense, and neither was Don. I thought about the killings the week before, and my apprehension increased with each step.

At some point, a young lad had fallen into line behind me unnoticed. I have no idea where he had come from. He was just suddenly there. He was about nine years old. I turned to look at him when I heard his footsteps and somehow imagined I saw mischief in his eyes. I could almost taste the tension. Three dead, three more to go? I was ready to run back to the helicopter. There was one problem: I didn't know how to fly a helicopter. Suddenly in a soft voice behind me I heard this little boy began to sing, in English no less, "Jesus loves me, this I know, for the Bible tells me so ..." I glanced back at him, and his eyes were dancing. I relaxed.

The men didn't show any signs of friendliness. After a short and difficult conversation through the little boy, we carefully walked back to the aircraft and offloaded more sacks of grain with the help of these colourful warriors, now without their spears. They still had their *simis* (two-edged swords) in scabbards on their naked hips. Now they had food to eat.

I had a quiet little conversation with God about Don Wederford. After all, Don was the guy who'd been shot down in a copter by rebels some years before and marched for miles through Ethiopian wilderness in his Dack's shoes. Perhaps he was dreaming of having another exciting experience. He seemed a bit of an adventurer. I tend to err on the side of caution—sometimes.

On the other hand, who was I to judge? I had done a few things which didn't make a lot of sense either, until it was all over.

Wisdom Gained: When sights, sounds, and emotions are disruptive to your normal, listen well to the voice from God, which ministers peace and calm to your soul. He is always with you and may speak to you in surprising ways.

60 PEOPLE OF INFLUENCE

I'VE NEVER SET out to befriend the rich, famous, or powerful. I don't belong in their company. Yet occasionally I have experienced situations where I have had little choice in the matter. Several come to mind. When some highly influential people are Christians, we have the opportunity at *100 Huntley Street* to get their unique perspectives on Christian life. David Mainse asked me to go and get some of these stories and interviews for the TV program.

President Frederick Chiluba of Zambia was one such.

President Chiluba had announced to the world that Zambia was a Christian nation. More easily said than done, I thought. I flew to Zambia to interview him. My son John, who worked in the production department of *100 Huntley Street*, was assigned to go to Zambia with me as my videographer. I appreciated that.

Rev. Joshua Banda, pastor of the large church in Lusaka, had made most of the basic arrangements in Zambia. He had also lined up an interview with Vice President the Hon. Godfrey Miyanda.

As we entered the grounds of the presidential palace, I was impressed with its grandeur. Kenneth Kaunda, the former president, had left an impressive place from which to rule the country.

We were led into a large stateroom, perhaps a ballroom, that was almost empty of furniture. One whole wall was made up completely of glass doors that were swung open to a beautiful view of the gardens, with peacocks and a few pieces of strategically placed garden furniture. We were told that this was the room where the interview with President Chiluba would take place. John set about preparing the camera, tripod, lights, and equipment, asking only for two chairs to be brought. One of the chairs was impressive. It had slightly longer legs. I was not the one who sat on it.

I was taken by an aide to President Chiluba's office, where I could brief him on the questions I would ask and get his okay on them. The officer led me through several remarkably extravagant rooms, and into a room within a room. It was a room with double walls, surrounded by guards and attendants. This inner room was the president's office. I was flabbergasted. Extravagant to the extreme.

The door was several inches thick, mounted in a wall that had at least 12 inches of reinforced concrete. The office walls and door were padded with rich red leather from floor to ceiling, stretched over some soft padding that itself was at least four inches thick. The leather was held in place by large leather-covered buttons such as you would find on a high-class leather sofa. It seemed to me that a cannon blast could not be heard once the door was closed. Perhaps that was the idea. It had the feel of a bunker. Mortars on the outside would not penetrate with sound or shrapnel.

The furnishings were lavish. The short man behind the massive desk seemed like a contradiction. President Chiluba, the most powerful man in Zambia, was diminutive. After a very cordial welcome and greetings, he apologized for the surrounding walls and furnishings, stating, "This is what was left for me by President Kenneth Kaunda."

We went over the questions, with which he had no problems. We chatted on for perhaps half an hour. We were notified when John had finished setting things up, and the president led me out to the great hall. As soon as John saw him, he decided that President Chiluba needed a higher seat in order to be on eye level with me. John went to great lengths to be deferential to the president. In every way, President Chiluba was agreeable and quite ready to follow John's suggestions.

The interview went well. At one point we had to stop the interview because of the raucous sound of the peacocks making their presence known. All the massive glass doors had to be closed.

For part of the interview, John squatted down to get a view upward of the president as he answered my questions. What I did not know until later was that when John crouched down with his knees apart to keep balance, the crotch of his black pants split wide open from the belt at the back, right down to the bottom seam. I had heard a slight ripping sound but hadn't thought much of it.

When the interview was concluded, both John and I thanked the president. President Chiluba must have though him the most respectful young man possible, as if backing out of his presence had to reveal his respect for the president. What it actually did was keep him from revealing his brilliant white shorts to the president through the gaping seat of his pants.

When the president was escorted away by an attendant, I helped John pack up his gear, and we left the palace and grounds and headed for the home of the vice president, General Godfrey Miyanda.

General Miranda's home was a much more ordinary house, though large. We were scheduled to have a half hour of his time. We were led into the house and met the very tall, broad-shouldered and solidly built general. From the start, he insisted I call him Godfrey. We sat down in his living room on a white leather sofa. John felt that the light and backdrops were perfect for the interview, so we decided that the interview should take place right there where we sat, relaxed. We were fitted with lapel microphones, then John began to set up his gear (he had changed pants) as the general and I began to chat, first about the interview, then about conditions within Zambia.

I was somewhat surprised and then shocked at the openness with which he spoke to me of the situation in Zambia. Matters of state seemed to be open for discussion. The matters of state and his personal faith in Jesus Christ were inseparable, it seemed. It was his custom to play the piano in a local Pentecostal church that met in a hotel in Lusaka. He would go out quite often on weekends to preach the gospel in various churches. He was a very deeply committed Christian. Two Christians at the helm.

While Kenneth Kaunda was still president of Zambia, Godfrey led a large contingent of Christian intercessors to a special temple Kaunda had built for his own personal guru he had imported from the East. The word was that Kaunda was somewhat under the strong, probably demonic influence of this guru to whom he went to for advice and guidance, even in matters of national importance.

Godfrey led this band of intercessors, all Zambians, as they marched around and around the temple and prayed loudly, calling on God and casting out evil powers in the name of Jesus. It caused quite an impact. It was plastered on the front pages of the newspapers in Lusaka. He was roundly criticized for what he had done but stated that his Christian faith demanded that he come against satanic powers in Jesus's name. He was unafraid, even under threats against his life. He told me of the midnight gathering of black Mercedes Benzes that drove into a large cemetery in Lusaka where demonic rituals were carried out. The horror of it was that many of President Kaunda's cabinet members were part of those rituals.

By the time Godfrey was ready to stop chatting and get to the interview, an hour had passed, and John was waiting patiently by his camera. I did not touch on those things in the recorded interview, but it certainly gave me a new edge for the questions I did ask.

When the interview was over, and John was packing up his gear, Godfrey's wife came into the living room and invited us to stay for supper. Godfrey insisted we stay. It was either that or a hotel meal. John and I opted for the wonderful smells coming from the kitchen.

It was one of the most delightful and certainly interesting meals I had ever had. Godfrey withheld nothing from John and me. The phone rang, and he was gone for some time. When he returned, he said, "I have just learned that Zambia Airlines has gone bankrupt. We were expecting this. We have some terrible corruption and mismanagement here in both government and industry."

One of the last things he told me was that the present hope was that President Chiluba would serve his predetermined two terms as president and that he would promote General Miyanda to the citizens of Zambia to be voted in as the next president. That did not happen, since President Chiluba tried to hold on to power beyond the two-term limit he himself had set in place. The overlong leadership of President Kenneth Kaunda had allowed corruption to develop and become entrenched in society.

In subsequent years, I had the privilege of welcoming quite a few students from Zambia to our School of Broadcasting at *100 Huntley Street*. They were very sharp and quick to learn.

Zambia is a unique country in at least one way. Seldom would anyone admit to being from any specific tribe, referring to themselves instead as "Zambians." Tribalism seemed one of the least of the problems at that time in Zambia.

Sierra Leone was convulsed with an attempted coup that involved the slaughter and mutilations of many Sierra Leonese. Arms and legs chopped off, including women and children, were among the most common atrocities.

Rev. Captain Moses Kargbo became senior chaplain after a semblance of peace had returned in Freetown, Sierra Leone. For his age, he is another outstanding man. And it all started so innocuously. He was a junior chaplain serving a contingent of Sierra Leone's soldiers who somehow got on the wrong side of the border into Liberia during the great horrors in Sierra Leone.

It was assumed that the troops for whom he was chaplain were all found on the Liberian side of the border in the bush to cause trouble for Liberia. That was not the case, but they were jailed in Liberia. Since Moses was the chaplain, they said he need not go to jail. Yet he insisted on being in jail with his troops. He wanted to continue ministering to them, encouraging them and helping in any way he could. Because of his request, he was able to join his troops in prison.

It's too long a story to tell, but through unwavering faith in God and untiring service to his troops, he was freed with all his soldiers. He was, after peace had returned, promoted to captain and became senior Christian chaplain to the Sierra Leone army. Moses had the authority and used it to appoint all Christian chaplains needed by the army. He chose exclusively born-again, Spirit-filled pastors as chaplains. And what a powerful force they formed. There was a Muslim chaplain as well, appointed for the small percentage of Muslim soldiers.

Again, my son John was sent with me as videographer. John and Moses were almost the same age and struck up an immediate friendship. Being brothers in Christ was a deep connection.

As a part of my responsibilities, not only did I manage the money donated for relief and development purposes, but I had to go to the various sites around the world to monitor and assess the effectiveness of the money we received from viewers of *100 Huntley Street*. Often, big money was involved.

It would have been much easier to stay in my office and send someone else to face the horrors. But since I was a known face on *100 Huntley Street* and sometimes host, I was personally responsible for each project. I also had to give video reports on *100 Huntley Street* as to how donors' money was being used.

Therefore, I had to go. Most of my trips the seventy-plus countries I have visited were in this capacity.

Some of the memories of those places stand out for their sheer horror, in contrast to the amazing optimism of the Christians involved in addressing the disasters.

I arrived in Sierra Leone with only a head knowledge of the atrocities being committed by the rebels.

My first introduction to Sierra Leone, West Africa, was while I was a missionary in Kenya, many years before. I was there as manager of Evangel Publishing House, finding distribution points for the literature we published. It was a tranquil and beautiful place.

Things had changed drastically since then. The rebels had indiscriminately and viciously hacked and chopped off the limbs of both children and adults. I was not prepared to see what I did see.

Lorna Dueck had brought the situation of Sierra Leone to our attention at *100 Huntley Street*. It was headline news in some papers. Viewers of *100 Huntley Street* grew concerned, and we got involved in financing the production of prosthetics for those who had lost an arm or a leg or both.

I visited a shop in Freetown, the capital city, that had been set up using basic local materials to assemble, produce, and fit the prosthetics in place, allowing a person to walk, and even some with both arms gone to work again. It was an amazing thing to see plastic ABS water pipes being used as the basic limb, with a variety of fittings, hinges, and springs to allow them to function. Simple genius.

We went to a slum camp in the middle of Freetown. It was not just the open filthy sewers, the makeshift cardboard houses, or even the conditions in which people had to prepare what food they had that sickened me. I had seen all that before. It was the limbless mothers, fathers, children, and even worse, little babies. I just somehow could not imagine the evil in a man's heart which would prompt him to hack off a baby's leg or arm, leaving a bloody pulp and shattered bone to heal into a mess of scars.

I was continually distracted by yet another even more horrible sight than I had already seen. I began to get nauseated. I wanted out of there! But the Sierra Leonean army chaplain, Rev. Moses Kargbo, kept urging me onward. He had a goal, a destination.

We stepped over dirt, garbage, and even people and finally arrived at a larger, somewhat better structure. It was made of tree branches, with former food sacks and ripped plastic tarpaulins draped over a roughly formed roof. It was all white material, so was quite bright inside. It turned out to be a church. It was also full. As we entered, the people, each missing a limb or two, broke out in songs of praise to God. The one man in the building with all his limbs was an army chaplain: Moses Kargbo. He had the joy of the Lord on his face as he led the people in praise to God.

You do have troubling personal thoughts when you see people in such dreadful conditions and needs, yet still able joyously and enthusiastically praise God. I wondered if I could, had I been one of their number. I had a difficult time shifting from the horror outside to the joy and peace inside that rickety church set in the middle of such devastation and pain. And I was supposed to greet them, meaning I was to preach a short sermon of encouragement. It seemed to me that they had no need of encouragement. They had more visible courage and faith than I did! I was encouraged by them.

As we were leaving, a man walked toward me. Both arms had been replaced by plastic ABS water pipes, levers and a pair of what I can only call "pincers" to replace the fingers of his hands. When he was told who I was, and that our ministry had sent the funds to provide him with the limbs he now used, he broke out in a glorious smile, threw his plastic "arms" around me, and gave me a hug. I wept.

His story was amazing. Since receiving his gift of arms, he had begun training to be a welder, no less. His plan was to open a school where he would teach others to weld. As I watched the way he handled things, even doing up the buttons on his own shirt, I realized his "hands" would certainly be steady enough to see his desire filled. I left that camp nauseated and encouraged.

But that was not the end!

I had to be introduced to "Rambo." Rambo was the nickname given to the man who led the rebel charge with his rabid troops into Freetown. It was his rebel group that had hacked and terrorized innocent citizens as the rebels fought their way into the government headquarters, stormed it, and took control of it. At that time, Rambo thought he should declare himself president of Sierra Leone.

He was the most daring leader the rebels had. He had gone through ceremonies with witchdoctors and was told that he could never be killed by bullets. He often ran straight into the gunfire of government troops and never once received a wound. He was convinced the bullets passed right through him or were diverted because of the power of witchcraft. He may even have been right. Witchcraft is a power to be reckoned with.

But the Rambo I met was a different Rambo. A big change! He had received Jesus through the ministry of Moses Kargbo. We met him at a displaced women's and children's camp. They were families or partial families. The husbands were missing civilians. I was introduced by Rev. Moses Kargbo to Idris Kamara, alias Rambo. He looked perfectly harmless to me and had a very calm, placid appearance. His eyes were soft and almost expressionless. He no more looked like an evil, demonic killer than I did. I treated him with some reserve. I just wasn't sure about him after all I'd heard of his vicious atrocities. What was *he* doing here?

I quietly asked Moses, "Why isn't he in prison?"

Moses answered, "I have vouched for him that God has changed him." He went on to state, "Sierra Leone has adopted a policy of forgiveness."

We had a meeting with the women and children under a very large, metal-roofed shelter. Some women shared their stories of having been brutalized, but when they gave their lives to Jesus and forgave their attackers who had done such horrible things to them, they knew the peace of God. They danced with great enthusiasm and played out, through drama, some of the horrors they had lived through. Seldom have I seen such release and freedom. It was filled with praise and joy. I felt my faith was shallow compared to theirs.

Chaplain Kargbo asked Rambo to lead in prayer. I was astounded, first because everyone knew him and his reputation of viciousness. He must have been reading his Bible constantly since he had received Jesus Christ as Saviour through the influence of Chaplain Kargbo. This kind of news is never reported in western journalism about Africa.

He didn't want to be called Rambo any longer. He was ashamed of what he had done. He had repented and was forgiven by God and his fellow men. He renounced witchcraft and was delivered from the power of demons. And he prayed. Oh, did he pray! He started off, in English, with the recitation of the complete Psalm 91, with vigor. Then he launched into an impassioned prayer for Sierra Leone and all the horrors they still faced in the work toward recovery and re-establishment of peace under the rule of Jesus Christ.

I spent quite a bit of time with Idris after that. He wanted to go to Bible college in Canada. I told him I would not support or approve this, since Canada could have a seducing effect on him. He understood. I personally undertook to pay for his three years in the Assemblies of God Bible College right there in Freetown, where he graduated. His high marks and progress were reported to me regularly. He is now in ministry, even though some are still trying to make him pay for what had been truly forgiven. I see some parallels between Idris Kamara and the apostle Paul.

I have seen what God can do through a yielded servant like Rev. Captain Moses Kargbo. God has some fine people in places of influence where situations and circumstances need such men. They are God's people in the right place at the right time.

Wisdom Gained: Famous people are only famous in the eyes of humanity, and often that assessment is a mistake. They are, in the eyes of God, on a perfectly equal level with you before God. Get to know them personally, and they are as common as you and me. Some just take advantage of their prominence.

61 SHOT OUT OF THE SKY?

IN MARCH 1997, I was flying into Sudan, illegally, to redeem slaves who had been captured by a combination of tribal militias from Muslim tribes from northwestern Sudan and soldiers of the National Islamic Front. I was flying into a humanitarian crisis. Not only had thousands of people been taken as slaves to the north of the country, but people were dying by the thousands through ground attacks, air attacks, and manipulated famine against the black and predominantly Christian south of Sudan. Their own citizens!

This was my first flight into southern Sudan. I was accompanying Lady Caroline Cox, and John Eibner, both leaders in Christian Solidarity Worldwide at the time. Lady Cox was a deputy speaker in the House of Lords in London, England. The previous October, when she was a guest on *100 Huntley Street*, Lady Cox had invited me to go with her.

Some time earlier, Lorna Dueck and I had discussed the issue of slavery in Sudan. Lorna read some excerpts from the *Baltimore Sun* newspaper. I had made the statement, "As Christians we cannot just sit and do nothing about this!"

On the way out of the studio that day, members of the TV crew handed me cash, some of it in big amounts. I was a bit bewildered. Within weeks, we had accumulated about $119,000 in donations from viewers without ever making an appeal for funds. As a result, we invited Lady Cox to appear on the program on her way to an official Senate hearing on human rights in Washington, where she would advocate on behalf of the southern Sudanese suffering at the hands of their own vile Islamist government in Khartoum. (This was years before South Sudan became an independent country.)

That led to her invitation for me to go to monitor the use of these Canadian funds in Sudan. Thus, I found myself flying over 500 miles into Sudan, illegally, to a destination called Nyamlel.

About a quarter of the way to our destination, Lady Cox leaned over and casually told me of her previous visit to Khartoum to challenge the government regarding its treatment of the black African population of their south. At that time, she had been rebuffed and told in no uncertain terms by the minister of state, "If you are seen flying into the no-go areas of the south, we will shoot you out of the air!"

Then she added. "That's the reason we're flying in low and just before sunset."

My eyes darted to the horizon in many directions. We were flying into totally forbidden territory. I kept my eyes on the horizon until we landed at dusk on a dirt runway about a mile from the ruins of Nyamlel. The Cessna Caravan dropped us off with our camping equipment and a large cargo of medicines. The pilot took off quickly so that he could fly back into Kenyan airspace under cover of dark. If caught on the ground, escape would have been most difficult for the pilots.

We hoped to see the pilot back in four days. Meanwhile, we would trek in the 126-degree (52 Celsius) heat for 13 miles to redeem slaves and then trek back a day or so later. The conditions were terrible, but we were determined. The full details of that trip and two subsequent trips into Sudan can be read in my 1998 book, *Let My People Go!* (Multnomah Publishing).

Wisdom Gained: Living a Christian life in today's world is both challenging and risky. Are you willing to risk your physical life to keep your eternal inheritance? Simple courage and determination can produce peace and divine tranquillity despite threats and ungodliness. God is always with you.

62 TERROR AND HORROR REIGN

IN THE NORMAL course of life most people don't come face to face with the atrocities of humankind and clear evidence of evil and demonic activity. In many ways, I wish I were one of those fortunate people who have been spared the horrors. But horror and atrocities do exist. Much of it is the direct activity and result of the evil that resides in some whose activities seem to be on the far outskirts of humanity.

Some horrors are the result of nature gone berserk. When I saw the results of Hurricane Mitch on Central America, I was appalled by the destruction of homes and lives when wind tore houses apart and the rivers swept people, towns, beasts, and property into oblivion. I can't imagine the shock and terror that overwhelmed those who were washed away into eternity.

Nature's ability to overcome all human efforts was seen in both the flood in Winnipeg, Canada, when the Red River drove people from their homes, and the ice storm in eastern Canada that left many hundreds of thousands without power and heat in the depths of winter. But these were the lesser degrees of displacement that I have witnessed.

Homeless and abused children on the streets of Lusaka, Zambia, and Nairobi, Kenya, were cause for weeping, needing compassion and action. In Zambia, my assistant, Rev. Jack Hawkins, put together what became known as the Lazarus Project. Children rescued from those mean and heartless streets were relocated to the countryside. There, they were placed in loving surrogate families who gave them food, clothing, and an education.

We worked with Charles Muli, who became a rich businessman in Nairobi. He had been a street kid himself and had risen from the streets to great financial success. God convicted him one day when he rejected the pleas of a poor, rag-covered child. God reminded him of his own hopeless beginnings on those same streets.

He turned his mansion in the countryside into a haven for street kids, providing himself as a father to all of them. There are now several villages of adopted street children outside of Kenya. He gave everything he had to the poor. After the total depletion of all his own riches, he experienced the miracles of God's provision. *100 Huntley Street* was one of those new resources that jumped into the gap. I had the privilege of seeing the beginning of this remarkable rescue of otherwise hopeless children. (The miraculous story is told in *Father to the Fatherless* by Castle Quay Books.)

One of the few times in our lives when Mary and I left North America for a holiday was to the Dominican Republic. While we were there, the Lord interrupted our holiday on the beach for an un-holiday in a slum not far from our suddenly disproportionately beautiful hotel.

We were invited to visit a barrio that stank of every form of human-made odor possible. Gutters full of garbage and human waste lined the trail we took to visit a new site being built by a Toronto businessman, Elio Madonia. He felt God had blessed him with riches through his business life, and he was to share with those in deep need. He too had gone to the Dominican for a well-deserved holiday. When Elio got there, his plans for a tropical retreat, and his life, were changed dramatically.

He found many people of Haitian origin running to the "safe" side of the island. In Haiti, they had lived in the brutal poverty brought on by the total corruption in the Haitian government and the overwhelming influence of voodoo. They escaped across the border to the Dominican Republic side of that beautiful island but simply found more poverty. They also settled into the role of becoming second-class people compared to the Dominicans, who themselves were poverty-stricken.

Because of my visit there, *100 Huntley Street* became involved in an extensive housing project, a dental clinic, and a water project to divert a filthy stream and install a safe water source. This was reason for rejoicing. People who had once been victims of avarice were now housed and healthy.

Had I known what I would see in Cambodia, I would have chosen to stay home! This was some time after the Khmer Rouge had killed almost all the intellectuals in this otherwise quite peaceful and civilized country. It was a lesson in how to regress to worse than animal behaviour.

When I saw lions in Africa kill their prey, it was a normal part of nature. When humans submit to evil, they kill and torture their victims with a godless glee. But Pol Pot was long gone when I saw the aftermath of his regime's crazed slaughter.

We had gone to Cambodia to do three things: build housing for the homeless after the massacre, get a Christian TV station up and running, and build a church in the housing development we were helping to set up. We did all that, and it was good.

Humans without God are only evil, the difference only being in degree. What I was seeing was the extreme of the extreme. Some things are just too dreadful to become calloused in heart about them. I don't know that I will ever recover from those sights.

Wisdom Gained: Never complain about the many injustices in life and around the world unless you are willing to do something positive about them. Christians belong in the public arena. As Jesus told us, it will sometimes be as victims, but other times as servant saviours.

63 AMBUSHED

I'D HAD GUNS pointed at me before, in Uganda forty years earlier, but this time I was in volatile, poorly governed Sudan.

Sudan has been a troubled nation. Divided between the Muslim north and the predominantly Christian south, it undergoes continual conflict. I had been to Sudan at least ten times before. This was to be a remarkably different venture into the chaos and lawlessness of the Sudan; South Sudan became the newest state in the world community of nations.

Sandro DiSabatino was my assistant in the missions department at Crossroads. We travelled together to Africa to monitor and expedite the development of two branches of the Savannah Farmers Cooperative in South Sudan. We always had to travel through Uganda, landing at the airport in Entebbe and then making our way north to the border.

We were travelling with Dr. Samson Kwaje, spokesman for the Sudan People's Liberation Movement/Army (SPLM/A), and Grace Garibani. Grace's husband was the head surgeon for the SPLM/A. Also there were our driver, Augustino, and a teenaged girl who was heading back to Yei, Sudan.

As usual, travel was slow over the unbelievably muddy and bumpy roads. About 19 miles before we got to Yei, we were ambushed.

We had slowed to a crawl to cross a washed-out piece of road through a stream bed with just a trickle of water. As we began to climb slowly out of the stream bed, a young man jumped from the tall grass with a rifle pointed right at the driver. He aimed and shook the rifle at us, ordering the car to proceed out of the water, then stop on the incline. We were all ordered out of the car and lined up on the vehicle's left side. Another young man appeared behind us with an AK-47. Two young fellows whom we had assumed were just meandering down the road ran to us and began to search us.

One of them saw my briefcase in the front seat, which had all my 35mm camera equipment and satellite phone in it, as well as all my papers. He took it, along with my CPAP machine. He stepped up in front of the car, holding my things, while the second fellow began to search me. He found my fanny pack. He grabbed at it. Before he could take it, I quickly unzipped the front pocket and picked out the money I had put in the front zippered compartment ($200 Canadian, including a $100 bill, and four or five hundred US dollars). I handed the money to him, hoping he would leave the fanny pack on my waist. He didn't. It had another US$3,000 in a hidden zippered section.

Dr. Kwaje volunteered his own wallet and handed it over. They also snatched his two-way radio. They found nothing else of interest and began walking up the left side of the road away from us. On the opposite side of the road the man with the rifle kept it pointed right at me now. He had dropped a black net over his face to conceal his features.

I'm not sure what came over me. When I realized they had my CPAP, I called out, "I need that machine, or I may die!" That was a bit of an exaggeration, but since I have sleep apnea, I wanted it. It never crossed my mind that I might not even be alive to be able to sleep that night.

Dr. Kwaje, who knew better than I what would probably happen to us, was whispering, "Cal, stop. Don't do anything! Be quiet, Cal!"

One of the bandits let me approach him and open the CPAP machine. When he saw what it was, something like a Darth Vader mask, he tossed it back into the Land Cruiser.

I realized my passport was in my briefcase, so I asked for it, even though he had walked another 15 feet or so away from us. He was rather naive. He opened the fanny pack and pulled out some papers, receipts, etc., offering them to me. I walked up to where he was, gingerly reached in, and took my passport and airline ticket out of the briefcase.

While he was looking at my Canon camera equipment, I put the papers under my left arm, then reached back into the briefcase and slipped the sat phone out right in front of his eyes and tucked it also under my left arm. He didn't even notice. I assume he was too distracted by the camera equipment.

Sandro told me later that the guy with the net over his face was shaking like a dog, pointing the gun directly at me while I walked back and forth between the bandits and our vehicle. He said that he feared the guy would shoot me more by accident than on purpose, he was shaking so badly. I didn't even glance at the men with guns.

I walked back to the Land Cruiser and laid the sat phone on the front seat with the papers. Suddenly I remembered that my medicines were in my fanny pack. I turned around and asked for my medicines. All the while, the guy with the net over his face was nervously shaking and saying what sounded like "Please, please, please!" pointing the gun at me. I never even looked at either of the men with rifles pointed at me.

When I mentioned my medicines, the young fellow with my stuff stopped and began looking in my briefcase again. He held up a bottle of headache pills. He was thirty feet away from me by this time. I said, "No, it's in the other!" and indicated with my hands at my waist that I meant the fanny pack. He didn't really seem to understand much English. He held up my fanny pack, and I nodded yes.

I walked up the road to him again and opened the two zippers in my fanny pack where my Zestril and other just-in-case dysentery pills were. I took them out. He looked into the fanny pack, which now appeared empty, felt it from end to end and, thinking it was empty, handed it back to me. He did not know it, but he had just given me back my Visa card as well as the $3,000 hidden in the back pocket. I took it and walked back to my companions, who were still standing by the car.

Dr. Kwaje was looking at me in sheer amazement. He must have thought I was crazy. Sando was wide-eyed with apprehension.

I began to wonder who was robbing who. I had conned him out of the $3,000. It was strange, but I did not have a tremor of fear through the whole interchange. I just calmly asked for what I wanted and took what I could at least pretend was vital to me.

Thinking about it later, I thought that perhaps my actions had put the onus for potential death on something other than the guns in their hands. I also am convinced that God prompted me do it.

By this time, the four ambushers were chattering excitedly, glancing up and down the road. It was not a heavily travelled road, but a bus driver had seen what was happening and stopped a long way up the rutted hill behind us. The thieves ordered us back into the Land Cruiser. The young girl in the back never did get out. Dr. Kwaje had said she had nothing—the only words uttered by anyone other than myself as far as I can remember, other than Dr. Kwaje's admonition to me.

We sat until we were told to drive away up the road. When I looked back, all four had disappeared with my camera, calculator, Bible, phone charger, and spare batteries. Samson Kwaje's wallet and high-performance two-way radio also went into the bush with the bandits. We drove about a kilometre, then stopped. Using the car's radio, we called ahead to Yei. The driver told them briefly that we had been ambushed. We also talked with two or three small groups of people farther up the road and gave descriptions and an account of what had happened.

An hour later, at mile 9 from Yei, the security for Norwegian People's Aid (NPA) met us. They had weapons sprouting out all the windows and on the back of their pickup. Samson, Grace, and the driver told them everything. Grace thought she had seen one of the four Dinka men before. This was about 400 miles from Dinka country. A few people came and discussed the whole matter in a local language. Then NPA security men took off toward the place where we had been ambushed.

By the time we got to Yei, it seemed everyone in town knew what had happened. Everyone was very apologetic, as if they had failed us somehow. From what they had heard from our vehicle by radio, they had jumped to the conclusion we were likely all dead by then.

Dr. Garibani, Grace's husband, was very apologetic and told us that we were lucky. Usually when things like that happen, they kill everyone and burn the car after looting it. We reported to the police. Dr. Kwaje made our statement and received effusive apologies. They used the word *sad* repeatedly. They also assured us the ambushers would be caught. Of course! *Yeah, sure,* I thought.

All I could think of was all those miles of empty bush where they could disappear across the border to either Uganda or Congo, with my camera and the little Bible I always carried with me on trips out of Canada.

We went to the NPA compound in Yei where we had arranged to stay, but I asked if we might get beds at the Karibu Kwa Yesu compound instead. They had flush toilets. I was not sure Sandro could handle the squat system. Didn't like it much myself, for that matter. While they were checking out that possibility, we watched CNN about Afghanistan and the search for Osama bin Laden. The TV set was hanging from some poles under the grass roof overhang. Their only power source was a generator.

Sandro and I wondered if we should call our wives in Canada and report this. After all, I did have my satellite phone back. We decided not to do so, since we did not want to unnecessarily upset them. It was not quite the welcome Sandro and I wanted to tell our wives we had received on his first trip to Sudan.

We were told that the robbers would be caught and that they would die in front of a firing squad. There were three crimes punishable by firing squad in southern Sudan: murder, rape, and armed robbery. I went to bed that night wondering if the robbers were caught and set before a firing squad.

That is not the end of the story. The thieves were captured when they tried to buy some beer with my Canadian $100 bill in a local bush brewery. The owner grew suspicious and sent for the police. They were able to retrieve my briefcase within a day, with all the contents except my small Bible, which I had travelled with for four decades. It is probably still out there somewhere doing evangelism. The camera was broken.

The thieves were being held at the border. We arranged to talk to the police when we crossed back into Uganda a few days later. I wanted to urge clemency for the young men. I couldn't bear the thought of them facing a firing squad.

I made my pitch to the authorities, and they listened. My briefcase, with every item inventoried, was given back to me. No money was returned. I have a suspicion that the money may have just found a new place with the police. They took us to meet the two men they had captured.

Speaking through an interpreter, I told them about the forgiveness of God through Jesus Christ. I told them that I forgave them. Then I discovered that they did understand English quite well. I got very serious with them and told them to put their trust in Jesus. A large crowd had gathered under a great mango tree to see this "confrontation" that was as far from confrontational as possible. They too heard the gospel.

They were then returned to a windowless mud-walled jail, shackled together at the ankles. That was the last I saw of them.

Later, I learned that one of them had faced the firing squad because it was discovered he had also shot a major in the SPLA army.

Not every story ends the way one would hope.

Wisdom Gained: When an impulse comes from God and you are certain, act, speak out, challenge! After a while you get to know when an impulse is from God. When you are serving God, He will guide, guard, and direct you. Fear will not be a part of it.

64 EMERGENCY FOOD DELIVERY

MANY WILL REMEMBER the devastating famine that struck Ethiopia in the early 1980s. Millions were at risk. Haile Miriam, a rebel and then current communist government leader, killed Emperor Haile Selassie. By doing so, he also ended the longest kingdom dynasty in history. The Ethiopian Empire began in about 1270. At the end of the empire, the communists shut down most if not all the churches. One of the largest was the Africa Inland Church in Ethiopia.

100 Huntley Street became involved in the famine emergency. Again, it was my responsibility both to relate to the public through the television program, to raise funds, and to administer the use of those funds in the feeding programs in Ethiopia. I worked in very close association with Rev. Don Raymer, already a close friend and associate. He oversaw the ERDO (Emergency Relief and Development Overseas) relief efforts of the Pentecostal Assemblies of Canada, and they, together with several other denominations, were working with the Canada Food Grains Bank.

The viewers of *100 Huntley Street* contributed about $3 million toward the Ethiopian emergency feeding operation. Through the Canadian International Development Agency (CIDA) and the Canada Food Grains Bank (CFGB) another approximately $5 million was made available for our use in the Ethiopian emergency. I had a job ahead of me, not to mention some rather life-changing experiences.

Someone somewhere was able to convince the communist government to allow churches (now banned, but still operating quietly underground) to reopen and provide the only effective infrastructure to oversee and administer the distribution of food.

Several times, shiploads of grains from various contributing countries sat on the docks by the Red Sea, rotting for lack of transport. We at *100 Huntley Street* had to decide how to distribute and monitor the use of almost $8 million.

Don Raymer, who was representing one of the member churches of the Canada Food Grains Bank, and I made several trips to Ethiopia. At *100 Huntley Street* we learned that in one area, hundreds of thousands would die simply because of the impossibly wild terrain. Imagine the Grand Canyon times a thousand. The area was simply inaccessible. Attempts were made (not by us) to sling sacks of grain over the backs of about one thousand donkeys and take it along the narrow, treacherous paths and down steep inclines to those who were starving in this maze of flat-topped peaks and plunging precipices. The donkeys all died. I'm sure hungry people got the food, but none of it reached its planned destination.

Our approach was to use helicopters. I inquired across Canada for a company that might be able to help us in the most efficient way to use the funds we had received.

I contacted Don Wederford, a man who had been flying helicopters in Ethiopia previously and worked out of Calgary, Alberta. He had been shot out of the air by rebels and had crash-landed and been taken captive. He walked for miles in a pair of dress shoes, over weeks of captivity, though he received civil treatment. He had written of his experience in a book of his own.

After Don took me for a demonstration flight into the Rocky Mountains and we landed back in Calgary, I decided to lease the Huey helicopter for use in Ethiopia. Don Wederford was contracted as a pilot.

It was while on monitoring trips in Ethiopia that I faced some stark realities. One of these realities is the pain and sheer horror of death by starvation.

My cameraman, Perry Mark again, was so horrified at what he was seeing that he resorted to his professionalism by insulating himself behind the eyepiece of the camera. It was the only way he could handle it. I, on the other hand, was stuck with the broader view. While Perry was shooting important detailed footage, I was standing aghast at the impact of real mass starvation.

In Ethiopia, Don Wederford maneuvered the helicopter down beside the sheer cliff of a canyon. We had six bags of corn still on board. I must admit, Don was taking chances when he gently landed on a flat-topped peak near where he had previously sighted people in desperate need. As the landing runners touched down, the helicopter began to lean to one side. There was just enough space to take one bag of grain off at a time and carry it on a narrow path with sheer drops on both sides, to a village of Coptic priests and their families.

When we arrived at their village, which was a combination of caves and simple mud shacks, we found 63 men, women, and children with nothing left to eat. They were too weak to go anywhere for food; there was nowhere to go in any case.

After we gave them the food, the women immediately began to prepare some. We sat with the priests and somehow communicated. We did not know their language, but they understood the language of love. Their deep appreciation was clearly reflected in their eyes, their handshakes, and the babble of their own language. We didn't stay long. There were others waiting.

When we prepared to leave, they would not allow us to go without pressing a gift on us, on me! I didn't want to take anything from them, but they insisted, and it would have been an insult if I had refused. They gave me a small empty beer pot with four straw spouts on the sides. One was partly broken. Communal drinking was their custom. I hated to think of what went up those straws and what might also have gone back down the straw only to be drawn up again on the next draw of beer by another person. I accepted it more for their sake than mine. I still have it, and I value it highly.

I've often thought of that little community of Coptic priests without any education, no Bible, and just some traditional rituals and teachings coming down orally over generations of past priests.

There were some areas where we were not allowed to deliver food. I never did find out a reason for such restrictions. We flew in there anyway. We would save lives. When we landed, we found a group of Doctors Without Borders from France. They too had been forbidden to go there, yet they had gone. The grass was parched dry, what there was of it. The people were obviously starving. The doctors had little satchels of medicines and were doing what they knew to do. We came with 50-kilogram bags of grain. It was received with stoic silence and little bows by the local people. The doctors said it was desperately needed. Many years later in Sudan, I heard the expression, "Food is the best medicine."

We had brought life-saving "medicine" to those isolated, marginalized fellow human beings.

Years later, the ambassador from Canada to Ethiopia declared that "at least 30,000 people's lives were saved as a direct result of *100 Huntley Street's* feeding program in Ethiopia." I've often thought of those we were unable to save, wondering what might have happened to them. We did make it clear that this feeding program was a gift from loving Christians who really cared.

The great revival in Ethiopia came some years later. I wondered if there was a connection between the compassion shown by Christians, and the people's readiness to accept the Jesus of the Christians. Compassion is often the first step in evangelism.

One of my most disturbing experiences in Ethiopia took place at a feeding station where I was obligated to monitor the distribution of food. We again came in by helicopter. It was in an isolated place almost impossible to reach by road, yet two trucks had finally reached the area, and offloaded about 50 tonnes of Canadian yellow corn.

As we were landing beside the compacted thorn-bush barrier surrounding the feeding centre, we saw many hundreds of people walking toward it. Some were literally crawling on hands and knees. There were already more than a thousand desperate people outside the compound. We landed and walked in through the only "gate," about five feet wide. As we entered, a man on his hands and knees was approaching the gate. He had knobby elbows and knees. His feet seemed too big for his frame, his legs and arms stringy and scrawny, his eyes sunken and almost lifeless. His strength was all gone. He was one of hundreds lined up waiting to be registered and fed. That kind of sight tends to persist in your memory.

We went in and talked with the administrator of the feeding centre, sitting at a makeshift table in the middle of the compound. As I talked with the visibly stressed administrator, asking the questions I had to ask, I happened to glance at the gate. A medic in a doctor's white frock was standing in the gate as people slowly approached from every direction. He inspected everyone and sent them either to the left, or to the right outside the compound. Most were sent to the left.

When I asked the administrator what the young man was doing, I was told that he was assessing who could be fed, and who could not. It was not based on whether they could be saved with food, but on the fact that they did not have enough food for everyone who was coming. He explained that they could probably feed everyone for a few days at the most, and sustain life, but they had an inordinate problem. No more food was scheduled to arrive for at least six weeks, possibly longer.

The medic was literally choosing who would live and who would die. I was horrified. Yet it was a fact of "life" in this wilderness of drought and starvation.

I don't remember very much of what went on after that. I do know that when we got back to Addis Ababa, I think I ate something, then went to bed. I did not sleep. I could not sleep. What an awful responsibility: choosing those who would live and those who would die. I hated the thought. By morning I had not slept a wink. But I had made a commitment to God. If ever I came across such starvation again in another country, I would do everything in my power to be a gatekeeper who sent everyone to a source of food. I have lived with that memory ever since. I have also lived with that commitment.

That's why I am raising funds to build farms for mass food production within Sudan. Too many people are still being turned away. The war is purportedly over, off and on, and a tenuous peace is not holding well in southern Sudan. The hunger continues. Darfur became a new problem, just as the war between the Islamist north and the predominantly Christian south began to wind down. A peace accord was signed between the north and the south of Sudan. As of 2021, South Sudan has collapsed and is a failed state. A high percentage of the population has fled to northern Uganda for refuge.

Yet, sometimes you win.

When I first got involved in Sudan, it was in the freeing of slaves. At one point I, together with John Eibner of Christian Solidarity International from Switzerland, and several Sudanese leaders, found it essential to somehow get into Kurmuk, on the extreme east side of southern Sudan. We wanted to investigate the violations of human rights being committed against the people of southern Sudan by their own extreme Islamist government out of Khartoum.

We had to go through Addis Ababa to enter eastern Sudan. Terrible floods were covering much of the land between Addis and the border of Sudan at the time. Kurmuk had been the centre of intensive fighting and had changed hands repeatedly between the black southerners and the Arab northerners. It seemed to be safely in the hands of Commander Malik Agar at the time. Malik was a black African army commander, trained and educated in Khartoum in the north to the point where he had thought himself to be Arab. He was a Muslim.

Some of his own black tribesmen had finally convinced him that he was a black African, not an Arab. When he was finally convinced, he raised a fighting force of 95 percent Muslims to resist the vicious attacks from the northern Islamists.

We flew from Addis Ababa to a landing strip that was not really a landing strip. In pounding rain, we landed at Asosa, Ethiopia. When we touched down, the grass was tall enough that it was slapping the leading edge of the wings, and the propellers were mincing it as we tore through it. How the pilot even found the place is beyond me. We'd flown through thick clouds, a storm with torrential rains, and big "potholes" in the air. It was rough.

We had gone through all kinds of hoops to get permission from the Ethiopian government to cross the border into Sudan. It was late Friday, and all the offices were closed. Yet one friendly officer in the ministry of foreign affairs went to great lengths to make it possible. Then he added, "They may yet stop you at the border, since we cannot overrule their decision."

When we landed, amazingly, a Land Rover was there to meet us. As soon as we were on the road, we headed toward Sudan. It was nearby. But the road was a highly rounded surface and as slippery as grease. It took hours to get to the border. On our way we had passed several very large refugee camps, one of them reportedly holding fifty thousand Sudanese who had fled from the predatory north. I have wondered many, many times why the world stood by so long while the government in Khartoum practiced genocide and pillaged their own citizens.

Immediately across the border was Kurmuk. It had stopped raining overnight. We met Commander Malik Agar, who gave us a tour the next morning through what was left of Kurmuk. He showed us the Catholic church that had been desecrated by the Arabs while they occupied Kurmuk at one time. Even Malik, a Muslim, was scandalized by the fact that they would desecrate a centre of Christian worship. Two of his siblings had become Christians.

Two children were panning for gold in the sand near the destroyed foundation of a building nearby. Gold figured largely in the equation at Kurmuk. There was a gold mine that had been run by the Chinese on behalf of the northern Khartoum government. Malik's troops overran the mine compound, and the Chinese managers and operators left their nice homes in the mine compound, escaped over a mountain into Ethiopia, and disappeared. The actual mine labourers were Sudanese and lived in the usual hovels common to the region, outside the compound.

Another of our purposes in being in Kurmuk was to find a way to bring food to hungry Sudanese in that area, displaced by the war and unable to grow food even in that verdant area. As it happened, Commander Agar had the answer. He had seized about 40 large transport trucks, among other things, such as tanks and personnel carriers, from the Islamists. He had the means to haul the food to the people. He told us that they averaged 40 to 60 people arriving and staying each day in Kurmuk, looking for food.

This one we won. We were able to ship food through Ethiopia where it was trans-shipped into eastern Sudan at Kurmuk.

Interestingly, an American called Tim was there at the same time purportedly looking for a way to ship out spent shell casings for recycling. A likely story! He gave me his card and said, "Call me anytime if you learn anything." What could I learn? And why would I call him? I had good reason to suspect he was CIA.

I'm a preacher, not a spy. Little did I know that I would soon be involved in exposing two al-Qaeda cells right in Canada.

Wisdom Gained: You will find that determination seasoned with discretion can carry you to your goals even though the road may be rough at times.

65 UNUSUAL SPIRITUAL REALITIES

LIFE HAS MOMENTS of great spiritual significance. I do not consider myself any kind of spiritual giant or a person of great spiritual insights. But I have had moments that I felt were just God and me. The most significant was that moment, at 14 years of age, when I accepted Jesus Christ as my Saviour. It took a while to learn that He was also Lord of my life. The reality of God the sovereign and omnipotent hit me.

While in college, I was driving my car from Peterborough, Ontario, to Toronto. As I drove along Highway 401, I spontaneously began to praise the Lord, an almost involuntary act from deep down in my being. Things had been tough, particularly my finances. I had been dwelling on the goodness of God and His provisions, which often came just in the nick of time.

My praise went from the heart level up to my mouth, and I began to extol the Lord with expressions of simple praise. As I drove along, a beautiful cloud formation with an interplay of light and dark clouds and rays of sunshine appeared as I glanced up at the sky. I was overwhelmed with its beauty. My mouth could not express the glory of the God who could create such beauty, and it seemed to be there just for me. I was overcome.

I began to weep as I praised, so much so that I had to pull off the highway because of the tears blurring my eyes. I sat in that old '49 Chevy and was broken before God as I worshipped Him. If a cop had come along to check me, he might have thought me to be lost or drunk. I knew differently. I was right on course! The presence of God was simply overwhelming.

On another occasion, as I was preaching a week of meetings for a pastor friend, Rev. Harold Minor, in Ancaster, Ontario, I had a strange, inexplicable experience. The meetings had been going well. On one evening, the altar was filled with people seeking and worshipping God in a deep and sincere way. I stood alone on the platform, right beside the pulpit. I too was praying with my arms raised to the Lord.

There were a few people in the service who did not live in Ancaster. One of them was a German lady who was a prayer partner on the telephone lines with *100 Huntley Street*. She had told me she was coming just to support me in prayer.

As I stood praising the Lord, I felt a hand placed on my right shoulder. It was warm and sent a sense of warmth through my whole being. For some reason I assumed it was the German lady. I hesitated, opened my eyes and turned to simply acknowledge her presence, but no one was there. The warmth of the hand remained on my shoulder. For a moment I was nonplussed. The door at the back of the platform had not been opened or closed, and that warm pressure on my shoulder remained. I could come to no other conclusion than that God had put His hand on me.

I continued to worship the Lord. There was a sense of God's presence that was unusual in the church that night. Why would a thing like this, so definite and real, even happen? I have no answers to many questions. This is one of them.

There have been other similar experiences. I mention them only because every one of these experiences happened when I was in an attitude of spiritual meditation, thinking about the things of God, or when I was in prayer.

Yet prayer is one of the opportunities God has given that we least use. I wonder why!

Wisdom Gained: Always leave the door of your heart open to God. Amazing events can emanate from a life given fully to God. And wonderfully, God is glorified as the result. That is what God wants!

66 ALL THINGS WORK TOGETHER

IN 2004, I was the speakers coordinator for Mission Fest Toronto at the request of Marie-Lucie Spoke, who was the CEO. I accepted the voluntary position, thinking it would be an easy matter, simply writing the official invitations for guest speakers. I had no idea the hours I would spend in volunteer work, the overseas calls at my own expense, the trips to Toronto from my home 100 kilometres away for meetings, and the hundreds of emails I would process.

Marie-Lucie received a request for one of our speakers, Tony Campolo, to preach at Mississauga Baptist Church. It was impossible to fit it into the schedule. Marie-Lucie asked me if I would speak at the church instead. Me? A substitute for Tony Campolo?

I was free that Sunday morning, so I told Marie-Lucie that I would be available if they wanted me. I did not know anything about the church, the pastor, or where it was located. Pastor David Russell thought I would be an adequate substitute and asked me to preach in both morning services. I agreed. My schedule was getting quite busy.

The further we got into Mission Fest, the busier I realized I would be. I began to dread having to get up early, drive to the church, preach twice and get back to the Mission Fest venue in time to fulfill my duties there. To be further pressured, not only was I asked to oversee the hosts of all the main speakers, but also to escort Dr. David Yonggi Cho personally while he was in Toronto. This was rather pleasant, since Dr. Cho had been a dinner guest in my parents' home some years previously.

We had made special security arrangements to keep Dr. Cho from being mobbed by those who would want to try to get some of his time. After all, he was pastor of a church of over 750,000 members. One man from the USA offered $20,000 to Mission Fest to have some time with Dr. Cho. His offer was declined.

I met Dr. Cho and his entourage at Pearson International Airport on the Tuesday he arrived. The local Korean Christian community invited me to have dinner with Dr. Cho and several pastors and workers. He was to preach the following night at a special Korean rally that was packed out. At Dr. Cho's invitation, I had a private lunch hour with him on Saturday. The food was unusual, simply bananas and water chestnuts.

We talked in detail about how his church of 750,000 people was organized. It was cell group–based, and he had many hundreds of assistant pastors. They held services Sunday through Wednesday. Each service had 50,000 in attendance. Every member got to church in the central complex weekly. Dr. Cho also started ministering live over the internet with about five million people from all over the world connecting. The church had sent out about 600 missionaries.

Dr. Cho had not heard some of what was happening in Sudan and asked me for more information. I told him as much as I could in the limited time I had, then went on my way until the evening service, when I would once again stand by his side, except at the pulpit.

On the Saturday evening, he preached a very straightforward sermon and prayed for those who wanted to accept Christ as their Saviour. On the way back to the car that would take him from the Metro Toronto Convention Centre to the hotel, we were on an escalator when Elder Shigaki whispered to me that it might be appropriate to say my farewells to Dr. Cho now, since they had changed their flight to 6:30 a.m. A moment or two later, still on a long escalator, Dr. Cho, whose eyes were closed it seemed in prayer, turned to me, and said, "Your work in Sudan is going to be very successful." Then, on the next escalator, he simply said: "Please be in touch with my NGO department!"

At the car, we bowed to one another in the Korean fashion, then Dr. Cho moved toward me, and we hugged one other. A huge smile was the last I saw of him after I had officially thanked him for coming to be the main speaker at Mission Fest Toronto 2004.

His departure at 6:30 a.m. on Sunday took a great deal of pressure off me, since I was scheduled to speak at the Baptist church in Mississauga. I arrived there a little early, and immediately sensed warmth from the few people who had already gathered. I set up a book table to sell some of the books I had written, then went into the sanctuary for the first service. Perhaps 120 people were there. I preached on the theme "You Are the Gatekeeper," based on Scriptures from Matthew's Gospel, and I related an experience I'd had in Ethiopia in the early 1980s.

The second service was a much larger congregation. Between services I had tended my book table. In the second service, I personally sensed a greater unction in my preaching but ended it the same as usual, urging the people to be gatekeepers who attract people into the kingdom of God and not turn them away because of their lifestyle or inaction in sharing the gospel.

As Rev. Russell went to the pulpit, I returned to the first row of the church, where we had sat together during the preliminaries. Then I remembered my book table, so I went to the back of the church, and began taking off my lapel microphone.

That's when things became a little strange for me. Pastor Russell was asking if anyone would like to become a Christian and receive Jesus as Lord and Saviour. No one seemed to respond. Pastor Russell then called a small worship team to close with some worship choruses. At that moment, the Spirit of God prompted me to return to the platform, where a young lady was leading in a closing chorus, her eyes closed. I wondered if I'd heard the Lord's voice or my imagination. I felt I was to give a salvation invitation, although the pastor had already done so. What was I thinking? I didn't want to try to upstage the pastor.

But I couldn't shake this strong urge. I reinstalled my lapel microphone and went tentatively to the front of the church again. With a nod of approval from the pastor, I returned to the pulpit. The young lead singer sensed my approach and stepped back as the chorus ended. I had never left the pulpit only to come back to say more in my ministry previously.

I told of an incident in Sudan when it had taken speeches from Lady Caroline Cox, John Eibner, and finally me to convince the 317 slaves we had bought back out of slavery that they were indeed free. They were free to go back to husbands and mothers, or whoever of their families had survived the slave raids.

Most of them were women and children. When they realized what we were telling them, they broke out in the first smiles we had seen from anyone under that big tamarind tree.

I asked the congregation a question. "If I had offered those slaves the alternative to go back into the slavery, terror, and abuse of their owners in the Arab north, how many would you suppose would have opted for a return to bondage of slavery again?" The consensus was clear on the faces of the standing congregation.

"No one!" I said. "Of course not; it would be a foolish choice! Yet there are some standing here right now who are ready to walk out the doors of this church back into the darkness of their sin, their slavery to habits, and the chains of sin. Don't do that! Please put up your hand if you want to receive Jesus and accept the redemption He bought for you on the cross at Calvary. Don't go out through that door back into slavery."

Six adults raised their hands. I asked them to come forward, explaining that I did not want to embarrass anyone, but I did want to pray with them. With tears running down the cheeks of several, they repeated a sinner's prayer as I led them. The joy of the Lord slowly blossomed on their faces, much as it did on the faces of those hundreds of slaves in Sudan.

What would have happened if I had been too shy or reluctant to obey the voice of the Spirit that day? I had done nothing like it ever before in my ministry.

After the service, a man came to me and said, "You will never know what you did in that service. Our church has had a troubled few months recently, and you addressed the situation accurately." I have no idea to what he was referring, but the pastor came to me a few moments later and said much the same thing.

I will never forget Mission Fest Toronto 2004.

God is in control and in love with those who obey Him. I have experienced in a clear way what the Scriptures mean when they state, "The LORD makes firm the steps of the one who delights in him" (Psalm 37:23). I am still learning to walk with the Lord to be as obedient a man as I can.

Wisdom Gained: Never fear getting involved in an opportunity to serve the Lord Jesus Christ. It will give a zest and purpose to your life, with great satisfaction.

67 OWNING A BARN CAN SAVE YOUR LIFE

I WAS NEVER a very willing city dweller. The 32nd floor of an apartment building was not my idea of a good place to raise two young children. We had to change. So we bought a semi-detached house in Agincourt, in the northeast of what is now called the Greater Toronto Area. There was a massive influx of people from Hong Kong living in the area near the end of the British lease of that colony. Even the street signs in Agincourt were reinstalled in Chinese characters.

Since *100 Huntley Street* was moving west of Toronto, we jumped at the opportunity to get out of the overcrowded city and perhaps get a little country place just west of Burlington, where the new Crossroads Centre was to be built.

Salaries in the late 1980s were only just adequate at *100 Huntley Street*, and both Mary and I had been working to keep everything in balance. We finally found what we wanted, better than we could have expected. We bought our new place in Onondaga in November 1988, just after we returned from a trip to Israel, leading a group tour for *100 Huntley Street*. We were sticking our necks out a long way financially, but we had a six-month closing date—plenty of time to sell our house in Agincourt.

With the help of a friend, Nancy Cheffero-MacBrien, who had experience with real estate, we put our house up for sale. We had paid $64,500 and thought it was an awfully high price. Houses around us were selling quickly to incoming immigrants. A Chinese real estate broker came, looked at our house, and agreed to a generous price for our house. She told us it was the twentieth house she had bought that day for people coming from Hong Kong.

We were dumbfounded by how much our house's value had gone up in just nine years. For four years in a row, our house increased in value through inflation more than our combined salaries!

The housing market crashed the next week, and prices fell overnight.

We wondered if the buyers would renege, but they didn't. We moved out May 31, stayed in a motel in Brantford that night, and the next day moved into our raised ranch house on June 1, 1989.

When we bought the house, it came with a two-storey barn, a broken-down chicken house, an outhouse, and rocks hidden in the long grass that was supposed to be lawn. After moving in, we discovered other oddities. That barn appealed to me. But the smell in the place was terrible. That was even before I installed a bunch of chickens. They added some stink too, but they also added some growth to my gardens with their by-product.

Why would a house seller tell me his well was pure drinking water just so he could sell it? *E. coli* and quite a few fast dashes for the bathroom later, we decided to bring drinking water from town. *E. coli* is not good. The house needed major repairs. Why would I want to buy it?

Because it had a barn!

And I wanted chickens. Of course, I got more than I bargained for. We had a billy goat that stank so much, we gave him to a farmer who had lots of land and a good breeze. We upgraded to two Angora goats and a pygmy goat. We had ducks too, but they greased up the lawns and fouled the water that was meant for the chickens. The ducks provided dinner for us long before we had planned.

With all my responsibilities at *100 Huntley Street*, this was starting to be fun. I think that barn probably saved my life. It provided enough physical work to keep me active, and enough chickens and eggs to keep all my family and relatives happy. I carried 100-pound sacks through snow for the chickens. I did not get 100 pounds of chickens and eggs for every 100-pound sack of feed, but I'm a preacher, not an economist. I became an "eggonomist"!

I built an office on the second floor of the barn. It was beautiful. I put a zebra hide on one wall and shelves of books down one 39-foot stretch. The large hide of an Eland hung on another wall. Spears, Maasai simis (swords), and gazelle horns from the plains of Kenya graced the other walls. Good used furniture was placed just so. Glorious! All that hard-physical labour had paid off.

And the squirrels really did appreciate it. They moved in behind the new insulated walls with which I had hidden the rough interior walls of the barn. They were on top of the insulation I had lovingly patted into place in the ceiling: they were everywhere. The smell grew. *Noxious* would be an appropriate word. *Obnoxious* would be another. Whatever we stored, the squirrels scored.

I decided I would use the ground floor of the barn for a woodworking shop. I slowly accumulated machinery, second-hand of course, from my brother-in-law and from a neighbour who seemed to have two of everything. I fixed and sharpened what needed it. I bought a new wood lathe. The squirrels chewed wood upstairs while I chewed wood downstairs.

My spare time seemed to shrink until I was left with only enough time to feed the chickens, pick up the eggs, and plant some gardens during the summer. I had built a greenhouse out of rejected scrap wood from a lumberyard nearby and large glass windows that people set out as garbage when they replaced them. Seedlings flourished in there, and my gardens abounded with cabbage, corn, tomatoes, beans, peas, raspberries, and fruit trees.

The squirrels appreciated the greenhouse too. It was always warmer than the barn on a cold but sunny winter day. Racoons fed on my chickens. Worms infested my apple trees. I cut down a tree, and it landed on the corner of the barn. I cut out scores of dead elm trees and used them for firewood.

We finally got a cat to live in the barn. The cat had kittens—many kittens. Most we gave away, but when kittens become cats, they are harder to give away. I could then say unhappily that the stink of rats and squirrels was being replaced by litter box odours.

A friend told me that if you see one rat, you can count on there being a hundred more. So I declared war. I set rat poison inside the walls. It did get 26 rats in one covert operation. The smell improved amazingly. And the consumption of chicken food was cut by at least a quarter.

A ray of hope developed later about the squirrels in the barn. We found the cats feeding on one, and a few days later I was sure I heard the demise of another squirrel somewhere in the upper realms of the barn.

All that physical activity probably improved my health. As Mary and I got older, the work on the property became too much. In 2018, we moved into a smaller place in the city of Brantford.

Wisdom Gained: Never vegetate! Movement and exercise make for good health. A remote in the hands of a couch potato leads to ill health. Never retire.

68 THE CRISIS CALLED SUDAN

I BEGAN TO wish I had never seen Sudan. Yet, what would be the fate of those to whom we brought freedom with western cash? I was torn. I wanted to hate. And I did hate the evil. Yet how can you dismiss those who do such things by merely hating them? A perverted form of religion has deceived them. These people have been brainwashed into thinking they are doing God a service by enforcing Islam and Arabisation through violence.

For years they have advertised that they will force Africa into Islam before the year 2150. This was and still is the beginning of that very long-range plan. Islam says it is a religion of peace, and to many of them it is. But the only peace the Islamists really refer to is the "peace" that will reign when 100 per cent of the world's population has been brought into the bondage of Sharia law, and no woman will dare expose her ankle; nor will anyone listen to non-approved music, and thousands of other irrational rules and regulations will hold sway.

Extremist Islamists claim that the West has become decadent. I cannot disagree. The West has wandered far from acceptable moral standards. Islamists have a point. But while they call their god merciful, benevolent, and supreme, their actions are anything but merciful or benevolent. Their god seems to have the characteristics of Satan himself. Whom do they really serve?

During five trips into southern Sudan, I met some people who became significant in my life and in my activities in Sudan. Steven Wondu was ambassador to the United Nations, Canada, and the USA on behalf of the Sudan People's Liberation Movement (SPLM). We became fast friends. He has helped me understand southern Sudan to a degree. I too have helped Steven through some of his own difficult times.

It wasn't long before Lady Cox and I became targets for a press campaign to discredit what we were doing for the south by freeing slaves. They were partially effective. The SPLM decided in a three-day conference that, though they would not *ban* slave "redemption," they would *discourage* it. Some of those making that decision had members of their own family and clan held as slaves in the north. Sometimes hard decisions have to be made.

Steven Wondu and I created a plan for agricultural development in southern Sudan. It involved the creation of the Savannah Farmers Cooperative (SFC). It would belong to no man, no group, and would be totally apart from any political or governmental involvement. The SFC would be run by a board of directors. Since at that time Crossroads (*100 Huntley Street*) would be the financial source, I became deputy chairman. Steven, who had been auditor general of Southern Sudan during the only eleven years of peace since 1956, became the chairman. Dr. Samson Kwaje, minister of information, became a member of the board. They were all members in their capacity as private citizens.

There were some significant challenges during those early years with the SFC. The board secretary was caught stealing from SFC. He also tried to hijack the Logobero farm by registering it under a slightly different name as his own. Then he and others had the temerity to take Steven and me to court for unspecified charges on several occasions, but they never turned up with any rational evidence of any kind of wrongdoing. The fact that I participated in financing the farms made it hardly likely that I was stealing the farm, as they finally claimed in one outburst in court. The whole thing was eventually thrown out of court.

The court did learn that 13 million Uganda shillings worth of food from the Logobero farm had disappeared into that farm's management's hands. The board dismissed the whole staff of that farm immediately.

We started four other farms at Morobo, Romogi, Moje, and Mogiri. They began producing food but not enough for the land they were using. I began to recruit Canadian farmers to go for set periods to teach and demonstrate modern farming methods. Production improved.

Initially, two farmers were of inestimable help. Clarence Persall, from the church I attend, went with me on several trips. He gave advice and help on the ground in Sudan and acquired good used implements that we sent to Sudan. The second farmer to go was Tim Vander Kooi from the Brampton area. He was faced with the most difficult situation possible. He went to the Logobero farm, which had been the subject of so much corruption and mismanagement. He had to rebuild the farm compound after the terrible neglect it had suffered and make it operational again. The next farmer, from Alberta, got production going.

The Hon. Zamba Duku, speaker of the legislative assembly of Equatoria State, had been involved with the SFC from the beginning and became a member of the board of directors. He eventually became the managing director.

I always hesitate when people say, "God spoke to me." But, 32,000 feet high over the Atlantic on my way to Sudan, a conviction began to grow in me that God wanted me to start 50 new farms of 2,000 acres each in southern Sudan in the next ten years. The implications of this never dawned on me until months later. I was almost seventy years of age. God was asking for ten more years.

But despite my own misgivings, I shared it in an SFC board meeting, and they saw it as possible. We decided to start a 2,000-acre farm at a new place called Bori.

At the dedication of the Bori farm, with pastors, local chiefs, and government personnel, they had the signing of the lease, at no cost. Just before Zamba was about to sign the lease as a private citizen on behalf of the SFC, he was asked to help them in another matter. He put down the pen and listened to their problem.

There was a large tract of empty but very fertile land between the Bori farm and the Uganda border. Ugandans had begun to encroach on the land and grow crops to sell back in Uganda. They had begun to build a road into the area. The officials in South Sudan did not want to cause any ripples with the Uganda government because Uganda had shown such significant moral and material support to the people of southern Sudan in the resistance to the military invasion from Khartoum. Zamba asked, "What can we do to help?"

The answer came quickly and clearly. "Along with the 2,000 acres for the Bori farm, we want to sign over by lease the whole area between here and the Uganda border. It's for the SFC if you agree." Zamba signed immediately. When

I was in Sudan in late 2007, I was informed that the land turned out to be about 100,000 acres. Good grief!

By 2017, all work on the farms had been suspended because South Sudan had become a failed state and was at war with itself. The responsibility has transferred from *100 Huntley Street* to Cal Bombay Ministries since 2003. Cal Bombay Ministries continues to help the hundreds of thousands of South Sudanese who have fled to northern Uganda because of the chaos and danger since South Sudan's collapse as a viable country.

Wisdom Gained: God is never done with a plan He calls into existence. No seeming failure is unredeemable. Patience, faithful waiting, and prayer bring all things into focus and fulfillment. There is always a door open to compassionate ministry.

69 CAL BOMBAY MINISTRIES

THE FOUNDING OF Cal Bombay Ministries Inc. was a mix of purpose, faith, hesitation, prayer, and thoughtful action. I was encouraged by Fred Vanstone, who was chief of staff at Crossroads Christian Communications Inc. It turned out to be clearly God's will.

When my employment at Crossroads Christian Communications had been terminated at age 66, I could not retire. I was not finished with what I felt I was called to do, particularly regarding South Sudan. What I started in southern Sudan while at CCCI, I was afraid, would be abandoned for lack of someone with the vision and burden to see it continue developing into a project of self-reliant continuation.

People were starving. Land was available in South Sudan, and many people of South Sudan were depending on me—yes, me, personally. I had no idea how to go about it, but I was convinced that I must.

The front-desk receptionist at Crossroads called my office. A visitor was there to see me. When I went down, it was a woman whom I had never met as far as I could recall. We sat at a table in the large dining room. We exchanged pleasantries for a while. Then she handed me a cheque for $1,000, saying, "This is for you to use to continue your work in South Sudan." My response was that it would go into the proper account here at Crossroads and be used as directed.

"No," the lady said, "I want it to go to you, to continue the work in South Sudan." We discussed it, but she seemed more than adamant that I personally must accept the cheque. It had been made out to me, not to CCCI.

I had not told anyone but the chief of staff of Crossroads, Mr. Fred Vanstone, that I was thinking about starting a new ministry to address the needs of South Sudan. I had asked Fred if he would consider being the chairman of the board for the new entity. He had agreed and was the person who insisted that I call it Cal Bombay Ministries because my name was well known across Canada through television.

This lady had no way of knowing what was in the works, nor did she have any connection with Fred. I finally accepted the money. I told her I could not issue a receipt for income tax purposes. It was that money that we used to register as a charity and as a corporation in Canada. We formed a board almost immediately, with Fred Vanstone as chairman, Mr. Jack Price, a well-known publicist, my son John, and me.

The founding of another charitable organization called Cal Bombay Foundation Inc. was incorporated on September 5, 2013. It serves charitable ministries we know and trust, in similar vision working worldwide.

Thus, when I concluded my work at *100 Huntley Street*, I was ready to start out on my own as God led me step by step. But that's possibly another book …

Although there are recorded incidents in this book of some things that happened in South Sudan, they were all during my time with Crossroads Christian Communications/*100 Huntley Street*.

I have semi-retired from Cal Bombay Ministries Inc., though I remain as president. My daughter, R. Elaine Bombay, was appointed by the board of directors as executive director in 2020. It was a challenging year for us all because of our federal and provincial government's poorly planned response to the pandemic.

I led the ministry for about sixteen years and during that time worked in South Sudan with total dedication and love for the people of South Sudan. I cannot include all that God did and is doing in South Sudan, since it would make this memoir much too large.

If God continues to grant me strength and length of days, I shall give an account of South Sudan in another book. Some of the most exciting, fascinating, dangerous, and rewarding years of my life have been these past sixteen years.

Meanwhile, thank you for letting me share my memories and observations with you. I trust what you have read causes you to bless God for what He has done.

The end ... maybe.

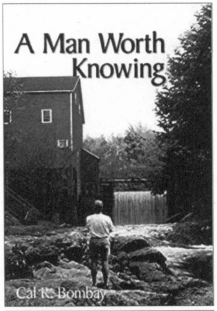

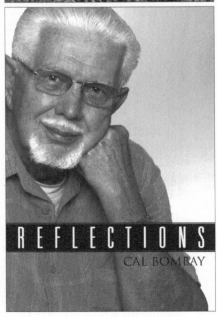

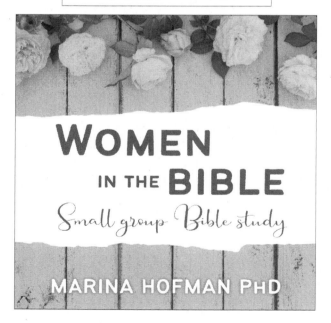

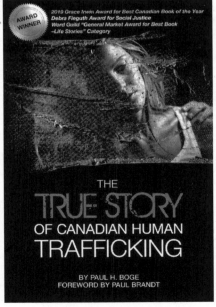